THE LONDON & SOUTH WESTERN RAILWAY

TO OLIVIA, MY WIFE
with memories of our
first railway journeys
together: Waterloo, 1935

THE LONDON & SOUTH WESTERN RAILWAY

O. S. NOCK
B.Sc., M.I.C.E., M.I.Mech.E., M.I.Loco.E.

LONDON
IAN ALLAN

First published 1965

This edition 1971

SBN 7110 0267 3

Published by Ian Allan Ltd., Shepperton, Surrey
and printed in England by
STAPLES PRINTERS LIMITED
at their Stratford, London, establishment

Contents

Preface

In writing a book about one of the old railway companies of pre-grouping days an enthusiast who can remember many journeys on the line, and what the locomotives and carriages looked like—not from the recollections vaguely aroused by photographs, but from vivid, evergreen memories—does so inevitably with some feelings of nostalgia. The London and South Western Railway was one of those that I knew from my earliest childhood, and that was in days when Dugald Drummond was in the chair, first at Nine Elms and then at Eastleigh. But as the story progresses one realises that it is not something that is working up to a finale, with the curtain falling on December 31, 1922. From the turn of the century South Western affairs are, one by one, building up towards a railway system of the future: Southampton Docks; the reconstruction of Waterloo; power signalling; and above all, electrification, on a very simple and quickly installed system.

The literature of the London and South Western is already considerable and I have referred freely to the books mentioned in the bibliography. The line also had, in the early days of *The Railway Magazine*, an ardent chronicler in one of its own servants, John Bosham; and I have referred to the many articles he contributed at the time. I have had the opportunity of studying extensively the train running records compiled in pre-1914 days by the late R. E. Charlewood. I am much indebted to Mr. G. J. Aston, the present owner of these records for a long-term loan of them. I am indebted to the British Railways Board for permission to use certain historical photographs, and to Mr. B. W. C. Cooke, Editor of *The Railway Magazine*, and to members of his staff for valuable assistance, and for permission to publish certain train running logs that were originally published in the *British Locomotive Practice and Performance* feature. I am also indebted to Mr. J. F. H. Tyler, Chief Signal and Telecommunications Engineer of the Southern Region, British Railways for his assistance in obtaining photographs of the low-pressure pneumatic signals, and interlocking frames at Basingstoke.

It is through the kindness and keen interest of Major-General Gilbert S. Szlumper that I am able to include the portrait of his father, A. W. Szlumper, the distinguished Chief Engineer of the line, and that of Sir Herbert Walker; and it is a pleasure to know that General Szlumper himself, the greatest surviving servant of the L.S.W.R., is still happily with us.

I am, as always, grateful to Olivia my wife for her help in typing the manuscript. The territory served by the old L.S.W.R. has particular memories for us both, and so I dedicate the book to her.

O. S. Nock
May 1965

Silver Cedars
High Bannerdown
Batheaston, Bath

I

The London and Southampton Railway

It is often difficult to picture the social and commercial conditions in most parts of England at the beginning of the railway age. In many places the gradual improvement in communications has entirely changed the face and heart of the country, to such an extent, indeed, as to make almost incredible to people living at the present time the state of isolation and lack of any development that prevailed 140 years ago. Some towns, like Crewe, were creations of the railway age; others were changed almost beyond recognition, and among these latter there is no more outstanding case than that of Southampton. It needs no more than a glance at the map to appreciate the well-nigh unique geographical situation of the town; but up to the year 1830 that situation had not been exploited to any extent, and it was then no more than a sleepy market town, far eclipsed in importance as a seaport by Poole on the one hand and Portsmouth on the other. As a naval base, then as now, Portsmouth was second to none.

Such being the case it is surprising that when railway promoters sought a route south-westwards from London to the coast they should have chosen Southampton as their coastal terminus rather than Portsmouth. In one respect the case was somewhat analogous to that of the South Eastern Railway. At Southampton no more than at Dover there was no trade to be attracted to rail transport; but it was, in fact, an even less obvious place for a terminus of a trunk railway. Dover was an established packet station and mail port. Southampton was neither. But its choice for a railway project had an older and more subtle origin. The English Channel was from time immemorial a difficult place for navigation in the days of sail, and the hazards experienced by shipping during the Napoleonic wars had only accentuated the conditions. There had been talk of making a canal for sea-going ships from Portsmouth to London—in fact things had progressed to the stage of a detailed survey of the route under the supervision of Sir John Rennie. The deep inlet of Southampton Water had suggested itself as the starting point of the canal, and then came the earliest railways—in each case connecting a seaport with an inland centre of commercial and industrial activity: Stockton-on-Tees, with Darlington and the Bishop Auckland coalfield; Liverpool with Manchester.

In one respect the coming of the railway age took the civil engineering profession by surprise. It was one thing for an enginewright of humble birth to build, by rule of thumb, these lumbering and inefficient steam locomotives; but when there were railway promoters who would entrust a man like George Stephenson with the construction of the railway itself things were going a little too far for the established professional civil engineers. They had a foretaste of what was to come with the Stockton and Darlington. Stephenson's success there could be attributed to local sentiment, and to the immense influence of Joseph Pease. But when the time came for the Liverpool & Manchester Railway to be projected the full strength of the professional opposition was massed against Stephenson. When Rennie had surveyed the route of the south-western canal he employed an engineer named Francis Giles to do the detail work. Giles happened to be a fluent speaker—unlike George Stephenson—and when Rennie was organising the opposition to Stephenson's route for the Liverpool and Manchester Railway he saw to it that Giles was called as a witness. In due course the Parliamentary Committee battle centred upon the crossing of Chat Moss, and on this subject Giles made some remarks that were to recoil on him like a boomerang in later years. He said:

> "No engineer in his senses would go through Chat Moss if he wanted to make a railroad from Liverpool to Manchester. In my judgment a railroad certainly cannot be safely made over Chat Moss without going to the bottom of the Moss. The soil ought all to be taken out, undoubtedly; in doing which, it will not be practicable to approach each end of the cutting, as you make it, with the carriages. No carriages would stand upon the Moss short of the bottom."

Giles went on to add that the crossing of the Moss would cost at least £270,000, whereas Stephenson had allowed no more than £400,000 for the whole line, including the laying of the permanent way. I need not enlarge here upon how Rennie and all the rest eventually failed to dislodge Stephenson, nor upon the difficulties he actually encountered in crossing Chat Moss. But although the situation at one stage appeared so desperate as to lead to a Board Meeting on the Moss itself, to decide whether to go on or not, the section of line over Chat Moss eventually cost £28,000, and this figure remained very clearly in the minds of many railway shareholders in Manchester.

Although Southampton was a place of very small significance at the time, support for a railway to London grew steadily, and a first meeting took place as early as 1831. It was an ambitious project, consisting not only of a main line between London and Southampton, but the construction of docks on Southampton Water and a 'branch' to Bath and Bristol. This branch was to be no mere offshoot from the main line, but diverging at Basingstoke it was to pass through Newbury, Hungerford, Devizes, and Trowbridge. These were all flourishing centres of population, by the standards of the day; in fact the 'branch' looked like bringing in far more traffic than the main line, which beyond Basingstoke served only Winchester on its way to Southampton. One feels that the interested parties in Southampton made a tactical error in the formulation of their excellent project. Cities of the status of Bath and Bristol would not look favourably upon a railway which placed them on a branch of a concern fostered in Southampton. Little support was forthcoming for the branch, and the

Bill eventually went to Parliament in 1834 for nothing more than the main line. With the support of the naval authorities, and certain shipping interests it encountered little opposition, and the Act was obtained in July of the same year.

Francis Giles was appointed engineer. When the line was still a proposal his estimates of the costs of construction were so moderate as to encourage many railway investors in Lancashire to support the scheme. In Liverpool and Manchester he was remembered as the man who had greatly over-estimated the difficulty and cost of crossing Chat Moss. He was regarded then as a very cautious and 'safe' man where railway estimates were concerned, and the moderate figure he quoted for the Southampton line probably influenced many hard-headed Lancastrians towards investing in it. Certain Scottish interests followed, and no difficulty was experienced in raising the authorised capital of £1 million. Fully half this amount came from Lancashire. Giles's estimate for the construction was between £800,000 and £900,000, for roughly 78 miles of line, compared to Stephenson's £400,000 for the 31 miles of the Liverpool and Manchester Railway. Considering that the Southampton line was to be carried through easy country, that there were not expected to be any excavations in rock, and no equivalent of Chat Moss the price seemed reasonable enough, and the London & Southampton Railway entered upon its corporate existence in high heart.

Francis Giles was then a civil engineer of 25 years standing, but in setting about the construction of the Southampton line he soon got into serious difficulties. Although he had been so critical of Stephenson at the time of the Parliamentary Committee on the Liverpool & Manchester Railway he succumbed to the very pitfalls for which Stephenson had been derided 5 years earlier. In scheming out the Liverpool and Manchester line Stephenson had purposely avoided finalising many points of detail, so far as bridges and small works were concerned, so that he could have a free hand in dealing with contractors as circumstances arose. His opponents seized upon such lack of detail as evidence that Stephenson did not know what he was about. But as things turned out, on a relatively small railway, with the work of supervision divided between three very competent resident engineers, Stephenson was able to get through. His 'free and easy' methods told heavily against him when it came to the building of the Grand Junction Railway, and at the same time Giles was failing just as completely on the Southampton line. Then the shareholders discovered to their mortification how it was that Giles had been able to quote so moderate a price for the construction of the railway.

In the 25 years of his practising as an engineer, in a considerable variety of works, he had come to know many contractors—principally local men in the south of England. Many of these were quite 'small' men, and with little in the way of establishment charges to cover they could quote low prices for specific works. The route of the Southampton railway was a splendid one, involving an almost perfect alignment and easy gradients.

But to obtain this state of affairs some very heavy earthworks were involved: unusually high embankments, deep cuttings, and some long tunnels in the chalk southwest of Basingstoke. In building such a railway, even though it ran through country that did not present any obvious hazards, the very volume of earth that had to be moved might have suggested to an experienced engineer the desirability of having a substantial reserve for contingencies; but Giles let his contracts to small men, in 'penny numbers' as it were, and the results as a whole were disastrous. A few did their work without incident or trouble; but where a local contractor with little capital or credit ran into difficulties, and was faced with using more men, and for much longer than he had anticipated he failed outright, leaving himself bankrupt and the railway company with an unfinished contract on their hands. These men had neither the experience nor the resources to deal with anything unexpected or novel, and if dangerous conditions developed the work just came to a stop.

The prolongation of the constructional work became a source of great anxiety to the directors, and was infuriating to the shareholders. Odium was heaped upon Giles. The original Act had given power to borrow £330,000 by loan, in addition to the authorized capital of £1,000,000. But the extra amount proved insufficient, and in 1837 a second Act was passed increasing the capital stock by £400,000 with authority to borrow a further £130,000. The shares slumped, and it was then that the Lancashire section of the shareholders took action. Among themselves they formed a committee, which demanded an examination of the accounts and the estimates, and a thorough enquiry into the state of the Company as a whole. Giles resigned, and at the strong instigation of the Lancashire party Joseph Locke was appointed engineer. At that time Locke stood second only to Robert Stephenson in status as a railway engineer, even including the brilliant though erratic Brunel. He had taken over from George Stephenson on the Grand Junction Railway, when Stephenson was getting into rather similar difficulties to those which beset Giles, and his rapid completion of the line from Birmingham through Stafford and Crewe to its junction with the Liverpool & Manchester at Newton-le-Willows had made a very deep impression upon the railway investors of Lancashire. In their eyes Locke was the only man for the job of getting the Southampton line completed.

In another respect too the year 1837 was a turning point in the history of the line that was soon to become the London & South Western. William James Chaplin, of the prosperous and well-established firm of road hauliers, Chaplin and Horne, had watched the inception of railways with great interest. Viewing the success of the Stockton & Darlington, the Liverpool & Manchester, and then the Grand Junction he realized that the completion of the line between London and Southampton would cut seriously into the family business. But instead of entering upon a diehard opposition, and doing all he could to harry and hinder the new form of transport he decided, even when construction and finances of the

Southampton railway were in so parlous a state, to put his whole weight behind it. He sold the greater part of his interests in the firm of Chaplin and Horne, and invested heavily in the railway. His action was electrifying. His wide business experience was immediately made available to the company; his financial backing had an immediate effect, and coming at the same time as the change of engineer the whole situation was transformed. But although things were very quickly put on to a sound financial basis the position, as finally revealed to the proprietors, was depressing in the extreme, so far as the prospects of early dividends were concerned.

Locke went about things with his usual immense energy. Although he was then no more than 32 years of age the successful completion of the Grand Junction main line was behind him, and he applied the same methods to the London & Southampton. Nothing was left to the discretion or whim of a contractor. Precise specifications were drawn up for every detail of the work still outstanding—and there was a great deal!—and the horrified shareholders were told that it would probably cost another £1,700,000! Even the entry of Chaplin and Locke into the ranks of the company could not offset such a shock as this, and the only way the money could be raised was by selling the £50 shares of the new capital at no more than £25. But now at last there was reasonable hope that the estimates would prove accurate, and there would be no more calls for money before the trains commenced to run. With Locke as engineer all the contractors knew exactly where they stood. His specifications were so precise as to leave no doubt, and with new and experienced firms on the job, the work went on steadily. It was supremely fortunate that the business acumen of Locke was available in the case of one particular contract, otherwise disaster might once again have overtaken the company.

In 1839 a further Act of Parliament had authorized a short branch from Bishopstoke, now Eastleigh, to Gosport on the western side of Portsmouth Harbour. In view of the importance of Portsmouth it is surprising that its first railway communication with London was established by the back door, as it were, involving the use of the ferry across the harbour to reach the railway station. But the authorization of the branch from Bishopstoke led to another important event in the history of the Company. The people of Portsmouth objected to being served by a branch of a railway named 'London & Southampton', and so in the same Act by which the branch was authorized the name was changed to 'London & South Western Railway'. The line never operated throughout under the original name, because it had not been completed beyond Basingstoke in July 1839. Nevertheless, for some time afterwards the line continued to be referred to as the 'London & Southampton'. The original London terminus was at Nine Elms, and the first section to be opened extended to Woking—originally known as Woking Common. This commenced working in 1838. The extension to Basingstoke was opened just over a year later.

Locke brought in that great contractor Thomas Brassey, and the combination of these two men produced some of the finest railway civil engineering in Western Europe. Brassey has been termed the 'Navvy King', yet anyone less like the swash-buckling, son-of-a-gun type of overseer would be hard to imagine. He was descended from a very old English family; and although no very great wealth was attached to his inheritance its longevity had bred that innate culture and quality that belonged to an English country gentleman of the old school. His contracts were sancrosanct. If anything went wrong he made it a point of honour to put things right, whatever it might cost; and the quality of his work was always of the very finest. Brassey established a reputation that spread far beyond this country, and in several important overseas projects where Locke was the engineer Brassey was the contractor. On the Southampton line he had the section between Basingstoke and Winchester which included the highest embankments and all the tunnels, and as expected he completed the work comfortably before the stipulated contract time.

Brassey was also contractor for the Gosport branch. One would not have thought there would have been any undue difficulty in this line of no more than 15 miles; but nearing Fareham the line, in pursuing the straight course characteristic of so many of the early railways, cut through a ridge extending westwards from Ports Down to the Meon Valley, and here there was a tunnel half a mile long. Here Brassey encountered a soil that defied all theory. In dry weather it was hard enough to need blasting, yet after rain it became little better than very fluid mud. Nothing remained stable. Retaining walls were built to contain the cutting slopes in the approaches to the tunnel, but in wet weather the soil just spewed over the parapets and on to the rails. It was bad enough in the open, but the greatest apprehension was felt for the stability of the tunnel. A small contractor would have given up the task and cut his losses. But Brassey and his men toiled on trying one experiment after another. It was still early in his great career as a railway contractor, and the prolongation of the work, and the replacements to which he had recourse nearly made him bankrupt. Then, when it was at last finished, Locke took fright and closed the line temporarily after no more than four days running. It was closed from December 2, 1841, until February 7, 1842.

Before the public opening of the branch the works had been closely examined by Sir Frederick Smith, Chief Inspecting Officer of the Board of Trade. He, of course, was aware of all the trouble encountered in the construction of that part of the line, and after referring to these in his report to the President of the Board of Trade he went on to make a very clear statement of the extent of the Government responsibility as a result of the inspection. While an inspector could refuse to sanction the opening of a line of railway the fact that a line had been passed did not mean that the Board of Trade took responsibility for the integrity of the works. Evidently Sir Frederick made his inspection of Fareham tunnel and the approaches on a good day; but his reference to it in the report is guarded in the extreme:

"I have not observed any cause for apprehension in respect of this tunnel in my present inspection of it, but in my former report I observed that the Lords of the Council (The Board of Trade) could take no responsibility in such work as tunnels, even under ordinary and favourable circumstances, as their officials have no knowledge of the efficiency of the sectional strength of the sustaining arches and side walls and of the inverts, or of the quality of the work of which they are composed.

The force of this observation applies much more strongly in such a case as the present where the work had already given evidence that it is exposed to great and sudden pressure and, therefore, the whole responsibility of using this tunnel must rest with the directors of the company, for they have had the means, by frequent personal inspection and by reports of their engineer, of arriving at a full knowledge of all the circumstances connected with this work and whether, if its form has undergone any change, that change has been to such an extent as to afford any grounds of apprehension for the safety of the work."

This was certainly an elegantly worded way of washing one's hands of the whole thing. The responsibility was placed fairly and squarely upon Locke, and one cannot blame him for being unduly cautious. Although there is no record of any subsequent mishap to a train on account of the extraordinary geological conditions at this location, the tunnel and its approaches proved a continuous anxiety and expense to the London & South Western Railway and in 1904 a deviation was built to avoid the tunnel altogether.

Reverting to the London–Southampton main line, the heavy earthworks have already been mentioned. In hilly country these characteristics of the work provided some magnificently broad vistas across the countryside. Amid the rich woodlands and open common land of West Surrey, and the rolling downs of Hampshire the London & Southampton is indeed one of the most beautiful railways in England, south of Derby. When my parents were living in Reading we used to enter upon South Western metals at Basingstoke when bound for holidays at Southsea or Bournemouth, and I can remember most vividly today what a tremendous impression the great earthworks made upon me, as a small boy. We joined the South Western train at Basingstoke, and were soon traversing the high embankments between Battledown Junction and the summit of the line at Litchfield tunnel. Then came the downhill run through the chalk, in deep cuttings the sides of which seemed well-nigh vertical. Again tunnels always gave a feeling of awe to me as a young traveller, and to emerge at Micheldever, and to see a wide expanse of level ground to left of the railway cut out of the gleaming white hillside immediately we struck daylight was always exciting. On the far side of this level ground, looking rather forlorn, was a line of old carriages, presumably condemned and awaiting disposal or scrapping. Nevertheless they always showed up well, with their orange-yellow upper panels prominent against the white background of the chalk.

After Micheldever, in preserving the continuously descending gradient of 1 in 250 the railway is on embankment and generally above the level of the countryside, and the prospects to both left and right of the line are exceedingly fine. On this magnificent racing stretch, where the Drummond 'paddleboat' 4-6-0s used regularly to knock up speeds of 80 m.p.h., the line is virtually straight from Litchfield tunnel to Shawford Junction, below Winchester. It has often crossed my mind in recent years that if the Southern had ever thought of challenging *Mallard's* world record this would have been the place to do it. But a railway however safe and suitable for 80 or even 90 m.p.h. can be quite different when speed climbs into the hundreds. It is not merely a question of straightness in alignment, and one has only to see the amount of rebuilding that has been necessary on the West Coast main line to make the track suitable for regular 100 m.p.h. running by the new electric locomotives to realize the preparation that must be made for high speed.

The section of the London & Southampton Railway south-west of Basingstoke is an enduring monument to Locke. The earthworks were very heavy to maintain that even gradient in hilly country, and one could well have imagined that the cost would have been high. The Southampton line, like the Great Western and the London & Birmingham belongs to that early period in railway history when it was believed that steam locomotives could not tackle any but the easiest of gradients. But the actual cost of construction, although more than double the original estimate prepared by the incompetent Giles, worked out at about £27,000 per mile. This was by no means an extravagant figure, and in other respects the Southampton line was built most economically. In his book 'History of the English Railway' published in 1851, John Francis quotes comparative figures for costs, other than those of actual construction, as follows:

COST IN £1 PER MILE

Railway	Law, Engineering Direction	Parliamentary	Land and Compensation
London and Birmingham ..	1,500	650	6,300
Great Western	2,500	1,000	6,300
London and Brighton	1,800	3,000	8,000
London and Southampton ..	900	650	4,000

The Southampton was thus, on every count, the cheapest of them all.

There was some criticism that in the interests of economy the London terminus had been placed too far out from the centre of affairs. A contemporary writer described Nine Elms as 'a low swampy district, occasionally overflowed by the Thames. Its osier beds, pollards, windmills and the river give it a Dutch effect, but the ground is fast becoming occupied with buildings, and losing its peculiar character'. The railway authorities made lavish provision for omnibuses to meet the trains, and there was in addition a service of river 'taxis' running in connection with each arrival.

One fears however that the speed of the river service was somewhat exaggerated in the advertisement: 'Passengers will be conveyed in small steamboats and landed *at any point* between Vauxhall and London Bridge *within a few minutes* of their arrival at the station. The two sets of italics are mine, for it would take a modern speedboat all its time to reach London Bridge 'in a few minutes' from Nine Elms, even if going non-stop! Nevertheless, although Nine Elms station lay on the south bank of the Thames the South Western management drew an interesting and amusing comparison between their situation, and those of the other main line termini in relation to the centres of business and social life in London thus:

COMPARATIVE DISTANCES IN MILES

From	Royal Exchange	Charing Cross
Euston	3·2	1·8
Paddington ..	4·3	2·75
Nine Elms	3·1	1·95

By this mode of reckoning there was little in it between Nine Elms and Euston, and the Southampton terminus was far more conveniently sited than Paddington!

At the Hampshire end of the line the straight alignment continued with little deviation to the shores of Southampton Water. This is a very gentle reverse curve taking the line slightly to the east between Winchester and Shawford. Today it might appear as though this had been done to join up with the Didcot, Newbury & Southampton line, which converges at Shawford Junction; but this connection was made many years later. The station at Eastleigh was originally named Bishopstoke, and as such became the junction for the Company's first branch line, that to Salisbury; and the terminus at Southampton was naturally sited near to the docks. At the time the line was built there was evidently no intention of providing for any westward extension through the New Forest. When the extension came to be made it was connected to the original line at Northam Junction by a very sharp curve which has been a bugbear in the operation of the Bournemouth service ever since. It only remains to add that the London & Southampton line was opened throughout on May 11, 1840.

II

Chaplin and the Gauge War

In studying the exciting times of the Gauge War it is always interesting to try and put oneself into the position of the various protagonists. The Great Western case is well known; and Brunel's good fortune in having such astute and loyal associates as Russell, Saunders and Gooch is widely appreciated. Equally it is known that the northern companies were out to damn the broad gauge at any price, and while Locke, Robert Stephenson and other engineers argued logically enough on the grounds of a *fait accompli*, in that there was a far greater mileage of narrow than broad gauge track in existence, the railway politicians like Hudson and Mark Huish used every wile in their respective armouries. The London and South Western case was rather different, and at the outset there was every sign that Chaplin would have been quite ready to settle down to a peaceful co-existence, and indeed to cooperate with the Great Western in providing an adequate railway network in the south and west of England.

It must not be forgotten that Chaplin was primarily a carrier. He was not a financier; not an astute draper caught in the maelstrom of railway speculation, nor did he nurse any dreams of a gigantic project of railway empire building. He was interested in the straightforward business of transportation, and all his early plans were based upon trade at the two extremities of the original main line. There is ample evidence in those early days of railways that the minds of most men in the industry were directed towards communication with London. In some ways this was natural enough, because then as now the Capital represented by far and away the greatest centre of population. London was the grand clearing house of trade, and at that time the London docks were the largest in the world. But Chaplin regarded Southampton as an equally important focus point of railway activity. The opening of the line saw the immediate transference of the Indian, South African, and West Indian mails from Falmouth to Southampton, and trade began to flow through the port in unprecedented volume. Chaplin began to visualize the Southampton of the future as one of the greatest ports in the country, and while he naturally paid every regard to the development of the traffic to and from London he also began to look farther afield.

The immediate opening up of trade through the port of Southampton made Chaplin look towards connection with the Midlands and the North. In the year 1843 the chain of once-independent railways between Bristol and Birmingham was nearing completion. This was regarded as of the greatest importance, because it would provide a route to the north that was quite independent of London. Furthermore, there was a useful connecting link from the south-east, in the form of the Cheltenham and

Great Western Union Railway, passing through Stroud and the Cotswolds to join the G.W.R. main line at Swindon. This of course was broad gauge, and had in fact been purchased outright by the Great Western in 1843. As yet the Birmingham and Gloucester was an independent line, and narrow gauge, and while the South Western people were at first most punctilious in avoiding any suggestion of trespassing into Great Western territory there is no doubt that eyes were being cast upon Swindon, and upon ways of bridging the gap between that town and their own line at Basingstoke.

But towards the end of 1843 events began to press upon the South Western, from a town lying almost on the direct line from Basingstoke to Swindon, namely Newbury. This historic old town had seen two fierce battles between Cavaliers and Roundheads in the Civil War, and while Newbury formed the focus point of a first encounter between the Great Western and the South Western in the Gauge War; skirmish though it was it did serve to rip the veneer of diplomacy from the relations between the two companies, and reveal them as the out-and-out rivals they were to be for many years afterwards. The first shots in the 'Third Battle of Newbury' were fired when a deputation from the town waited upon Chaplin to discuss the possibility of a railway connection. It was known that they were also negotiating with the Great Western, and the latter project could mean only one thing—connection towards London. Chaplin felt that so far as Newbury itself was concerned the interests of the town lay much more with the Great Western than with the South Western; the distance to London would be much shorter than by a route via Basingstoke, and that this attempted flirtation with the South Western was no more than a means of obtaining better terms from Paddington. Because of this Chaplin turned it down flat.

On further reflection however the South Western management began to see the broader aspects of the proposed line from Basingstoke to Newbury, particularly when it was learned that the Great Western proposal to meet the wishes of the town was to be nothing more than a short branch line from Pangbourne. This latter would follow the pattern of other and subsequent Great Western offshoots from the main line, such as Cholsey to Wallingford; Uffington to Faringdon, and Dauntsey to Malmesbury. The line from Pangbourne to Newbury would have no strategic value whatever to the railway network of the country as a whole, and unless express trains were to be stopped at Pangbourne—which was most unlikely!—the service to and from Reading would be slow. In the South Western proposals greater emphasis was placed upon the connection with Southampton. It was pointed out, for example, that coal coming by sea to Southampton and conveyed thence by rail could be sold in Newbury at 30s. a ton, compared to the existing price of 40s. And with a line from Basingstoke to Newbury in operation the South Western would be well launched on the way to Swindon and eventual connection with the line to Birmingham.

When the South Western submitted a Bill to Parliament in 1844 for the line from Basingstoke to Newbury the fat was fairly in the fire. Charles Russell, the celebrated Chairman of the Great Western, took up a very pained attitude, as much to the citizens of Newbury as to the London & South Western Railway. He pointed out that the Great Western had always intended to make the connection from Pangbourne, and had in fact drawn up plans in 1838 and again in 1840. He was however in some difficulty to explain why his Company had so far done nothing about it! Things were made still worse when the Parliamentary Committee of 1844 unanimously turned down the Great Western proposal, and again unanimously accepted the South Western one. The House of Commons passed the Bill by a large majority, but it came to grief in the House of Lords. In reversing the decision of the Commons it was pointed out that so far as Newbury itself was concerned it would be much cheaper to make the connection to Pangbourne than to Basingstoke; but in referring to the broader aspects of the South Western scheme the Committee of four peers who examined both projects made this rather extraordinary statement:

> "Further, as regards the interests of the country at large they are of the opinion that the communication by railway between the north of England and the towns of Southampton, Portsmouth etc., and the southern coast will be hereafter more usefully effected by the contemplated lines in connection with Pangbourne than by an extension of the Basingstoke and Newbury line to Swindon."

On the face of it one might indeed ask how on earth a short branch line from Pangbourne to Newbury would facilitate connection between Southampton and the Midlands! But there is no doubt that after the first shock of the South Western proposals the Great Western had done some fairly intense lobbying, and by the time they came to consider the Basingstoke and Newbury proposal the House of Lords Committee was aware of the broader strategy being developed by the Great Western, and they turned the South Western scheme down in the light of Great Western plans that had not yet been publicly revealed. The immediate outcome was, of course, that with the end of the Parliamentary session of 1844 the town of Newbury was no nearer to getting a railway. Parliament had scarcely risen however before Charles Russell announced the Great Western proposal that eventually became the Berks & Hants Line, namely a two-pronged branch from Reading—the 'Berks' section running up the Kennet valley to Newbury, and the 'Hants' section running through Mortimer and Bramley to a junction with the South Western at Basingstoke. Thus despite the comments of the Lords' Committee the 'contemplated lines' had no connection with Pangbourne at all!

The Great Western idea of a north to south connection lay clearly via Basingstoke, Reading, Didcot and Oxford; and in outlining proposals for the 'Berks & Hants' Line Russell added that to complete the scheme it would involve building 50 miles of further line to join up with the London & Birmingham, and with the Midland at Rugby. A glance at the map is enough to show that between Basingstoke and Didcot the route is reasonably direct. Although it made use of some 17 miles of the Great Western main line the direction of the latter in the Upper Thames valley is more northerly than west. Nevertheless the South Western saw grounds for opposition in that Newbury was located at the end of a branch line, whereas in the rival scheme they put forward, to go through from Basingstoke to Didcot, Newbury would be situated on a main artery of traffic. The mileage between Basingstoke and Didcot by either route would have been much the same. But all this 'cut and thrust' business, in which a Hudson or a Huish would have revelled, was not all to the

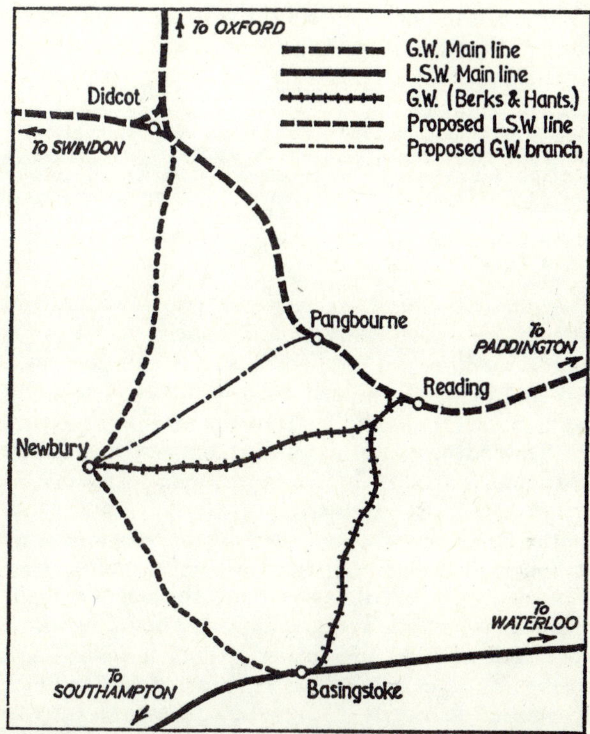

liking of Chaplin, who was above all anxious to get on with the job of transportation; and while the rival proposals for the lines between Basingstoke and Didcot were in no more than Parliamentary stages, in the first weeks of 1845, a meeting was arranged between representatives of the Great Western, and the London and South Western to discuss the whole question of future railway development in the south-west of England.

Apparently this meeting was on the most cordial terms. The South Western people were anxious to avoid all the trouble and expense of costly Parliamentary warfare, while the Great Western, realizing by that time that they would soon have a full-scale 'war' on their hands north of Oxford and Gloucester were ready to secure peaceful co-existence with the narrow gauge neighbours on their southern flanks. The immediate terms of agreement were that the South Western would withdraw its opposition to the Berks & Hants project, in return for which the Great Western would relinquish its lease of the Southampton and Dorchester line. Furthermore the South Western undertook to promote no competing lines west of Salisbury or Dorchester. This would have left the Great Western and its broad gauge associates in absolute possession in the West of England. From this it would seem that the South Western had received by far the worst of the deal, and speaking at the half-yearly meeting of the L.S.W.R. on February 13, 1845, Chaplin said:

> "We might have driven a harder bargain with the Great Western Company, but you may generally observe that any hard bargain is a bad bargain. I do not know what the Great Western feel, but I am sorry that we had not more to give them. They have entered into friendly relations towards us with a good grace, and it is our duty to observe good faith with them. We have arranged that if the requirements of the country generally should, at any future period, show that it ought to be accommodated with railway communication, then we go hand-in-hand with the Great Western to hear what these requirements are and mutually make the extensions under the sanction of the Board of Trade."

The idea of the two companies working 'hand-in-hand', in such close harmony during the stormy railway atmosphere of the years from 1845 onwards sounds a trifle naïve; and the peaceful situation that it envisages was wrecked in less than eighteen months. Instead of going amicably 'hand-in-hand' with the South Western the Great Western, entirely on its own, put forward a bill for extending the Berks & Hants line from Hungerford to join the Wilts & Somerset line at Westbury. Chaplin was furious, though the Great Western argued that this extension was a domestic matter of their own, and outside the scope of the agreement. Seeing that the Berks & Hants itself had been authorized as an express result of the G.W.R.–L.S.W.R. agreement, this argument did not carry much weight with the South Western Board. They drew the attention of the Board of Trade to what they called a breach of the agreement; but while admitting the force of the South Western contention that august body neatly washed its hands of the whole affair, and declined to take any positive action. It was then Russell's turn to be annoyed, and he accused Chaplin of 'an unexampled breach of faith'. The Agreement of 1845 was now little more than 'a scrap of paper', and from the autumn of 1846 the gloves were off in earnest.

In my previous book 'The Great Western Railway in the 19th Century' I have told of the repeated attempts made by Paddington to secure a direct route to Exeter, short-circuiting the long detour via Swindon, Bath and Bristol, and how the shareholders of the Bristol & Exeter, in adopting a very narrow-minded outlook, did more even than the London and South Western Railway to secure the rejection of the 'Exeter Great

Western' Bill in 1846. Although in the present book I am looking at things from the South Western angle one must admit that the proposal would have made a splendid line, serving Frome, Yeovil, Crewkerne, and Honiton en route to the west. It is true that Taunton would have been left 'out in the cold' as it were, on the old roundabout route; but the 'Exeter & Great Western' as it was originally planned by Brunel, would have made things much easier for the re-shaping process now being so painfully undertaken on British Railways.

It is worth dwelling on this very important event; for although it could be considered as a purely Great Western matter, seeing that it was the action of the Bristol & Exeter shareholders that finally and decisively tipped the scales, it was nevertheless a vital point in London & South Western history. Had the Exeter Great Western been authorized its construction would virtually have sealed off the West of England beyond the Wilts, Somerset & Weymouth line. All the independent railways beyond Exeter would eventually have fallen into Great Western hands, and it is most likely that Salisbury and Dorchester would have marked the westward extremities of the London & South Western. Two years later the Great Western succeeded in getting authorized the lines that came to make up their shortened route to the west, via Castle Cary and Langport. But the powers conferred by Parliament were allowed to lapse, through lack of funds to construct the line, and it was not until 1906 that this route was actually completed. But even if these lines had been built in 1848, or shortly after, they would not have blocked the South Western advance to Exeter. They took the line via Taunton, and all the country west of Yeovil was still left wide open.

Thus it was the spring of 1846 that proved an outstanding milestone in South Western history, a point that decided whether the company was to be a compact unit, confined in its westward extent to the countries of Hampshire, Dorset and the south-east corner of Wiltshire, or instead to be a long-drawn-out, straggling concern extending to Plymouth and North Cornwall, and a perpetual thorn in the side of the Great Western. There is however no doubt that in the mind of Charles Saunders—a most upright and straightforward man—the Great Western were the injured party in the breaking up of the Agreement of March 1845. The suspicions of Paddington had been aroused in no more than a few months after the signing, when Joseph Locke was giving evidence before the Gauge Commision. In addition to being Engineer of the London & South Western Railway Locke was M.P. for Honiton, and he had been active in the investigation of railways in the south-west of England—not as yet in direct association with the L.S.W.R. On August 8, 1845, the Commissioners had asked:

> "Suppose that the narrow-gauge lines, which you have projected in the district of country between the South Western and the Great Western, were not to be formed, but the portions were to be made from Chippenham to Yeovil, would it not be an evil to compel the Great Western to change their gauge at Chippenham or Corsham, and to transfer their passengers from the narrow-gauge carriages at Bridport and Trowbridge?"

Locke replied:

> "There is no doubt, if you say that the traffic of this district of country, including Exeter and Sherborne, is always to be taken round by the Great Western Railway, and is not to have the benefit of the shorter railway, which is projected with a chance of its being carried out, it would be an evil to have a change of gauge; but it would be better to keep a uniform gauge with the line which has been already projected, by Salisbury and Yeovil, to Exeter; for the crossing of that line by lines of a different gauge would be more inconvenient to the public than the change that I am proposing to be made at Corsham; and for this reason, the people from Weymouth and Dorchester and Yeovil, in addition to those from Exeter, have an opportunity of getting to London 20 miles shorter than by going round Corsham; and to those people it would be a hardship if they were drawn round 20 miles further, simply because this railway was made on the wide gauge instead of the narrow."

The critical phrase is clearly:

> ". . . the line which has already been projected, by Salisbury and Yeovil to Exeter."

Apparently the news of this piece of evidence from Locke did not reach the Great Western officers immediately, or alternatively the significance was not at first fully appreciated by them. The main body of their evidence was given between October 17 and 25, when Gooch, Seymour Clarke, Saunders and Brunel appeared before the Commissioners. None of them took it up, but on November 1st 1845, Mr. Thomas Whitaker, Surveyor of Bridges to the County of Devon, and Surveyor to the City of Exeter was called as a witness, and he revealed himself as engineer to a proposed railway from Exeter to Yeovil exactly along the route eventually taken by the L.S.W.R. main line. He had reckoned upon a direct end-on connection with the South Western at Yeovil, thereby envisaging an extension of that system from Salisbury. But the most interesting part of this project was that there was to be no connection with the broad gauge at Exeter. This line was to have a station in the centre of the city, and then on the way to link up with a project known as the Cornwall Central it would cross the Bristol & Exeter somewhere near St. Davids Station on a viaduct 40 or 50 feet high. Whitaker revealed also that he had been closely associated with Locke in this project, and stated that it was supported by 'the landowners upon the line, nearly the whole of the way through; people resident in the towns, who want a line of railway in that neighbourhood: I believe it is well supported; we have gone through the whole district without any difficulty or opposition from any landowner'.

Clearly there was some very strong opposition to the Great Western brewing down in South East Devon, and it was after digesting this piece of evidence, in conjunction with what Locke had previously said, that Charles Saunders asked to be heard again. Then on November 22, 1845, he stated before the Commissioners:

> "I observe, with reference to some evidence given before this Commission by Mr. Locke, that the South Western Railway Company have it in agitation to make lines by Salisbury through Yeovil to Exeter. He refers to an agreement that was made last year between the two companies under the sanction of the Board of Trade. That agreement specifically undertakes, in consequence of the Great Western Company

having given up the line from Dorchester to Southampton into the hands of the South Western, that no line beyond Salisbury and Dorchester is to be carried on by them, it being left to the Great Western Railway Company to fill up the district beyond the Wilts & Somerset for the accommodation of the public, a junction of the Wilts & Somerset being formed with their line at Salisbury. Under the same agreement it was arranged also, with the sanction of the Board of Trade, that from Basingstoke to Salisbury, or from Basingstoke to Portsmouth, or in that direction, a line should not be undertaken from the Berks & Hants Railway by the Great Western Railway Company, but should be left entirely to the South Western Railway Company. Whatever steps may now be taken by the South Western Railway Company to violate that agreement must be brought before a Committee to be considered in Parliament during the next year. We wish it to be understood by the Gauge Commissioners specifically that those were the conditions of the agreement, and that the agreement is in writing, and that the Board of Trade have recently refused to declare that the South Western Railway Company are justified in proceeding beyond Salisbury towards Exeter, while it is well known that, instead of the Great Western Railway seeking to prevent any more direct communication to Exeter, they are themselves forming that which it was understood was to be formed by them. I give this evidence in consequence of what has been stated by Mr. Locke before the Gauge Commissioners, which is calculated to leave the impression on their minds that it was an open question, whether the South Western Company were to carry their lines beyond Salisbury and Dorchester or not."

The Commissioners then asked:

"Did not Mr. Locke in that evidence state specifically that the South Western Company were not the parties that were enganged in that scheme?"

Saunders replied:

"He stated in that evidence, if I remember rightly, that he was pressing the South Western Railway Company to be parties to it; that he had disapproved of the agreement when it was made; that he was himself the engineer of a line for one of the purposes from which they were prevented acting; but it is their own responsibility in breaking that engagement. With reference to the evidence of Mr. Locke, this evidence was previous to a decision being come to by the Board of Trade; but the arrangement of which I speak has been made since the answer of the Board of Trade. What I wish to state to the Commissioners in observation upon this answer is, that in the first place there was no question whatever about the preamble of the Wilts & Somerset Bill being passed upon the condition that we were not to oppose a South Western direct line. What was done in the House of Lords was this: while that Bill was before the Committee of the Lords they required a declaration from us that the line so made should not prevent a direct line being made to Exeter. This was the condition, and we were willing to do it; they had themselves urged that the country should be provided with a railway. The difficulty, as we told them, was that we were not at that time prepared to go further. The promise that we would not prevent a direct line being made was given immediately in the Lords, for it was always intended by the Great Western Company that the Wilts & Somerset should form part of the direct line towards Exeter. The agreement between the two Companies was not that the South Western Company should never, under any circumstances, go 'beyond Salisbury or beyond Dorchester' but that they should not go, 'except under such a completely altered state of circumstances as should induce the Board of Trade to say that the principles which guided them in the decision of last year were no longer applicable to the case'. Those are the words of the agreement. It was left to the Board of Trade to say whether there had been such a completely altered state of circumstances. The Board of Trade have refused to say that there is such a completely altered state of circumstances and the South Western Company have written a letter, in consequence of that, to say that they take upon themselves the responsibility of breaking the agreement made in January last, while, at the same time, they keep possession of the Southampton & Dorchester line transferred to them, the price paid by us for the other conditions of arrangement."

Before the agreement of 1845 it seems that the South Western had been actively considering some westward extension from Salisbury, and when Locke went some way towards revealing the intention it is to be supposed that Chaplin and the L.S.W.R. had confidently assumed this would be one of the projects—namely the opening up of the country west of Yeovil—on which the two companies would go 'hand in hand' to the Board of Trade. Saunders clearly took a much more serious view; but as the Agreement specifically mentioned Basingstoke he seems genuinely to have felt free to project an extension of the Berks & Hants westward from Hungerford without consulting the South Western. Saunders was a man whose word was his bond. Even Huish had to admit that! But unfortunately the South Western people thought otherwise, and on the maxim of what is sauce for the goose is also sauce for the gander they projected their own line west of Basingstoke.

In this period of suspicion and uncertainty, before the open breach between the two companies, it is interesting to study Chaplin's evidence before the Gauge Commissioners. It was unusual in containing some definite expression of transport policy. He admitted to feeling some regret at first that the South Western had not adopted the broad gauge but he added:

> "I think the principle of managing railways is altering. We used to think it was a bad thing to increase the number of our trains; I think now, every one must feel, that to make more frequent departures, and go quickly, and avoid double and treble engines, is a very much better way; therefore I think the narrow gauge comes better into play, because you can do that with less expense."

The Commissioners then put this point:

> "The Broad Gauge advocates state that they are enabled to carry less expensively by working larger engines, and that they thereby supersede the necessity for the greater number of trains which must be drawn upon other lines?"

Chaplin replied:

> "Yes, but I think that will not be the proper course; everyone must feel that the more frequent the communication the more trade it creates. If you wish to avoid those very lengthy trains, the narrow gauge works more economically; at least that would be my view of it. I believe it gives more general accommodation."
>
> "You therefore think"—the Commissioners continued "it more economical to work trains with small carriages than trains with large carriages?"
>
> "Yes", replied Chaplin "I think frequent departures are a desirable measure for the public accommodation; and if you do not require immense trains, by having frequent departures the narrow gauge is more advantageous to work."

A good deal of the subsequent questioning dealt with problems of the break of gauge, at junction points with the Great Western, and of the difficulties of transhipment of goods. But towards the end of his evidence there was one answer that could be taken as rather amusing. The Commissioners said:

> "It appears that the number of miles run by the Great Western engines in the course of the half-year was 13,119 by each engine, whereas upon the South Western it was 15,765; so that, of course, each of your engines worked 2,500 miles more for the half-year than the engines of the Great Western."

Chaplin was very guarded in his reply:

> "It would not lead to that difference, if there be that difference. I cannot correctly answer that."

But then the Commissioner queried:

"Your repairs per mile are more than double those of the Great Western, as stated?

To this Chaplin made the classic answer:

"I should imagine that that had more to do with the manner in which the accounts are kept than with the positive nature of the repairs."

And what was the outcome of it all in the West of England? Even before the Gauge Commissioners had made their report and recommendations first the shareholders of the Bristol and Exeter Railway, and then financial stringency baulked the Great Western management in their efforts to get a direct route to Exeter, avoiding Bath and Bristol; but although the country was thus left wide open for the South Western, progress west of Basingstoke was slow. Financial difficulties following the 'mania' period even led to another truce with the Great Western which in its turn had been unable to complete the Wilts, Somerset & Weymouth line. The South Western was constantly being urged to proceed with the line west of Basingstoke; but the cost was very high, and in 1851, a proposal was made to build the line right through from Basingstoke to Exeter as a single line, though constructing all the bridges, earthworks, and so on, wide enough to take a second line of rails when required. At a time of financial difficulty this seemed a very reasonable proposition, and in October 1852 the Board put the proposal to the shareholders. The South Western proprietors proved as shortsighted as those of the Bristol & Exeter had been over the Exeter Great Western project in 1846, and turned the single line down. In consequence Chaplin resigned from the Chairmanship, though retaining his seat on the Board.

This episode really ended the period of the Gauge War, so far as the South Western was concerned, and although the next chapter tells of further vicissitudes that had to be endured before the line was completed to Exeter I may conclude here by relating that it was not until the following much deferred dates that the narrow gauge reached the important centres of population in Wilts, Dorset, and East Devon.

Basingstoke to Salisbury	1857
Salisbury to Gillingham	1859
To Yeovil	June 1860
To Exeter	July 1860

III

Build-up of the System

During the 'forties' of last century such episodes as the Gauge War and the Railway Mania occupy such an outstanding place in history that one can well imagine that directors, managers, and secretaries had little time to devote to anything else. Actually, under Chaplin's wise leadership, a steady and sagacious build-up of the system was in progress nearer London, while the repeated quarrels with the Great Western over the territory west of Basingstoke and Salisbury were in full blast. There were some colourful episodes in the campaign to give a better railway service to the town of Portsmouth, with the South Western not always in the right, and gaining the ascendancy more by luck than anything else; but in the London area and in its western approaches the Company scarcely put a foot wrong.

Despite all that had been said in defence of the location of the original terminus at Nine Elms it was not an ideal spot, and in 1845 the L.S.W.R. obtained its Metropolitan Extension Act, authorising an eastward extension to a site near the south approach to Westminster bridge. Even this was not considered to be the ultimate eastward extent of the railway, and in the following year a second Act was obtained for the continuance of the line to a site known as Humphrey's Wharf, near London Bridge. But before any contracts could be entered into for the construction of the latter line the Railway Mania had ended in the inevitable crash, and money for any form of railway development became very scarce. Meanwhile construction of the line between Nine Elms and Waterloo was proceeding. It was an expensive job, for the entire line, 1¾ miles long, was carried on arches. With the example of the Greenwich Line in mind, no doubt, it was hoped that the arches could be made a source of revenue, by letting them as warehouses and such like.

The work apparently took a great deal longer than was expected, and cost more than half a million pounds per mile. The shareholders became anxious and critical, and eventually extracted a promise from the Board that the line would be completed and opened by the end of the first half year of 1848. In order to redeem the promise given to the shareholders the last stages of the work were very hurriedly done. It was not that the basic construction of the arches was unsound, but that the permanent way was roughly laid, and almost without ballast. The Board of Trade Inspector was invited to see the work and pass it fit for traffic, but this rough finish to the job created a bad impression and made him suspicious of all the work. His suspicions rose when he came to examine the 90 ft. span bridge over the Westminster Bridge Road. This had a very shallow arch with a rise of only 9 ft. It was the slenderest arch this particular inspector had ever seen, and to the consternation of everyone he refused to pass the line.

Everything had been rushed to the last minute. Capt. Laffan, the Government Inspector, did not finish his inspection until June 29, and the Company had already announced that the line would be opened on June 30th. No wonder there was consternation. An urgent letter was sent to the Board of Trade pointing out the difficulties that would arise if the line was not opened and Capt. Simmons, the Chief Inspector of railways at the Board of Trade took the matter into his own hands. The principal objection was undoubtedly the viaduct over Westminster Bridge Road, and while sanction could obviously not be obtained in time to open the line on June 30, Capt. Simmons immediately arranged for some deflection tests to be carried out on the bridge. In a week's time he was able to report that all was well, and the line was opened on July 11, 1848. From this time Nine Elms as a passenger station was closed, and activities there confined to goods.

From the outset there were four running lines in the approach to Waterloo Bridge, as the station was at first known. In 1846 occurred the first step in the build-up of the huge layout now so familiar as Clapham Junction. In that year the Richmond Railway was opened, from Battersea, —the present Clapham Junction—to Richmond. The South Western took steps to acquire this small independent railway, and in the following year an extension was projected, to carry the line out as far as Datchet. This was known as the Windsor, Staines & South Western Railway. But although the traffic from the Richmond branch cannot have been very heavy apparently some difficulty was experienced in the junction working at Battersea, and the extraordinary decision was taken to give the Richmond trains tracks of their own to Nine Elms. This decision was extraordinary only in the time at which it was made. The provision of quadruple tracks from Clapham Junction to Nine Elms and later to Waterloo Bridge was fortuitous to the last degree as things turned out, and the elevated four-track line into the terminus was constructed at a mere fraction of what the cost would have been to widen the line in later years. From the outset, and ever since, the pair of tracks on the north side have always been known as the Windsor lines.

In discreet seeking of Royal favours at Windsor the South Western came into competition with the Great Western, and the Commissioner of Woods and Forests cashed in upon this railway eagerness to secure an agreement whereby the Great Western and the South Western were respectively required to pay sums of £25,000 and £60,000 not for any privileges they might receive, but towards the construction of new *roads* and road bridges, and improving the approach to the Castle! Originally the South Western was to stop short at Datchet, a point not very convenient for the town, but the nearest the Commissioner of Woods and Forests would permit. But in 1848 Queen Victoria gave permission for the line to be extended across the Home Park right into the town. This extension was duly legalised by Parliament, and when it was completed the Queen regularly used the South Western line for her journeys to and from London.

The Windsor line soon became the means of important connections with other railways in the west of London. The act authorising the section

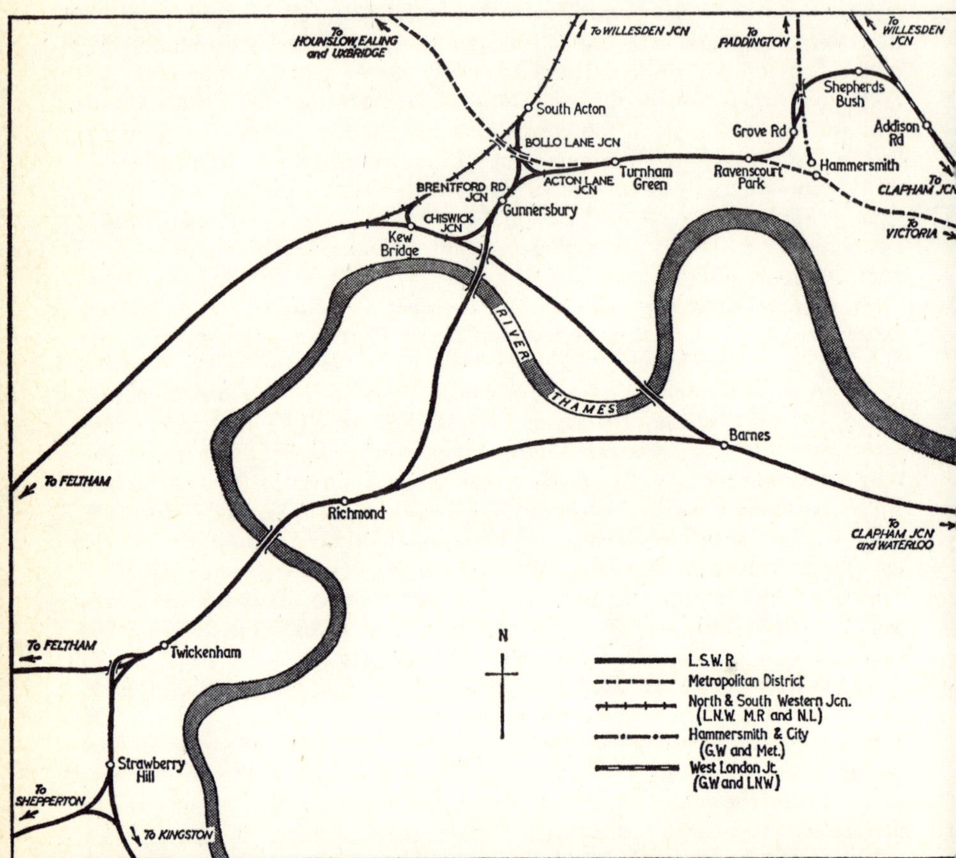

of line between Richmond and Datchet also provided for a loop leaving the original Richmond & Battersea line at Barnes, crossing the river Thames at Barnes Bridge, and in a wide sweep to the northwards including Chiswick, Kew Bridge, Brentford, Isleworth and Hounslow before joining the main Windsor line again at what is now known as Feltham Junction. By the year 1850 it was becoming apparent that the general scheme of railways around London, whereby each line remained independent and isolated, running like spokes of a wheel into a central hub, was not ideal for interchange of traffic, and one of the first attempts to provide north to south connections came in 1853 when the North & South Western Junction Railway was opened, between the L.N.W.R. at Willesden Junction and the Chiswick-Brentford loop of the L.S.W.R. Windsor lines, at Kew Bridge. This line crossed the Great Western at the west end of what is now the Old Oak Common depot, and provided a most useful connection to the north. It was worked jointly by the L.N.W.R. and L.S.W.R., though after the Midland had completed its London extension line they constructed a connecting link from Cricklewood to join the N.S.W.J.R. at Acton Wells Junction—almost at the point where the-line crossed the G.W.R., and from 1871 the N.S.W.J.R. became a joint concern of the L.N.W.R., the Midland, and the North London Railway.

Although it is taking things somewhat away from true chronological order two further developments in connection with the Windsor line may now be mentioned in order to complete what may be termed the 'Strategic' picture of the London & South Western Railway in the western approaches to London. In 1856 what was called the Staines, Wokingham & Woking Junction Railway was opened, providing a line from Staines, through Ascot to join the Reading branch of the South Eastern at Wokingham. There was originally intended to be a branch passing through Chobham to join the Southampton main line at Woking, but this section was not constructed. On completion of the line to Wokingham the South Western obtained running powers over the South Eastern line into Reading, and there promptly ensued a war of fares with the Great Western for the London–Reading traffic. Although it is a much longer route that of the L.S.W.R. runs through much more attractive countryside, via Ascot and Virginia Water, and the service was always very smartly worked. When my father's business was in Reading, in days before World War I, we lived for a time at Hurst, and I used Sindlesham Halt for my schoolboy journeys to and from Reading. We used to see the Drummond 0-4-4 tanks come flying through in tremendous style, in strong contrast to the progress of the lethargic S.E.C.R. locals that I had to use.

But the so-called Staines, Wokingham & Woking came to have a greater significance than that of a pleasant alternative route to Reading. The line to Chobham and Woking was never built, but in 1866 a connection with the main line was made by constructing a branch from Virginia Water to link up with the Chertsey branch and to make a triangle junction with the main line between Weybridge and Byfleet. It should be mentioned in passing that although the Staines, Wokingham & Woking was worked by the South Western from the outset it remained an independent company, leased by the L.S.W.R. until 1900, when it was purchased outright. The line from Byfleet to Virginia Water and Staines gradually assumed major importance as a route for freight traffic to and from the northern lines, and in 1903 the down line from Staines was carried under the main lines at Byfleet Junction in a burrowing connection to avoid conflicting movements from heavy down freight trains crossing and consequently delay to main line trains. This line was to assume an even greater importance when the large mechanised marshalling yard at Feltham was built just after World War I.

While there were a number of branch line constructions in the London district during mid-Victorian times two in particular need special mention because of the connections they involved with the London Chatham and Dover Railways. Even before these however more links were forged in the connection of the L.S.W.R. with the northern lines. The West London —'Punch's Railway'—had been in operation between Willesden and Chelsea since 1844. It had been leased jointly by the Great Western and the L.N.W.R.; but in 1859 an extension was authorised to connect its southern end with the Brighton & South Western lines near Clapham Junction. This extension was also a joint affair owned in the proportions of one third by the L.N.W.R.; one third by the G.W.R.; and one sixth each by the Brighton and South Western. There were eastward and westward connections with both the southern lines, and the eastward connections to the L.S.W.R., at West London Junction, was used for one of the most curious 'round London' passenger train services ever to be introduced.

The eastward extension from Waterloo had never materialised. Although it had been authorised the powers obtained by the Act had been allowed to lapse through lack of money; but when, in 1859, the London Bridge & Charing Cross Railway was authorised, and the proposal was taken over by the South Eastern, in 1863, the South Western management saw an easy opportunity of securing an access to London Bridge, since the new line was to pass 'through their back garden' as it were, at Waterloo. So arrangements were made to build a single line connection to join the new line. This ran over what is now part of the main concourse at Waterloo, and which is now used as a connection for passengers between the two lines. The line was completed in 1864, though at first there was no passenger station on the South Eastern line at the point subsequently known as Waterloo Junction. Then in the following year came the curious 'round London' service referred to in the previous paragraph. It was worked by the L.N.W.R., from 1865, from Euston, Willesden, Addison Road, West London Junction, Waterloo, and thence over the single line bridge to the South Eastern line to terminate at London Bridge. Stranger still, it was the *only* regular passenger service worked over the connecting bridge at Waterloo Junction. The L.S.W.R., which at one time had been so anxious to enter the City, never showed any inclination to work a service of their own to London Bridge.

They were to get enough of entanglements in the City in the years immediately following. The Company had been induced to advance substantial sums of money towards the Metropolitan Extension of the London Chatham & Dover Railway, and in return for this help the Chatham company granted running powers to the L.S.W.R. to run to Ludgate Hill. This time there was no question of a 'round London' service, but rather the provision of a series of residential trains from the rapidly-growing western suburbs to a station in the heart of the City, on the north side of the Thames. To exercise the running powers that were made available a new connection was made at Clapham whereby up L.S.W.R. trains could transfer to the down Chatham line, at Factory Junction, and eventually proceed, via Herne Hill to Blackfriars Bridge and Ludgate Hill. A service of trains from Kingston to Ludgate Hill was inaugurated in April 1866, and in 1869 another one was put on from Wimbledon to Ludgate Hill, via Tulse Hill. The Kingston trains originally ran by the direct line to Clapham Junction, and then took the new spur to Factory Junction; but from 1869 they took a considerably more roundabout route.

Despite the connection with the northern lines provided by the West London Extension lines at Clapham Junction the South Western management felt that a connection from the West London direct to their Richmond and Windsor lines was desirable, and in January 1869 a branch was opened from Kensington (Addison Road) through Turnham Green, Gunnersbury and Kew Gardens to Richmond. At Addison Road this junction was such as to make a trailing conection with south-bound traffic. Thus any trains from Richmond that were bound for the north would have to reverse direction at Addison Road. But from 1869 advantage was immediately taken of this line to route the Ludgate Hill trains via Addison Road, utilising the connection with the L.C.D.R. at Longhedge Junction. From Richmond to Ludgate Hill by this route was nearly 15 miles, and took about an hour. But the L.S.W.R. must have found some virtue in it, because they operated a service of about 10 trains a day for many years, and it was not finally abandoned until 1914. What is perhaps not generally realised today is that the line between Ravenscourt Park and Richmond so familiar as part of the electrified District line, was not originally an 'Underground' line at all. It was owned by the L.S.W.R., and it was not until 8 years after its opening, when the 'District' extended its line to Hammersmith, that the Underground trains from Mansion House began to run over it, by virtue of running powers granted by the L.S.W.R. In later years the South Western, and eventually the Southern must have derived a far greater revenue from running powers than from any traffic of their own, particularly after the District extended its lines from Turnham Green to Ealing and Hounslow. Such, in broad outline, were thus the ramifications of the London & South Western Railway in the London district.

It is now time to look at Portsmouth. In the boom years for railway development, which eventually led up to the 'Mania', plans for railways in every direction were being made, and it was not altogether surprising that the people of Portsmouth felt they were being left out in the cold. All they had were a few crumbs from the rich man's table, in the form of a branch line from the London & Southampton, which in any case terminated on the wrong side of Portsmouth Harbour. Then came a general scramble to provide the town with something more appropriate.

Three schemes were projected. Two of these involved those roundabout routes that were so common in the early days of railways, when apart from the establishment of great trunk routes the main consideration, even with promoters like Hudson, seemed to be to get a line of rails, no matter how meandering the course may be. One of the Portsmouth schemes was a connection to the Brighton line along the coast through Chichester, while another was to carry a line from Guildford through Midhurst to join the existing Gosport branch of the L.S.W.R. at Fareham. Thence there would be a 'branch' into Portsmouth itself. But, one would query, if coming down through Midhurst why on earth go to Fareham first? Why not straight into Portsmouth, with an offshoot to join the Gosport line?

Strangely enough the L.S.W.R. gave whole-hearted support to this curious proposal; but the issue was complicated by a proposal which would, in itself, have been more attractive than either of the others had it not embraced the Atmospheric principle. The name of the company was 'The Direct London & Portsmouth Atmospheric Railway'. It was examined and backed by Joseph Cubitt, son of Sir William, and in the period of the Mania it actually got authorised. Fortunately for the promoters however the powers were allowed to lapse, and at the end of that troubled period only the Brighton scheme remained to provide a lengthy route from London via Worthing and Chichester. In dealing with Portsmouth, Chaplin began to apply the same technique that he had tried with the Great Western over potentially competitive traffic. An agreement was made between the two companies that there should be only one line running into Portsmouth itself, and this should be joint. There would, in future, be two routes from London, one via Basingstoke, Eastleigh and Fareham (95¼ miles) and the other via Brighton, Worthing and Chichester (also 95¼ miles). The two would converge at the Farlington, Cosham, Portcreek triangle junction. These lines were completed and South Western trains began running into Portsmouth in October 1848.

The centre of interest next moves, for a time, to Guildford, where South Western interests were to some extent linked with those of the South Eastern Railway. Apart from the original line from Woking in the first extension actually to be constructed was the Farnham branch. But there was also what remained of the scheme to build a Portsmouth line via Midhurst. This was eventually reduced to no more than a branch southwards from Guildford terminating at Godalming; but both the Farnham and the Godalming branches had a strategic value in that they were to be used, by running powers, by the Reading, Guildford, and Reigate section of the South Eastern, from Shalford Junction to Guildford, and from Guildford to Ash Junction. These lines were both opened in August 1849. The former section was hurried forward, largely to oblige the Reading people, and the short tunnel under St. Catherine's Hill, near Shalford Junction, gave a great deal of trouble, to such an extent

Waterloo: A very early photograph showing the original "A" signal box.
[*British Railways*

Eastleigh, soon after opening of the line appears to be much the same today.
[*British Railways*

2–4–0 express passenger engine No. 31 *Leeds*, built 1852 at Nine Elms.

2–4–0 6 ft. 6 in. express passenger engine *Locke* built 1870.

2–4–0 No. 280 built by W. G. Beattie in 1873 as rebuilt by W. Adams.

[*All L.P. Co.*

Meldon Viaduct, near Okehampton, Exeter—Plymouth line.
[*British Railways*

owley Bridge Junction, near Exeter showing B. & E. line to right, and L.S.W.R. line to left, both laid with mixed gauge. [*British Railways*

The Royal waiting room entrance at Windsor.

[*British Railways*

The Colonade at Gosport: the elaborate station used for Queen Victoria's journeys to the Isle of Wight.

A view looking east at Exeter Queen Street. [*L.G.R.P.*

Southampton old station (Bletchynden) looking east—almost on the site of the present Central station. [*L.G.R.P.*

Top. A Beattie 2–4–0 suburban tank, No. 314, originally built 1874, here shown as rebuilt by Adams in 1889. [*L.P. Co.*

Centre. Dugald Drummond's private engine and coupé, built 1899. [*L.P. Co.*

Lower. One of the surviving Beattie 2–4–0 tanks as working at Wadebridge in 1959. B.R. No. 30587. [*O. S. Nock*

Weymouth train near Bournemouth hauled by Adams Class "460" 4-4-0 No. 474, originally built in 1874.

Up local train near Haslemere, hauled by Adams 7 ft. Class "T6" 4-4-0 No. 686. (Note the variety of coaching stock.) [*L.G.R.P.*

Top. An Adams "Jubilee" Class 0–4–2 No. 645 at Waterloo.
[*L.P. Co.*

Centre. Drummond large-boilered mixed traffic 4–4–0 No. 403, built 1903.
[*Real Photographs*

Bottom. Drummond small-boilered mixed-traffic 4–4–0 No. 391. Class "K10" fitted with cross water tubes; built 1902.
[*L.P. Co.*

that the line had to be closed for a time. There was an occasion also in 1895 when the line had to be closed temporarily, and single line working used for some months afterwards. But apart from the facilities these lines in the Guildford area afforded to the South Eastern, that short branch southwards to Godalming was inevitably a pointer towards future developments, namely a direct line to Portsmouth.

The initiative in this direction did not come in the first place from the L.S.W.R. An independent company, without any particular allegiance, calling itself the 'Direct Portsmouth Railway Company', obtained authority to build a line from Godalming to Havant, on the Brighton line from Chichester to the Farlington–Cosham–Portcreek triangle. It was built purely as a speculation. Thomas Brassey was the constructor, and the promoters evidently intended to sell the railway when it was completed to the highest possible bidder. The party most interested was the London & South Western, but the promoters also had their eyes on the South Eastern. The latter company's westward extension to Reading, and their presence at Guildford made their participation quite likely. Anyway, work was pushed ahead with the line. The fact that Brassey had built it ensured a first class job, but there were certain features in its construction that are of considerable historic interest. It traversed a very hilly stretch of country. Some stiff gradients were involved, but had the contractors followed certain notorious advice they might have been worse still.

It will be recalled that the original proposal for a direct line from London to Portsmouth involved use of the Atmospheric principle. This of course made light of gradients, or was supposed to; and it was this theory that ensnared Brunel into the building of the South Devon line on such an extraordinary profile. But after the abandonment of the Atmospheric project for the Portsmouth Direct Line another scientific theorist entered the field, in the person of Dr. Dionysius Lardner. At this distance in time it is difficult to understand how any practical men came to take any notice of the words of this extraordinary man, at any rate so far as railways were concerned. He was called as an expert witness over the proposals of Brunel for the construction of the Box Tunnel, and talked pure rubbish on the dangers of such a gradient as 1 in 100. Yet when it came to proposals for building a line from Godalming to Havant, and crossing the North and South Downs en route, one finds him putting forward this illuminating idea:

> "The resistance produced by steeper gradients can be compensated by slackening the speed, so that the power shall be relieved from as much atmospheric resistance as is equal to the increased resistance produced by the gravity of the plane which is ascended. And, on the other hand, in descending the plane the speed may be increased until the resistance of the atmosphere is increased to the same amount as that by which the train is relieved of resistance by the declevity down which it moves."

How Dr. Lardner got away with such absolute *tripe*—one cannot really find any other word for it!—passes comprehension. Incidentally, to add to his reputation, he 'proved conclusively' that it was impossible for a steamship to cross the Atlantic just before Brunel's famous vessel the *Great Western* successfully performed the feat, in 1838.

But enough of Dr. Lardner, and all his kind! When the Portsmouth line came to be built there was more than a suggestion of Locke's influence in the engineering and the gradients. Locke and Brassey worked together in close friendship for many years, and the moderated form of an undulating line, which Locke afterwards used with such success on the Salisbury–Exeter road, is also in evidence between Godalming and Havant. Although impetus cannot be used in climbing northwards from Havant to Buriton Tunnel, and only to a limited extent between Godalming and Haslemere, the section between the two summit points could be taken at maximum speed, and I shall never forget an experience on the footplate in Southern Railway days when I was riding a 'School' on one of the up Portsmouth 90-minute non-stops. The engine was 'let fly' down through Petersfield; touched 83½ m.p.h. at the foot of the descent, and cleared the long climb over the North Downs at 48 m.p.h.—all this with a maximum load train, of all but 400 tons.

But to revert to the 'eighteen fifties', as the time approaches for the completion the Direct Portsmouth Railway Company began to look seriously for a purchaser, and by way of an overture to the South Eastern they proposed to build an independent line from Godalming to link up with the Reigate and Reading section of the S.E.R. at Shalford Junction. By so doing they would be independent of the Godalming–Guildford line of the South Western. Parliamentary powers were granted for this northward extension, while beyond Havant running powers were granted over the existing lines into Portsmouth. This forecast a possible association with the South Eastern and Guildford, and definitely involved association with the Brighton and with the South Western in Portsmouth. There was a curious clause in the agreement to award running powers, in that the Brighton & South Western could demand that the Direct Portsmouth built a separate station at the terminus if the other two companies demanded it. For once however the South Eastern refrained from fishing in what might have become very troubled waters, and declined to have anything to do with the 'Direct Portsmouth'.

This is not at all what that company had been hoping for. Having witnessed other railway battles they had hoped to see the South Eastern and the South Western bidding against each other, and eventually to strike a good bargain with one or other of them. Funds were running short. Only a single line of rails was being laid, and they were glad enough when the South Western decided to take a lease of the line, and to open it to traffic in January 1859. The 'Direct Portsmouth' thereupon dropped their idea of an independent line from Godalming to Shalford Junction. But at the southern end of the line there was trouble brewing. It was one thing for the Brighton railway to grant running powers to an independent company over the line between Havant and Portcreek Junction, but quite another thing when that line was leased and worked by the London & South Western. Whatever the state of the 'Direct Line' in 1858 it was potentially a serious rival for the London–Portsmouth traffic having a mileage of only 73, against 95 by both the existing L.S.W.R. and L.B. & S.C.R. routes. The Brighton people left the South Western in no doubt as to their attitude to this new development, and when a trial trip was arranged for December 28, 1858, the South Western approached Havant fully expecting to meet trouble. The train was indeed manned by a considerable force of navvies.

In reviewing what followed, in his book 'The History of the Southern Railway', C. F. Dendy-Marshall finds it rather strange that the Brighton and the South Western should have carried things to such extremes, to quote his own words 'seeing that both of them had been running into Portsmouth for ten years, the last portion of line being jointly owned'. But an amicable existence was quite possible when both companies ran from London to Portsmouth by widely separated routes, of almost identical total mileage, and each serving on the way busy and prosperous areas where the business was in no sense competing with that of the other company. The leasing of the 'Direct Line' by the South Western completely upset the balance of power, and the Brighton were determined to do everything in their power to 'seal off' the South Western at Havant, and make the new line virtually useless as a through route. They adopted the most simple method of 'sealing off', by chaining an engine to the track and removing some of the rails. When the South Western train arrived from Guildford and the navvies on board began to clear the obstruction, up came a superior force of Brighton navvies, and the famous 'Battle of Havant' ensued. The South Western folk had to withdraw; but having failed in the field they won in the Law Courts, and the first train from the Direct Line arrived in Portsmouth on January 24, 1859. The tremendous advantage in mileage thus obtained by the South Western was to some extent countered in 1863, when the Brighton opened the 'Mid-Sussex Junction' line, from Pulborough to Ford. This meant that the Portsmouth trains could thenceforth leave the main line at Three Bridges, and travel via Horsham and Arundel. This reduced the overall mileage from London to Portsmouth to 85—still a good deal more than by the South Western 'Direct Line'.

The Portsmouth Direct Line involved the South Western in what might be termed a neat, compact campaign in a limited area, albeit a very important one. But while it was in progress the company was involved in a much more complicated affair in the 'debatable land' lying between the London & Southampton main line and the River Exe. The failure of the Great Western and its broad gauge allies to make use of the Parliamentary powers conferred upon them by the Acts of 1848 had left the countryside wide open, save for the Wilts, Somerset & Weymouth line. Even this line, although authorised in 1845, had not been constructed beyond Frome. In the period of great financial stress following the Mania there had been a truce between the Great Western and the South Western, and the latter company had held up its plans for extensions west of Basingstoke and Salisbury. In the preceeding chapter I referred briefly to the events that led to Chaplin's resignation as chairman, over the proposal to build a line from Salisbury to Exeter; but the whole question was thrown into the lap of his successor, the Hon. F. Scott, in 1853, when a proposal for a so-called 'Devon & Dorset Railway' was made, with strong Great Western backing, for a line from Exeter to Dorchester.

With the support it had the Devon & Dorset was naturally proposed as a broad gauge line. The South Western opposed it tooth and nail; but opposition in itself was no good. In the Committee stage of the Bill the necessity of providing railway communication through this area was emphasised, and there was considerable hestitancy in rejecting the Bill. The railway would have provided a useful alternative through line to Exeter, via Westbury, Yeovil, Dorchester, Bridport, and Honiton. It would, of course, have been no more 'direct' than the existing Great Western line via Bath and Bristol. But in the Committee stage of the Bill the South Western stated that they were planning an extension of their own from Dorchester to Exeter. There was strong pressure from the military and naval authorities to have a narrow gauge line, to avoid the troubles of a break of gauge in the transport of troops in emergency; and having received from the South Western a promise that a Bill for an extension from Dorchester to Exeter would be introduced in the next session they rejected the broad gauge proposals. In fulfilment of this pledge a Bill was prepared and submitted to a special meeting of the shareholders in November 1853; but to the chagrin of the Board a majority of the shareholders repudiated the pledge made to the Devon & Dorset Parliamentary Committee, and rejected the proposed Dorchester & Exeter line out of hand. There was nothing for it but for Scott to resign, and with him went four other directors. The Company then called once again upon Chaplin, and he took office as Chairman for the second time, in February 1854.

The affair caused intense indignation at the time. There were suggestions that Scott and his fellow directors had pledged the company to the Exeter extension for their own ends; that they had obtained support for the stand they took in the Committee stage of the Devon & Dorset Bill by unfair means, and that the Exeter extension would be nothing but a drain on the shareholder's pockets. There was a strongly-worded article in *The Times* that included this passage:

> "We have surely heard of such a thing as tampering with some votes and creating others of a fictitious character, for the purpose of carrying out any scheme upon which a body of railway directors may have set their hearts. In the absence of direct evidence, all we know is that the directors of the South Western assert that their shareholders gave their authority to make a bargain for them, and the shareholders came forward and said they did nothing of the sort."

This article was considered to make such serious reflections upon the character of Scott and other L.S.W.R. directors that proceedings for libel were taken against William Harrison, printer and publisher of *The Times*. In due course—but after the briefest consideration by the jury—Harrison was found guilty and fined £100.

This affair did not advance the prospects of railway construction west of Dorchester however, and strong pressure was brought upon the South Western from Parliament to redeem the pledge and promote the line from Dorchester to Exeter. There were threats of stopping all dividends until it was done. One can nevertheless appreciate that among the more far-sighted shareholders there was a reluctance to go ahead with an extension beyond Dorchester. A line to the west which would have snaked its way from Southampton via Ringwood and Wimborne, Wareham and Dorchester, and then make a hilly course from Bridport to Axminster and Honiton was far from ideal. The obvious way to the west was the direct one from Salisbury to Yeovil, and then straight on to Axminster. Locke was thoroughly out of patience with the delays in forming a resolute policy on these extensions and he resigned his position as consulting engineer to the company, leaving things to his partner J. E. Errington. Locke however was engineer to an independent company, the Salisbury & Yeovil, which was authorised by Parliament.

The Salisbury & Yeovil, with the influential backing of Locke, was so obviously a pointer towards the future that the directors of the L.S.W.R. at last began to consider the possibilities of a Yeovil-Exeter line as an alternative to the Dorchester Scheme. Furthermore the gap that had formerly existed between Basingstoke and Salisbury was in process of being closed, by an excellent direct line. And so in 1856, the L.S.W.R. went to Parliament with a Bill for the Yeovil–Exeter line. It passed through with very little difficulty, except that a stipulation was made that the line should be completed in 5 years. In such a chain of diverse circumstances was one of the finest main lines in the country built up. Although constructed as a series of disjointed units the line from Basingstoke to Salisbury and Exeter forms incomparably the best line from London to the West; and the fact that it is such a good route—so free from curves and petty restrictions—owes much to the massive influence of Joseph Locke, whether as engineer or as Member of Parliament for Honiton. But neither Chaplin nor Locke lived to see the line in operation. Chaplin resigned the chairmanship in 1858 because of ill-health, and he died in the following year. Locke died in 1860, at the early age of 55.

IV

The Beatties, Father and Son

In a book of this kind it is never possible or even desirable, to maintain a strict chronological order of events, and in this chapter I am turning from the story of the gradual build up of the line itself to mechanical engineering. And in what may be called 'the middle ages' of the London & South Western Railway the work of Joseph Beattie, and to a lesser extent his son 'W.G.', stands out. But to appreciate rather more clearly what Beattie the elder did for the South Western it is necessary to make a quick survey of the motive power stud from the opening of the line until Joseph Beattie took office, in 1850, and began the régime that lasted for 27 years. Actually Joseph Beattie had been with the company from its very inception, for he joined as an assistant to Locke, in 1837. He had thus witnessed the gradual build up of the locomotive stock, and the development of the traffic from the outset, and his remarkable career as Locomotive Superintendent can be seen thus against this invaluable early experience.

In its first days the L.S.W.R. was in the same position as the great majority of early railways, in that it was dependent upon contractors for both design and supply of locomotives. The first superintendent was Joseph Woods, but he seems to have been no more than a running and maintenance man. There is no record of his having contributed anything to the design of locomotives. The enthusiasts of 60 and 70 years ago who compiled the earliest locomotive histories are at pains to point out the discrepancies that exist in some of the early records—particularly in that the totals of locomotive stock quoted in some reports usually amount to no more than actual engines the construction and delivery of which can be traced. In the case of the London & South Western Railway there is nevertheless a most comprehensive acount in *The Locomotive Magazine* of every known design from the opening of the line down to the end of the Adams régime; in that journal the series extended from January 1903 to the end of 1908, and a great number of the early types are illustrated by excellent line drawings. In this account however the name of the first locomotive superintendent is given as Henry Wood, whereas C. F. Dendy Marshall quotes him as Joseph Woods!

One can only be thankful for, and delight in the scholarship and research work of the anonymous railway enthusiasts who produced these long and fascinating serial articles in *The Locomotive Magazine*. Today one can turn through these old volumes, and by studying the drawings alone obtain a very clear picture of what the motive power stud of the South Western was like in early days. Woods was succeeded by John Viret Gooch, brother of the great Daniel of the G.W.R., in January 1841, and to him belongs the credit of having designed the first engine to be built at Nine Elms works, a 6 ft. 6 in. 2-2-2 single named *Eagle*, in December 1843. In the matter of priorities it is remarkable to find that Nine Elms was actually ahead of both Crewe and Swindon. The *Columbine* was not turned out at Crewe until 1845, and Daniel Gooch's 'colossal locomotive', the *Great Western*, was completed in 1846. Before J. V. Gooch's arrival on the South Western an assortment of inside cylinder 2-2-2 engines had formed the backbone of the motive power stud. In November 1841 a return issued by the Board of Trade stated that the company owned 48 locomotives.

The 2-2-2 engines can be classified as follows:

Year Built	Maker	Driving wheels ft.	in.	Cylinders dia. stroke in.	Position of cylinders
1838	G. & J. Rennie	5	6	13 × 18	inside
1838	Tayleur & Co.	5	6	13 × 18	inside
1838	Sharp Roberts	5	6	13 × 18	inside
1838	Rothwell	5	6	13 × 18	inside
1839	Tayleur & Co.	5	6	13 × 18	inside
1840	Fenton, Murray & Jackson ..	5	6	13 × 18	inside
1843	Fairburn & Co.	5	6	13 × 18	outside

From this it appears as though certain basic dimensions were specified, and the details of construction left entirely to the contractors. Only the Fairburn lot differed from the rest in having outside cylinders. All the inside-cylindered engines had outside frames and outside bearings to all wheels. The early records do not give the boiler pressures of all series down to and including the 1840 lot, from the Leeds Foundry of Fenton, Murray & Jackson; but the Fairburn engines of 1843 carried a working pressure of 75 lb. per sq. in.

All these early engines were named, and like those of the Great Western at first they had no numbers. Some of these old names raise a smile today. Mythological and astronomical titles were popular, such as *Minerva*, *Pegasus*, *Mars* and *Jupiter*; one is not surprised to find *Chaplin* and *Locke*; but why *Sussex*! Then there were *Wizard*, *Comet*, *Vesta*, *Vivid*, while *Tartar* might have been chosen in anticipation of the locomotive superintendent who came to succeed J. V. Gooch. But perhaps the oddest of all was one of the 1839 batch built by Tayleur & Co.—*Sam Slick*! What the origin of this name was I have no idea. It could quite well have been a racehorse belonging to one of the directors. The only other engines to be mentioned were four little 2-2-0 Bury's, and a few 0-4-2s. Such was the locomotive stock of the L.S.W.R. at the time of J. V. Gooch's appointment.

The first engines to be built at Nine Elms seem likely to remain something of an enigma to locomotive students of the present day. Although a glowing reference to them is made in the series of articles in *The*

Locomotive Magazine as 'some very fine expresses' they remain one of the very few classes that were not illustrated, either by line drawing or by the reproduction of a photograph. So that we do not know what these epoch-marking engines looked like! They were evidently a considerable advance in size on earlier South Western locomotives, and their driving wheels, of 6 ft. 6 in. diameter were the largest that had then been used on any narrow gauge engine. Otherwise all that is reported of them is that they had outside cylinders, 14¼ in. diameter by 20 in. stroke and were named *Eagle*, *Hawk*, *Falcon* and *Vulture*.

Although there is thus a notable gap in a chronicle of locomotive building that is otherwise very complete we can, nevertheless make a pretty shrewd guess at the appearance of these first Gooch 2-2-2s. From 1845 onwards he produced a series of express passenger locomotive designs all having a strongly family likeness, and of gradually increasing dimensions. These designs, taking their names from the first engine of each class, can be summarised as in the accompanying table. I have also added the *Eagle* of 1843.

Date	Name of 1st engine	Driving wheel dim. ft.	in.	Cylinders Dia. in.	Stroke in.	Number in class
1843	*Eagle*	6	6	14¼	20	4
1843	*Snake*	6	6	14¼	21	2
1845	*Mazeppa*	6	6	16	22	8
1846	*Alecto*	6	0	15	22	10
1848	*Rocklia*	6	6	16	22	6
1849	*Vulcan*	7	0	15	20	8

Line drawings of all these engines, except for the *Eagle*, are available, and they all show certain marked characteristics. The smokebox and cylinders are completely ahead of the leading wheels; the leading and trailing wheels have outside bearings, whereas the driving wheels have only inside bearings. The connecting rod is within the outside frames, but the running plate is carried at a height considerably above the frame, and leaves a portion of the driving wheel exposed. When the engine was in motion the movement of the connecting rod could be seen both above and below the outside frames, and behind it. The running plate was carried forward from the cab above the springs of the rear wheels, over the uppermost position of the big-ends to a point at the front end where the driver had easy access to the forward oil cups, and other points needing occasional attention while running. The portion of the driving wheels above the running plate was encased in a handsome slotted splasher. The *Mazeppa* class had domes of the Sharp type on the first ring of the boiler; the two engines *Snake* and *Serpent* had domeless boilers, and the later engines had large domes on the firebox.

There were certain other features of these Gooch 2-2-2 engines that are worthy of particular note. In all cases the cylinders were mounted above the frames, and slightly inclined, in a strong mechanical position between the top of the frames and the outward curve of the smokebox. This also permitted a very short and direct exhaust passage from cylinders to the blast pipe. Another interesting feature was the design of the firebox, the top of which was raised above the line of the boiler top. This was a feature common to Gooch's brother's engines on the Great Western, and was an excellent point in providing additional steam space in the hottest part of the boiler. Joseph Beattie continued the practice on the L.S.W.R., but on the Great Western Daniel Gooch's immediate successors abandoned it, leaving it to be revised in a modern form in the magnificent range of standard boilers designed at Swindon in Churchward's time.

The names of the Gooch engines on the L.S.W.R. are worth recalling, as many of them became very familiar in later years—not on the South Western but on the North Western. I may add that the two engines of the 'Snake' class of 1843, *Snake* and *Serpent* were strictly speaking the first new locomotives to be built at Nine Elms. They were actually the first completed, but requiring some adjustments to their boilers they were held in the works, and the *Eagle*, was the first to be turned out and put into traffic. The other four classes were as follows:

1845:	Mazeppa Medea Medusa Mentor	Meteor Sultana Sirocco Sappho
1846:	Alecto Acheron Achilles Actaeon Aeolus	Apollo Argus Ariel Alaric Arrow
1848:	Rocklia Avon Test	Trent Stour Frome
1849:	Vulcan Stromboli Volcano Etna	Vesuvius Hecla St. George Britannia

Having made his mark in no uncertain way on the L.S.W.R. J. V. Gooch resigned, to take up a similar position on the Eastern Counties Railways. At the time of leaving the South Western he was no more than 38 years of age, and he was to live another 50 years, although he stayed for no more than 6 years on the Eastern Counties. He was there long enough to exert a marked influence, and Robert Sinclair's famous 2-2-2s of 1862, in their frame design, position of cylinders, and their high raised firebox might also have been designed by J. V. Gooch.

On taking over the locomotive department at Nine Elms Joseph Beattie made immediate provision for more powerful engines in the form of a class of 2-4-0s with inside cylinders; but he is best remembered by his development of the Gooch outside-cylinder designs. As space does not permit of a reference to all the locomotives he put on the road I will confine attention here to his 2-2-2s, 2-4-0s, with outside cylinders, and the 2-4-0 suburban tanks. The year 1912 saw *The Locomotive Magazine* reach the heights of lavish presentation, and in that one year there were no fewer than eight magnificent colour plates, reproduced from the ever-famous series of oil paintings by 'F. Moore'. In that year those plates included not only some of the latest British express locomotives, such as the Great Eastern '1500' class 4-6-0, a North Eastern 'Z' Atlantic, and a North Stafford 4-4-2 tank, but an equally gorgeous representation of one of Joseph Beattie's 7 ft. 2-4-0s, the *Ariel*. Nevertheless, feasting one's eyes on this positive apparition of a locomotive one realises that even this was a sobered-down edition of what these engines looked like originally. For the plate in *The Locomotive Magazine* shows *Ariel* in her later condition.

Joseph Beattie has sometimes been represented as a prolific, even fanciful inventor, who having a very strong will of his own played ducks and drakes with the locomotive stud of the L.S.W.R. by fitting all sorts of fearful gadgets. But in making a modern appraisal of his work one must take into account the degree of freedom enjoyed by many high-standing railwaymen of the period. Who was there to say them nay! Although some of his more complicated inventions did not quite turn out as intended Beattie was a strong and effective administrator, and carried his men along with him. In his day locomotive performance on the L.S.W.R. was some of the finest in the country, and was without any doubt the most economical. He succeeded J. V. Gooch at a time when there was urgent need to reduce the operating expenses of railways, and one obvious way in which locomotive engineers could assist in this was by modifying their engines so as to burn ordinary coal instead of coke.

This was easier said than done in the early eighteen fifties. The opponents of railways in the early days had made such play with the evils likely to arise from emission of smoke from locomotives that coke was used instead of coal. Any engine that belched black smoke after the fashion of some latter-day habitués of the main line from Waterloo would have brought the direst trouble upon the railway management concerned. But coal was becoming a necessity, and so locomotive engineers on many railways began experimenting with different kinds of fireboxes, in order to secure complete combustion of the fuel, and a clear exhaust. Joseph Beattie was well to the fore in this respect, and he fitted a number of locomotives with a most elaborate design of boiler and firebox. This included a double firebox each having its own firedoor. In this boiler there was also a combustion chamber, in which was mounted a thermic syphon to improve the circulation of water in the boiler.

The method of working was to keep a bright intensely-hot fire in the front firebox, and do all the heavy firing in the rear one. The latter would have produced much black smoke, but the unburnt fuel in the smoke causing the discoloration was burnt as the exhaust passed over the forward firebox, and the gases were completely clear at the top of the chimney. These boilers must have been difficult and expensive to maintain; but they enabled the South Western express locomotives to use coal freely, and with good economy. Beattie may have been a strong willed martinet, but there was sound engineering behind the devices that are sometimes lightly dismissed as 'gadgets'. He was one of the earliest experimenters in the field of feed water heating, and the first engines so equipped were distinguished by having the condenser mounted vertically on the smokebox, immediately in front of the chimney. This tall pipe gave the engines so fitted a most peculiar appearance. Some engines even had twin condensers. But whatever their appearance the arrangement worked well, and resulted in a notable economy in fuel. The coal consumption on fast express duty between London and Southampton was given as 17 lb. per mile—a remarkably good figure for the eighteen-sixties.

In developing the Gooch express engines to his own needs Beattie abandoned the rather peculiar style of running plate, and reverted to a more orthodox style. To provide the necessary clearances for the connecting rod and its big-end he introduced a second slotted splasher concentric with the main one for the wheel itself. This handsome detail was also used by Robert Sinclair in his famous 2-2-2s for the Great Eastern Railway. Another unique feature of Beattie's express locomotives both of the 2-2-2 and 2-4-0 type, was the arrangement of bearings on the leading wheels. These had inside bearings designed to take most of the weight, and small outside steadying bearings the support for which were hung on the underside of the slide bars. This arrangement was also used on the 2-4-0 London suburban tank engines, and could be seen on the three survivors that remained at work on the Bodmin & Wadebridge line until quite recently.

In their most ornate days the Beattie express engines had their huge domes—likened to an inverted Grecian vase—of polished brass. The safety valve was also polished, and in successive batches of locomotives was located at most unlikely positions on the boiler. In later years, as depicted in F. Moore's magnificent painting of *Ariel*, they were painted over, albeit in the rich purple-brown that so distinguished South Western engines in the days of Joseph Beattie. The copper caps to the chimneys remained, and even though the boiler mountings were painted over there was still plenty to be polished. In the later form of feed water heater the condensing pipe was carried horizontally along the boiler. On many of these engines the names of the old Gooch 2-2-2s were perpetuated. Beattie was a man who evidently loved engines for their own sake, and so far as handsome appearance was concerned he was ably seconded by his son 'W.G.', who eventually succeeded him. Joseph Beattie's express passenger 2-2-2 and 2-4-0 locomotives can be summarised thus:

Year First Built	Type	Name of first engine	Driving wheel dia. ft.	in.	Cylinders dia. stroke in.	Number in class
1853	2-2-2	The Duke	6	6	15 × 21	1
1856	2-2-2	Harold	6	6	15 × 21	5
1857	2-2-2	Eugénie	6	6	15½ × 21	5
1859	2-2-2	Victoria	6	6	16 × 21	1
1859	2-4-0	Clyde	7	0	17 × 22	12
1859	2-4-0	Undine	6	6	16½ × 22*	48
1862	2-4-0	Eagle	6	0	17 × 22	2

* Later engines of class all had 17 in. cylinders

From the time of the first Beattie outside cylinder 2-4-0s, in 1859, there were three standard classes, with 6 ft., 6 ft. 6 in., and 7 ft. coupled wheels respectively. The 6 ft. 6 in. class was by far the most numerous—in fact, until the year 1868 there were only three 6 ft. engines, and seven 7 ft. In catholicity of choice their names rivalled those of the L.N.W.R. Those of the 6 ft. 6 in. outside cylindered 2-4-0s are worth recalling in full.

Year	Name
1859	Undine
	Psyche
	Circe
	Ariadne
	Atalanta
	Electra
	Cupid
	Sylph
	Zephyr
	Nymph
	Naiad
	Hebe
1863	Falcon
	Argus
	Alaric
	Arrow
	Apollo
1864	Ariel
1865	Wildfire
	Harpy
	Hornet
	Herod
1866	Sultana
	Siren
	Saracen

Year	Name
1866	Shark
	Stentor
	Sirius
1869	Vesuvius
	St. George
	Britannia
1870	Sussex
	Mercury
	Mars
	Tartar
	Locke
	Cossack
1871	Albert
	Briton
	Princess
	Queen
	Reindeer
	Prince
	Gazelle
	Etna
	Ganymede
	Minerva
	Leeds

One can smile at the readiness with which the name selector, whoever he was, changed from goddesses and nymphs to characters like *Alaric*, *Herod*, and *Stentor*. The curiously incongruous name *Sussex* appears again, with such diversities as *Vesuvius*, *St. George*, *Tartar*, *Locke*, and *Minerva*! The name *Albert*, used on one of the engines of 1871, was undoubtedly in memory of the Prince Consort who died in that year. Taken all round the Beattie 2-4-0s were excellent engines, and many of them ran nearly a million miles. One of the most interesting events in their career was the celebrated series of interchange trials with the South Eastern Railway in which two of the 6 ft. 6 in. engines *St. George* and *Vesuvius* worked on the Continental boat expresses between Charing Cross and Dover. The loads were very heavy for that period, being usually between 190 and 200 tons. The run of 78½ miles was done in about 96 min., on a coal consumption of 23 lb. per mile, average, for the series of trials. The trials lasted a full month. On six days out of the seven each week *St. George* made the running for the L.S.W.R. *Vesuvius* was the stand-by engine, and did the work on Sundays, which was shed day for the *St. George*.

During Joseph Beattie's time a number of other engine classes were introduced, including 2-4-0 and 0-6-0 goods engines, but apart from the outside cylindered express engines of the 2-2-2 and 2-4-0 types the best known were the celebrated 2-4-0 well tanks, with 5 ft. 6 in. coupled wheels. These engines, of which the first were delivered by Beyer, Peacock and Co. in 1863, were a development of a Nine Elms product of 1858, having 5 ft. coupled wheels. The well-tanks of 1863, having 15 in. by 20 in. cylinders were some of the prettiest little engines working in the London suburban area. They had most of the external characteristics of the express engines, in the way of ornamentation, except that the decorative slotted splashers were replaced by the traditional Beyer-Peacock brass band, with the maker's name prominently displayed on it. Fifty of these excellent little engines had been supplied by Beyer, Peacock & Co. up to the end of the year 1871. In that year Joseph Beattie died, and was succeeded by his son.

At first the changes were superficial rather than anything else. For example, construction of the standard 6 ft. 6 in. passenger engines was continued until January 1875; but many of these engines were unnamed, and an ugly development was the use of a long continuous splasher with a square front covering both pairs of driving wheels and the lower side of the cab. In these engines 'W.G.' continued all the mechanical details of his father's engines, but those splashers profoundly altered the general 'look' of the engines. They took on yet another 'look' in the 'eighties' when William Adams rebuilt some of them with orthodox domed boilers and his own pattern of stove pipe chimney. They were very smart little engines in this form with a character all their own, and having absolutely nothing of their original Beattie flavour. Adams, of course, was an artist as well as an engineer and his rebuilding of the Beattie 2-4-0s provides one of the very few cases where a renewal of a very celebrated engine design resulted in a very handsome and new-looking creation.

The last of the Beattie 2-4-0s built new at Nine Elms was No. 43, *Milo*, in January 1875. In naming this engine W. G. Beattie displayed his sense of the historic. Despite the long rectangular splashers it was unquestionably a Joseph Beattie engine, and was indeed the last of the line—the last new engine to be built at Nine Elms for many years. But it cannot have been a mere coincidence that it was named *Milo*; for that was also the name of the engine popularly supposed to be the very first built by Joseph Beattie at Nine Elms, a 2-4-0, with 5 ft. 6 in. wheels and inside cylinders, in 1851. *Milo* certainly belonged to his first class, and according to the records published in *The Locomotive Magazine* was the third engine, dating from December of that year. This engine was scrapped in June 1880, so that the name was probably removed in its last few years of existence.

By that time a most definite change was beginning to come over new locomotives delivered to the L.S.W.R. In 1872 Beyer, Peacock & Co. delivered the first of a new series of 0-6-0 goods engines, with conventional domed boilers, raised round-topped fireboxes, on which were mounted Ramsbottom type safety valves. These engines had double frames and were generally finished most ornately. A development of this class followed in 1874, with inside frames only, and on these latter engines, at last, the polished brass dome disappeared. Another innovation was the purchase, also from Beyer-Peacock & Co. of six 4-4-0 tank engines of the 'Metropolitan' type, though with standard L.S.W.R. fittings. At that time the locomotive stock was still being painted in Joseph Beattie's standard livery. These engines had ordinary single fireboxes, whereas all other engines continued to have the double one, and carried nameplates with the words 'Beattie's Patent' on the cab sides.

In 1876 W. G. Beattie broke clean away from established tradition on the L.S.W.R. and introduced the 4-4-0 type, with outside cylinders, for heavy express work. Twenty engines, Nos. 348 to 367 were delivered from the works of Sharp, Stewart & Co., and these were the forerunners of a notable series of 4-4-0 designs, with outside cylinders. In these engines Beattie used his ugly continuous rectangular splasher, and so spoiled the appearance of what would have been an elegantly proportioned engine. They had stove pipe chimneys, a shapely dome, and the running plate was curved gracefully over the coupled wheel bosses. Unfortunately the splashers were not the only thing that was misproportioned on those engines. The cylinders were far too large for the boiler; the design of the piston valves was faulty, and they were frequently in trouble with broken valves and bent spindles. These troubles could have been cured, by lining up the cylinders, and modifying the valve design; but these engines had another fundamental weakness that could not be cured.

At the time of their introduction the limitation of weight imposed by the permanent way engineers were severe, and in producing a potentially more powerful locomotive W. G. Beattie was much restricted. The use of steel in locomotive construction was in its infancy, and so a designer had to rely upon wrought iron, which requires a greater weight of material to provide the same tensile strength. Beattie handicapped himself in another way by putting the coupling rods next to the wheels. The connecting rods were outside and this required the centre lines of the cylinders to be spaced farther apart, and this increased the stresses in the frames. From one point of view this arrangement of the rods was advantageous in that it gave completely free access to the big ends; but in his 4-4-0s W. G. Beattie saved weight by skimping material in the frames, and as a result the engines were always in trouble with cracked frames in addition to their other defects.

These unfortunate engines constitute a classic example of an attempt to enlarge, and produce a powerful machine, when it seemed that the designer did not appreciate the principles underlying successful locomotive design. It might have been thought that W. G. Beattie, having been associated so long with the work of his father, should not have slipped up on fundamentals. But it is easy to be wise after the event and the '348' class 4-4-0s eventually proved to be not the only case of this peculiar phenomenon on the London & South Western Railway. In the year following the introduction of these engines Beattie's health gave way, and in 1877 he retired, only 6 years after the death of his father.

V

The lines west of Exeter

It is extraordinary how early memories of railways remain fixed in one's mind. I encountered the L.S.W.R. quite early in my boyhood, when I used to travel from Reading with my parents to Southsea and Bournemouth for holidays. Sometimes we used the through trains from the north, and joined them at Reading West, but at others we changed at Basingstoke, and I have an awed and rather terrifying memory of seeing an up West of England express hauled by an enormous engine bear down upon Basingstoke and roar through the station at a speed that made the Great Western non-stops through Reading seem pedestrian by comparison. I think it must have been the strange, and to me extraordinary shape of the engine that left so vivid an impression. The date would have been 1911 or 1912, and that engine was almost certainly one of Dugald Drummond's "Paddleboats" in its original condition. But I was even then a reader of *The Railway Magazine*, and the photographs of F. E. Mackay were familiar to me. I devoured the L.S.W.R. captions: 'Padstow and Bude Express': 'Up Torrington Luncheon Car Express' and so on, and in my childlike imagination those North Cornwall resorts loomed as tremendously important places. They must have been important to need such huge engines pulling the trains!

My exploration of the L.S.W.R. lines west of Exeter did not begin until many years later, not until indeed the South Western had become part of the Southern Railway. Even then my first trip came in a manner that was not premeditated. I had to go down to Plymouth to meet one of the 'A' ships of the Cunard Line on the Canadian service, and all arrangements had been made for me to travel down on a certain Friday evening to meet the ship when she arrived in the Sound next morning. Then at the last minute news came that she was a whole day late. It was midsummer; on that Saturday there were many available trains by either route, and I decided on the spur of the moment to go down Southern. With the whole day at my disposal I went to Waterloo and boarded the first train of which the engine looked interesting. The weather was bad, with high winds and pouring rain, and I gained no more than the vaguest impressions of the northern slopes of Dartmoor, as our little Drummond 4-4-0 fairly sailed up the heavy gradients from Yeoford Junction. But those western lines are a fascinating group, and in no respect less than in their diverse origin.

To present day enthusiasts the Bodmin & Wadebridge line became an object of exceptional interest, because it provided the spectacle of no fewer than three Beattie 2-4-0 tank engines continuing in active service. But this was also of special interest as it constituted the oldest part of the London & South Western system. The Bodmin & Wadebridge was in fact opened to traffic before the London & Southampton had been authorised by Parliament. The main line was but 7 miles long, and there was a branch 6½ miles long up the Camel valley to Wenford Bridge. The traffic for which it was intended was, strangely enough, sea sand of which large quantities were required inland for manure. Passenger business was meagre from the very start, and the staple traffic for which the line had been built yielded disappointing results. By the year 1845 the company was on the verge of bankruptcy. One of the western associates of the Great Western, the Cornwall Railway, offered to buy it; but a company that had been promoted to build the so-called Devon & Cornwall Central came forward with a more attractive offer, which the Bodmin & Wadebridge accepted. But at that time the Devon & Cornwall project came to nothing—save that the still-born railway had the bankrupt Bodmin & Wadebridge on its hands. The situation was saved by the action of the L.S.W.R., which acquired the B. & M. even though it was 200 miles away from the nearest South Western metals. The situation was even more incongruous, because the L.S.W.R. took no steps to get Parliamentary authority for the purchase! The transaction was in fact not legalised until 1886.

The purchase of the Bodmin & Wadebridge Railway might have seemed an extraordinary plunge into the unknown for a railway with a host of problems on its immediate doorstep, without venturing into the north-west of Cornwall. But the management of the South Western was nothing if not ambitious, and in the general scramble of the Gauge War, and the recurring disputes with the Great Western two lines had been authorised in 1848 that would have brought the narrow gauge to Exeter. Like the Great Western and the Bristol and Exeter schemes for a short cut to the west the powers granted by Parliament had to lapse through lack of funds to build the Salisbury & Yeovil, and the Yeovil & Exeter. At the same time other interests west of Exeter were acting independently, and this eventually led to a minor battle of the gauges in the fair land of Devon, between the Taw and the Exe. But the South Western lines west of Exeter are not among the most familiar ground to railway enthusiasts, and it will perhaps be best to sketch in details of the complete network as it was at the turn of the century, and then to mention particular points in its build-up rather than to trace chronologically the many vicissitudes that were experienced between 1845, when the Exeter & Crediton was authorised, and 1899, when the L.S.W.R. eventually reached Padstow.

The one-time Exeter & Crediton Railway forms the springboard for a group of lines that has a particularly sprawling and indirect appearance on the map. Everything travelling west of Exeter has to travel over the 10·3 miles between Cowley Bridge Junction, on the Bristol and Exeter, and Coleford Junction. Some trains of composite destination were run combined as far as Yeoford, 9·3 miles, and divided there. It was the practice to run these trains double-headed from Exeter and then one engine could take the Taw Vale portion, and the other the through coaches for either Plymouth or Cornwall. The northward fork at Coleford Junction led over the summit by Copplestone and then into the Taw valley, which was followed to Barnstaple. The Taw Vale Railway, as this part of the line was originally known, continued from Barnstaple along the south side of the Taw Estuary to Fremington Pill, and was later extended to Bideford. This latter extension was completed in 1855, but the better known line from Barnstaple that strikes off along the north shore of the Taw estuary, to Ilfracombe, was not completed until nearly 20 years later—in 1874.

The inland section of the line, between Exeter and Barnstaple, running through a deeply rural countryside does not pass any outstanding scenery in a county so generally beautiful as Devon. But the lines on both sides of the Taw estuary have the charm of wide prospects and a glimpse of the open sea; and while the Bideford branch swings round from the estuary of the Taw to that of the Torridge the Ilfracombe line turns almost due north to climb on fearsome gradients to Morthoe, and to descend no less precipitately into the terminus at Ilfracombe, high above the town. It was over this line that I had an unexpected and fascinating run on the footplate of an L.S.W.R. engine. It was just after the end of the second World War, and I was making a number of runs on Bulleid 'Pacifics'. My journeys took me west of Exeter, and on one occasion I stayed overnight at Barnstaple prior to footplating on the 9.50 a.m. from Ilfracombe to Waterloo. I had intended to ride from Barnstaple to Ilfracombe on our own engine, which would be travelling light; but having arrived at the shed in good time I found that a Drummond 0-4-4 tank, No. 670, was also leaving to Ilfracombe, and going some 20 min. ahead of our own engine, and so I rode on her instead of the Pacific.

What a delight that little engine was! She was painted plain black, and was decidedly grubby; but mechanically she was immaculate, and we skated along beside the Taw estuary rounding curve after curve at a merry 55 m.p.h. She rode superbly, and as we 'floated' round those curves without a suspicion of a jolt or the merest beginnings of a roll I could not help recalling William Stroudley's notable exposition of his idea in giving the famous 'Gladstone' 0-4-2s front-coupled driving wheels. We were stopped by signal at Braunton to receive a message, and then puffed merrily up the 1 in 40 bank to Mortehoe. I must say I enjoyed that ride on No. 670, light engine, as much as I was intrigued by the first experience I gained that week-end of the Bulleid 'Pacifics'. From Mortehoe the line descends at 1 in 37 into Ilfracombe, thus making a holy terror of a start for up trains, coming on to this gradient immediately off the platform end.

Reverting now to earlier days on the line between Barnstaple and Exeter, had things been managed more astutely it could easily have fallen permanently into the Great Western empire. Both the Exeter & Crediton, and the Taw Vale were authorised in 1845. The latter was a very modest affair centred upon Barnstaple, contrived in the first place for local purposes, very much after the style of the Bodmin & Wadebridge; but the Exeter & Crediton involved a junction with the Bristol & Exeter, and both companies had the same chairman. At first the gauge of the Crediton line was not specified, but the Act provided for the line to be purchased or leased by the B. & E. and at the outset a broad gauge line seemed a foregone conclusion. The Crediton line was authorised in 1845, but at first little was done towards construction. In the meantime the very alert South Western management had its finger on the pulse of events west of Exeter; it was learned that the Crediton company was preparing to advise its shareholders to sell out to the Bristol & Exeter, and accordingly things were very neatly worked. The provisional agreement for sale to the B. & E. was offered to the Exeter & Crediton proprietors in January 1847, and to the astonishment of the Chairman and the Board was flatly rejected.

Railway shareholders in the West of England had a way of running counter to what their directors desired, as in the famous case of the Bristol & Exeter, rejecting the Exeter Great Western project. The Crediton case was however more complicated, and also involved the Taw Vale. The latter company was proposing to apply for powers to make an extension to join the Crediton. This was opposed by the Bristol & Exeter, but in due course this opposition was withdrawn on the understanding that after completion the B. & E. would take over and work the line. Consequently, when the Crediton shareholders turned down any suggestion of their line being leased or sold to the Bristol & Exeter the fat was in the fire. The Railway Board, which at that time played the role of a Parliamentary watchdog on railway development, investigated the affair, and it was found that a large number of the shareholders whose votes had secured the veto had been on the books less than a week! Further inquiry revealed how it had been contrived. The South Western had advanced a sum of £30,000 to the Taw Vale, and with this money 1700 shares in the Exeter & Crediton had been bought—ample to sway the meeting!

As a result of this 'fiddle' the South Western stood arraigned before Parliament, but despite all the Exeter & Crediton decided to lay its line on the broad gauge. One can appreciate that this was a matter of practical politics. Their Act provided for an entry into Exeter over 1½ miles of the B. & E. line. At that time there were no narrow gauge tracks nearer to them than Salisbury, and they were anxious to get the line finished and start business. The decision of the Crediton people to go broad gauge caused a violent reaction in Barnstaple. The Taw Vale was already in the London & South Western pocket, and on every score seemed much more anxious to align itself with Waterloo rather than with Paddington, and the Broad Gauge alliance; and now the prospect of a broad gauge 'buffer' between Exeter and their own territory seemed to seal off any prospect of an eventual link-up with the South Western, when the narrow gauge reached Exeter. There were petitions and memoranda, and the Bristol & Exeter told the Taw Vale, in decidedly brusque terms, that they would be taking a lease of the line and reminded them that there was no narrow gauge railway within 100 miles of their territory.

Then, in the autumn of 1847, it was learned that Bills for two narrow gauge lines were being prepared—the Salisbury & Yeovil, and the Yeovil & Exeter—which would not only bring the narrow gauge into Exeter, but which had influenced the Crediton line to the extent of causing it to begin changing the line to the narrow gauge. A memorandum was immediately sent to the Railway Board, and in January 1848 Capt. Simmons, one of the inspecting officers of the Board of Trade, was sent to Barnstaple to look into things on the spot. The result was the very opposite of what the Taw Vale people had hoped for. Having examined the lines around Barnstaple, and seen the unfinished works of the Exeter & Crediton he confirmed that the latter company was indeed altering the gauge, and that they were not intending to run into the existing station at Exeter. Instead they were building a temporary station at Cowley Bridge, nearly 2 miles from the City centre. He further commented that as the Crediton line had not been offered for inspection it had no voice in determining what its gauge should be!

Captain Simmons clearly found the whole situation west of Exeter most unsatisfactory, and seemed to be very much on the side of the broad gauge. In his report he expressed the opinion that the Taw Vale case for linking up with the proposed narrow gauge lines from Salisbury to Exeter would be very much weakened by the construction of the 'direct' broad gauge lines which the Great Western and the Bristol & Exeter were projecting—the Berks & Hants Extension to Westbury, and the Bristol & Exeter line from Durston to Castle Cary. He went so far as to say that these latter, on easier gradients, would prove the principal routes from London to the West; and as a result of this report the Railway Board told the Taw Vale, to its chagrin, that it must be a broad gauge line. I have already told how both the rival direct lines to Exeter, Great Western and South Western, were authorised by Parliament in 1848, but how neither came to be built until many years later. For similar reasons—lack of money—things moved very slowly west of Exeter; and after all that had gone before it is amusing to recall that the Crediton was, after all, leased to the Bristol & Exeter, and was opened as a broad gauge line in 1851. The Taw Vale extension to join it, which provided through communication between London and Barnstaple, was not opened until 1854, and then also as a broad gauge line.

Once the South Western got through to Exeter, as told in Chapter 3, the whole situation changed. The new line via Salisbury, Yeovil and Honiton was incomparably more direct than the broad gauge route via Bristol, and the argument put forward by Capt. Simmons for the Taw Vale to team up with the Bristol & Exeter fell to the ground, for the simple reason that the narrow gauge had secured their direct line from London to Exeter and the broad gauge had not. Taw Vale sympathies, and indeed direct interests had always lain with the South Western, however the Crediton people may have vacillated; and with the South Western now at Exeter nothing could stop this natural alignment from blossoming. In 1862 the lease of the Crediton line was transferred to the South Western, and in the following year the Taw Vale also came within the fold. The latter line, leased in 1863 was purchased outright in 1865, though the Crediton line did not come finally into the hands of the South Western until 1876, the year in which the Bristol & Exeter was amalgamated with the Great Western. One last link in the chain of narrow gauge communications between London and the North Devon coast needs to be mentioned, namely the steeply-inclined connection between the South Western and the Great Western stations at Exeter, which was opened in 1863. Queen Street station had originally been built as a terminus, and successive changes eventually resulted in an inefficient jumble of a station, which was not rebuilt until Southern Railway days.

The arrival of the South Western at Exeter put new life into a number of early schemes for railways in north-west Devon and Cornwall, which had languished since the days of the Mania. There is no doubt that the management of the L.S.W.R. had their eyes upon the Far West. The key to the situation was the West Cornwall Railway, from Truro to Penzance, which was then *narrow gauge*. If the South Western could get through to Truro any further extension of the broad gauge could be sealed off. Prior to this the Taw Vale had changed its name to the North Devon Railway. After leaving Crediton it turned to the northward at Yeoford, and by striking westward from this particular point a line could be envisaged skirting the northern slopes of Dartmoor, passing Okehampton, and continuing straight on, in a west-south-westerly direction to Launceston. Once there they would be well placed for an advance further west. The situation seemed propitious, because friction was developing at Truro between the Cornwall Railway and the West Cornwall due to the break of gauge. The Cornwall Railway had the right to demand the conversion of the older West Cornwall line to broad gauge, and the South Western felt that if they could get to Truro before that threat became an actual demand they might be able to prevent it altogether.

The trouble was of course finance. It was one thing to promote lines in the prosperous farming lands of Dorset and East Devon, but quite another to strike through bleak, hilly country such as that lying beyond Launceston. Nevertheless the Okehampton Railway was authorised in 1862, leaving the North Devon line at Coleford Junction, and in the following year the Act was obtained for an extension to Lydford. Here a junction was planned with the broad gauge Launceston & South Devon line. Then in the two succeeding years the associates of the L.S.W.R. obtained authority to extend their lines from Launceston to Truro. The first stage was the incorporation of the Launceston, Bodmin, and Wadebridge Junction Railway, and next, in 1865, an extension from the end of the Ruthernbridge branch of the Bodmin & Wadebridge to Truro. It might have seemed that the Truro extension was too late even when it was projected; for in 1864 the Cornwall Railway, exasperated by the break of gauge troubles at Truro had exerted their rights, and demanded the conversion of the West Cornwall Railway to broad gauge. Nevertheless the narrow gauge parties continued to press ahead, and at the time the Ruthernbridge–Truro line was authorised the name of the whole undertaking west of Launceston was changed to the Central Cornwall Railway. Quite apart from finance however the weakness of the scheme as a through route lay in the use of the broad gauge link from Lydford to Launceston. Even granting that this could readily be changed into mixed gauge it would have involved a reversal of direction at Lydford.

In any case railway politics entered once more into the province of straightforward development. Realising that Cornwall provided yet another field for wasteful competition the four established companies most deeply involved—the Great Western, the Bristol & Exeter, the South Devon, and the London & South Western—got together to formulate what is sometimes called the Quadruple Treaty. It was a sound practical working arrangement to which all the interested parties were ready to agree. In it however Parliament sensed the chance of a railway monopoly being established in the west, and sanction for this working arrangement was refused. Nevertheless what the broad and narrow gauge companies were forbidden to do by overt treaty they seem to have achieved pretty successfully by private arrangement, and from the mid-sixties onwards there was reasonably cordial cooperation between the western associates of both the Great Western and the South Western. So far as the Central Cornwall line was concerned the opening of the various sections took place as follows:

Coleford Junction to North Tawton ..	1865
North Tawton to Okehampton.. ..	1867
Okehampton to Lydford	1874

There had originally been branch lines authorised from the Devon & Cornwall, as this group of lines became known, to Bude and Torrington; but these had been allowed to lapse. They were revived in 1873, and the Bude branch was constructed as far as Holsworthy in 1879. This diverged from the 'main line' at Meldon junction, in wild moorland country high on the northern slopes of Dartmoor where the line to Lydford attains an altitude of 950 ft. above sea level. This eventually proved to be the highest summit level anywhere on the L.S.W.R. Near to the junction the line crosses the West Okement river on a lofty viaduct of the Bouch type. It will be familiar to many who have not travelled that way, as it is one of the most photographed spots on the western lines of the L.S.W.R. In fine weather the prospect of the Dartmoor heights is magnificent with Yes Tor and High Willhays near at hand. One does not ordinarily associate the London & South Western Railway with high wind-swept mountain slopes; but there is certainly more than a taste of it on the line between Okehampton and Lydford. The gradients are appropriately severe.

From Meldon Junction the Bude branch wriggles its way over Bradbury to Halwill, where the line originally did no more than bifurcate. The South Western would gladly have abandoned their power to provide a branch to Torrington from this direction. As the management once aptly stated, branch lines originally intended as 'feeders' to the main system can all too easily prove to be no more than 'suckers'—a prediction that has been verified all too forcefully in our own times. In the case of Torrington however Parliament would not permit of the abandonment, and so a line that was probably unremunerative from the outset was built from Halwill Junction on a meandering course that passed no place larger than Hatherleigh on the way. From Halwill it is convenient to mention the westward extensions of the system, that came from 1886 onwards. The Lydford route was never a convenient way for the South Western to reach Launceston, and if traffic to the west was to be developed seriously an independent route was desirable. So a new line was constructed south-south-east from Halwill, and although this involved a longer mileage than via Lydford it was a much better route from the L.S.W.R. point of view.

From Launceston, reached from Halwill in 1886, the line was extended stage by stage until Wadebridge was eventually reached, and physical connection established at last with the patriarch of all lines in the L.S.W.R. system, the Bodmin & Wadebridge. The dates of completion of the various sections was as follows:

To Tresmeer	July 1892
To Camelford	August 1893
To Delabole	October 1893
To Wadebridge	June 1895

Finally, in 1898, the Holsworthy branch was extended to Bude, and in the following year the picturesque final stretch of the Devon & Cornwall line beside the estuary of the Camel, brought the L.S.W.R. into Padstow. But having achieved this it must be remarked that the lines west of Exeter did not constitute an easy economical unit to manage. To reach the resorts on what the Southern came to call the 'Atlantic Coast'—Ilfracombe, Bude, Padstow, meant the working of three separate branch lines, with a fourth if connections had to be provided for Bideford and Torrington. They were not short lines like the Great Western's to Falmouth, Helston and St. Ives, or even those to Looe and Perranporth.

A westward extension was not the only objective of the line skirting Dartmoor and coming eventually to Lydford in 1874. Here a junction was made with Launceston and South Devon branch of the South Devon Railway. This of course was a broad gauge line; but the spirit of cooperation between the different railway interests in Devon and Cornwall began to blossom. The South Devon had applied for Parliamentary powers to lay in mixed gauge on the Launceston branch whenever the Devon &

Cornwall Railway asked them to do so. Once in Lydford the L.S.W.R., which had by that time absorbed the Devon & Cornwall, applied for the mixed gauge to be laid. The South Western built a station of their own at Devonport, and in 1876 for the first time there was through communication between London and Plymouth by the narrow gauge. At that time the broad gauge companies were handling all their passenger business at Millbay; but the new station at North Road was put in hand in anticipation of the L.S.W.R. traffic, to be a joint station built entirely at the expense of the South Western. It was opened in March 1877. When the L.S.W.R. trains first came into Plymouth and Devonport they travelled from Tavistock down the Plym valley line passing through Yelverton and Plym Bridge, and joining the South Devon main line at Tavistock Junction. Thus originally they entered Plymouth from the east, and ran through to Devonport.

This entry to Plymouth, welcome as it was, could be regarded as no more than a temporary expedient, because the single-tracked Launceston branch of the Great Western was hardly ideal for what was hoped to be an important developing traffic. So the South Western built an entirely independent line, from Lydford, running closely parallel to the G.W.R.

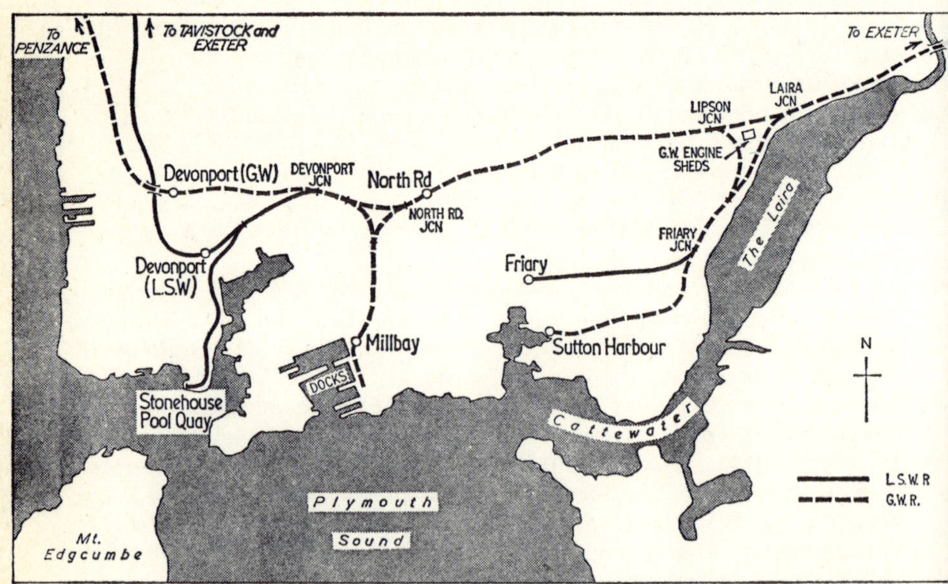

Launceston branch almost to Tavistock and then swinging away southwestwards to pass through Bere Alston and Bere Ferrers, and then follow the left hand bank of the Tamar. It passed beneath the Royal Albert Bridge opposite to Saltash, and entered Plymouth from the west. This line was opened in 1890, and had the curious effect of bringing *down*

L.S.W.R. trains into North Road in the same direction as *up* Great Western trains. The final development at Plymouth, so far as the L.S.W.R. was concerned, was the opening of the Friary station as the passenger terminus. This had been made possible by the Great Western constructing the curve between Lipson Junction to Mount Gould Junction—the third side of the triangle enclosing the G.W.R. Laira running sheds. The first L.S.W.R. trains used Friary station in July 1891.

Although the Great Western had facilitated the South Western entry into Plymouth, albeit at very little cost to themselves, and with the convenience of a new station thrown in free of charge, which was to avoid the inconvenience and delay in reversing all trains for Cornwall at Millbay, it was not long before the South Western came to be a very restless bedfellow in Plymouth. The day indeed was not far off when the two companies would be engaged in a 'stop-at-nothing' competition for the Ocean traffic between Plymouth and London. But a very curious outcome of the opening to Friary was the inauguration of a through carriage service with the Midland, and for the significance of this to be appreciated I must for a moment step outside the counties of Devon and Cornwall. The big broad gauge merger of 1876, by which the Great Western and the Bristol & Exeter were amalgamated, caused a flutter in many a railway board room, and one line lying almost within the folds of the Greater Great Western was the Somerset & Dorset. Its management half anticipated a 'take-over bid'. The conditions for one were certainly favourable, and as the London & South Western came to be involved the story may be told in outline here.

In the financial crisis of 1866 the railway was thrown into Chancery; but then, after its release in 1869 business boomed to such an extent that the very expensive extension from Evercreech Junction to Bath was undertaken. This line was opened in 1874, and proved so serious an incubus that the management made overtures to both the Great Western and the Bristol & Exeter. In the spirit of the Quadruple Treaty the two broad gauge companies told the South Western about this. Now the Somerset & Dorset provided a link with the Midland Railway, and Archibald Scott, General Manager of the L.S.W.R. saw an opportunity to realise an ambition cherished by the South Western since the days of the Gauge War, namely to establish direct communication with the Midlands, via the Midland Railway rather than by the Great Western. It is to be feared that all ideas of the Quadruple Treaty were temporarily thrown aside, and Scott went straight to Derby. The Midland were only too glad to enter into an alliance with the L.S.W.R., and the two companies jointly offered to take a lease of the Somerset & Dorset on such excellent terms that the poor little struggling company was glad enough to accept at once. It was not surprising that the Great Western were very annoyed!

Midland ambitions in the West Country were shown immediately the South Western had their own line into Plymouth by the introduction of a through carriage service from Leeds. In 1891, when Friary station was opened this could not have been done in any other way; for although the Great Western had laid in mixed gauge as far as Exeter there remained the purely broad gauge 'bloc' between Exeter and Truro. The Midland through carriages to Plymouth travelled via Birmingham, Bath, Templecombe, Exeter Queen Street, Okehampton, and Tavistock. From the point of divergence from the present route from the Midland to the west, Mangotsfield North Junction the mileage to Plymouth North Road was 166, as compared with 133·2, via Bristol, Taunton, and Newton Abbot. As far as I can trace the service lapsed very soon after the Great Western had abolished the broad gauge, after which Midland through carriages could be worked by the direct route.

VI

Bournemouth and Southampton

In the history of the London & South Western Railway there is no more curious passage than the way in which the railway reached Bournemouth. At the same time when one speaks of Bournemouth in the nineteenth century it is not to visualise the vast residential area that has grown up behind that wonderful stretch of golden sand that stretches from Hengisbury Head, to the east, to the entrance to Poole Harbour. It is rather the Bournemouth of the Wessex novels of Thomas Hardy, thinly disguised as 'Sandbourne', that is the place that at first seemed to be deliberately avoided by railways. It was as though Bournemouth was some hostile, impregnable fortress. The railway first took a wide sweep around it to the north; then there was a long-drawn-out flanking movement from the east, followed by another from the west, and it was not until 41 years after the opening of the Southampton and Dorchester line, from 1847 to 1888, that the line as we know it today, passing from east to west through the northern part of town, was completed.

The fact is that Bournemouth was a place of no importance to early railway promoters. The 'Southampton & Dorchester' was a strategic line in the gauge war, and when it fell to the South Western the route settled upon was designed to serve as many centres of population as possible Charles Castleman, a Wimborne solicitor, who in later years became Chairman of the L.S.W.R., was one of the moving spirits. The line must of necessity pass through Wimborne. Then there were Ringwood and Wareham to be served, while instead of making straight through the New Forest from the head of Southampton Water to Ringwood the line was carried in a wide sweep to the south to pass through Brockenhurst. The result was an extraordinarily sinuous route, aptly named "Castleman's corkscrew". Christchurch and Poole, no less than Bournemouth were completely by-passed, and the situation at Poole was an almost exact counterpart to that of Portsmouth in that this ancient seaport, standing on a fine harbour, was served no more than indirectly by a branch line from Hamworthy Junction that terminated at Hamworthy, on the wrong side of Poole Harbour. Poole itself had to be reached by ferry, and to reach Bournemouth one had to charter some road conveyance from Poole. It was probably quicker to get out of the train at Wimborne and travel by road across country.

The first step towards the improvement of communications in this area was the projecting and authorisation, in 1859, of the Ringwood, Christchurch and Bournemouth Railway—another curiously roundabout route, as can be seen from the map. But once again railway pioneers seemed loath to approach the 'impregnable citadel'! Construction of this line was authorised only as far as Christchurch, and after the opening of this line from Ringwood things went no further for several years. It was not until 1870 that the section between Christchurch and Bournemouth old station was opened. On the western side the approach was equally timorous. For example, in 1866 a branch was authorised from Poole Junction (now Broadstone) into Poole, with a continuation to what is now Bournemouth West; but for several years nothing was done. What really put the jerk into things on the west side of Bournemouth was, strangely enough the completion of the *northern* part of the Somerset & Dorset line, as told in Chapter Five of this book. By this a direct connection was established between Wimborne and the Midland Railway, at Bath. In readiness for this work was pushed ahead with the Poole and Bournemouth extensions, and by the end of 1874 through carriages from the Midland could be worked into Bournemouth West.

This development went some way towards realising Chaplin's ambition of a connection from Southampton to the Midland line; but when the service from Bournemouth was first operated the trains ran via Wimborne and had to reverse direction there. The direct connection from the Somerset & Dorset, from Corfe Mullen Junction to Poole Junction was not made until 1886. While connections were being improved on the western side the route from London still remained via Ringwood, Christchurch and into the old station, known as Bournemouth East. Until 1878 there was a further hindrance in the journey. At Southampton the Dorchester line had been constructed to terminate at the original station of the London & Southampton Railway, and reversal of direction was also necessary there. The northern curve, to provide direct running from London to Bournemouth, was opened in 1874. At that time, too, the site of the present Southampton Central station was anything but central, and it was occupied by a country station on the outskirts named Blechynden.

It is said that certain influential residents of Bournemouth opposed the coming of the railway, as others of their kind had done at Northampton, Stamford, and elsewhere; but there is no doubt that there was a conspicuous lack of drive and purpose in the higher management of the L.S.W.R. It was indeed once apostrophised as the worst managed railway in Britain. Such an indictment is nevertheless unfair to Archibald Scott, who, for 32 years had the unenviable task first as traffic manager, and then as general manager, of running the railway. His resignation, in November 1884 seems to have taken the Board by surprise, for they did not appoint a successor till March of the following year. Scott had all the burden of affairs through the most tiresome years of rivalry with the Great Western, and the worst that could really be said of his management was that he considered the shareholders more than his customers. In 1868 'Punch' had sarcastically commented that the L.S.W.R. 'had put one fifteenth per cent. into the pockets of 20,000 shareholders by destroying the comfort and crippling the accommodation of as many million passengers'. On his retirement Scott joined the Board of Directors.

After casting the net far and wide for likely candidates for the general managership the choice fell upon Charles Scotter, Goods Manager of the Manchester, Sheffield & Lincolnshire Railway, who was then just 50 years of age. Like most nineteenth century general managers Scotter had climbed from the lowest rung of the ladder, having risen from junior clerk in the Hull goods depot of the M.S.L.R. Prior to joining the South Western all his career had been spent on that line, where his abilities had caught the eye first of James Allport and then of Sir Edward Watkin. At the early age of 25 he was appointed Passenger Superintendent, and subsequently he played an outstanding part in the development of traffic through the port of Grimsby. His work in the fostering of rail–sea trade on Humberside was a striking prelude to the great development he was to initiate on Southampton Water. He came to the South Western well known as a man of immense enterprise—an apt pupil of Allport and Watkin, with the sagacity of the former and the vision, though not the buccaneering instincts of the latter. On hearing of his appointment a wit among the shareholders is said to have remarked: "Scott, now Scotter—I suppose the next G.M. will be Scottest!"

The new general manager was no believer in cheese-paring methods to scrape a meagre dividend; immediately he put his whole weight behind major development projects, and one of these was the development of Bournemouth. It was certainly time to do something better than the existing roundabout route via Ringwood, and plans were put in hand for the construction of a new direct line from Brockenhurst to Christchurch, via Sway and Hinton Admiral. The old Bournemouth East station, a terminus, was replaced by a fine new station arranged for through traffic from east to west, and in March 1888 the direct route was opened throughout, with a connection into Bournemouth West station. With such facilities Scotter could begin to develop an excellent passenger service, which benefited Weymouth as well as Bournemouth. From 1890 onwards a Pullman car was run, though in South Western days these facilities did not attract business to the same extent as they did on the neighbouring Brighton railway. Many years were to pass before there was to be a 'Bournemouth Belle'.

The new 'direct' line to Bournemouth ran through pleasant country, touching the fringe of forest country again at Hinton Admiral. But one section originally proved a point of great anxiety to the engineers. After leaving the old route at Lymington Junction the new line climbs over open heathland to Sway on a gradient of 1 in 100, and near Sway itself there is an embankment 60 ft. high. The local soil is blue clay, and in early days there were frequent slips in the bank due to the crumbling nature of this soil. Over the years the natural soil has been largely replaced by chalk and Portland stone added to form a hard and stable foundation for the line. The connection to the Ringwood line at Christchurch was laid in for reasonably fast running, though the curve through Christchurch station remained. I speak feelingly of that curve! In the days of the

Drummond 4-4-0s the old drivers showed it no respect. They used to come down Hinton Admiral bank like the proverbial bomb, and take the Christchurch curves at full speed so as to get a 'run' at the sharp rise through Pokesdown. In the old South Western coaches the lurch as we hit the reverse curve in the platforms can be better imagined than described. They were not the smoothest riding of carriages anyway, but from my experience on the footplate many years later I should imagine those fine engines took the curve much more comfortably than the carriages!

From the complicated, and roundabout nature of its build-up the Bournemouth district eventually had quite a comprehensive network of

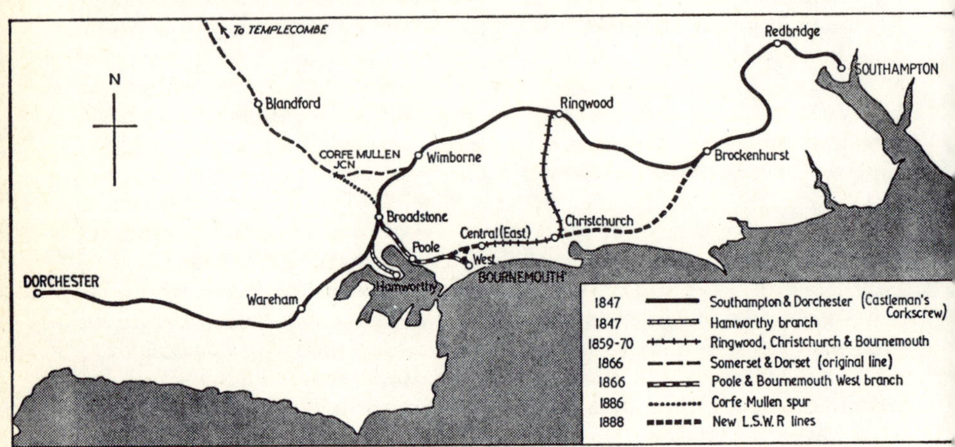

railways. The last link was the construction, in 1893 of the Holes Bay curve, to permit of direct running from Bournemouth and Poole to Dorchester. From this time onwards the present pattern of train services developed, whereby expresses from Waterloo included portions for Weymouth and Bournemouth West, which were combined or divided at Bournemouth Central. Use of the old line via Ringwood diminished, though at first there were a few trains to Swanage and Weymouth routed that way to avoid the Bournemouth district. Today it is used at busy holiday times for block-load trains, though I have known this cause complications through drivers not 'knowing the road', and needing a conductor beyond Brockenhurst. From the 'nineties' of last century Bournemouth came rapidly to the fore as one of the most potentially valuable sources of South Western holiday traffic, and through services were eventually established via Basingstoke and Reading West, to Birkenhead, and to as far afield as Newcastle-on-Tyne.

While the principal source of income to the L.S.W.R. from the Bournemouth district was in passengers Scotter was quick to appreciate the far more diverse possibilities of Southampton. Here it was the maritime side of railway enterprise that claimed his attention, and from his previous experience at Hull and Grimsby he saw a great opportunity for the L.S.W.R. The affairs of the Southampton Dock Company were in a very poor state. A policy of stagnation over many years had led to serious losses of trade to more enterprising concerns. Despite the tremendous possibilities of its situation the port of Southampton had not advanced with the times. Nothing had been done to provide for the larger ships that were being introduced on the great trade routes of the world; silting up continued, and eventually there came the blow that made even the most supine of managements to realise their plight—the great fleet of the Peninsular & Oriental Steam Navigation Company was moved away from Southampton. Far-seeing men had clamoured for deep water in vain. Now it seemed that nothing could save the port from falling into disuse, except for a small amount of coasting trade.

The state of this port was not the only reason for the removal of the P. & O. fleet—in fact it was not the principal one. The opening of the Suez Canal had led to many changes in the shipping arrangements to India and the Far East, and the P. & O. was faced by new lines carrying cargoes at highly competitive rates. Many of these shippers that had been placing their cargoes with the P. & O. worked from London, and no objection was raised to the cost of rail carriage between London and Southampton. Then the Post Office decided to speed up the Imperial Indian Mail by sending it overland from Calais to Brindisi, instead of through Southampton. This change was made in 1881, and was the final factor that led to the P. & O. decision to make London the terminal point; combined with the loss of cargo to other lines which docked in London and avoided rail charges, plus the condition of the port itself it was enough to cause this drastic decision. It was a bitter enough blow for Southampton, but so far as the L.S.W.R. was concerned salt was rubbed into the wounds of lost traffic by the inward bound P. & O. liners calling at Plymouth, and handing over their London passengers to the Great Western Railway!

Then upon this dismal scene came Charles Scotter, and on his recommendation an arrangement was made, in 1892, for the L.S.W.R. to purchase the entire estate of the Southampton Dock Company. Never was there such a transformation! The overdue dredging was put in hand at once; the defeatist attitude vanished overnight, as it were, and the Company started campaigning for business in addition to improving its own steamer services to Havre, the Channel Isles, and the Breton packet stations. It so happened that the Mersey Docks and Harbour Board was just then resting upon its laurels. It was not that the Liverpool Docks were inefficient; the port was then so full of traffic that the Board saw no reason to make any special efforts to assist the enterprise of individual shipping lines. There were disagreements with the Liverpool Corporation, and although the arrangements for conveying passengers from Lime Street to the Landing Stage were most comprehensive there was all the trouble of transferring the luggage of ocean passengers from train to omnibus, and then of repeating the process at the quayside. Charles Scotter who had come to Waterloo straight from Manchester was well enough aware of this, and of the dissatisfaction among the shipping people; and he proceeded to 'cash in' upon the vastly more favourable situation at Southampton, where the trains could be brought alongside the steamers.

The real turning point in the fortune of Southampton as a great port came in 1893 when the Inman Line decided to transfer the terminal port for its transatlantic services from Liverpool to Southampton. This move was also the first nail in the coffin of Merseyside as the premier port of Great Britain for first class traffic to America. The capturing of this business was a great triumph for Scotter, because at the time the Inman crisis blew up in Liverpool there had not been much time to rehabilitate and modernise Southampton. Enthusiasm and enterprise by themselves cannot deal with large Transatlantic liners. The Inman Line had to make their decision upon what Scotter promised, rather than what he had actually available; but within five years everything promised had been done, and by the end of the year 1897 Southampton was the regular calling port of the Royal Mail, Hamburg-America, North German Lloyd, Nederland, General Steam Navigation, Rotterdam Lloyd, and the two South African lines that were then separate—the Castle, and the Union, later to combine as one of the most famous British steamship lines, the Union Castle. In addition there were several companies sailing in the narrow seas, such as the City of Cork, the British and Irish, and the Liverpool Bristol & London.

All this was a great triumph for Scotter; but things did not stop when promises to Inman had been fulfilled. Reclamation work was started on waste ground to the west, known locally as the 'Mudlands', and by that same year, 1897, Southampton had what was then the largest graving dock in the world. In 1894 the great natural advantages of Southampton, and the unbounded enterprise of the London & South Western Railway so impressed the military authorities that they decided to transfer the service of transporting troops from Portsmouth. Only a few years later, with the onset of war in South Africa, Southampton had its first big test, and this was no more than a small rehearsal, as it were, for the tremendous task that was to come in 1914. So far as general business was concerned the upsurge in traffic through the port after the South Western acquired the docks could well read like a fairy tale. In no more than *six months* after the change in ownership imports were up by 32 per cent., exports by 56 per cent., and passenger traffic by 25 per cent. The town itself benefited by all this increased activity, and in 1895 public gratitude to the L.S.W.R. and to Scotter in particular found expression when the citizens entertained him at a great banquet.

In November 1897 *The Railway Magazine* commenting upon Scotter's forthcoming retirement said:

Waterloo: approach lines, and "A" signal box, taken just after the 1892 remodelling.
[*British Railways*

A period piece on No. 1 main line platform, prior to the departure of the 11 a.m. Plymouth Express. [*British Railways*

Circulating area.

The main line cab yard. [*British Railways*

A panorama of Waterloo station in 1904 after the

ebuilding had commenced, taken from "A" signal box. [*British Railways*

On the Windsor side, 1915: a view taken between Nos. 12 and 15 platforms.

On the concourse, July 1919, showing unfinished work on the north side of the station.
[*British Railways*

A Bournemouth express of pre-1914 days in Earlsfield cutting, hauled by "T9" 4-4-0 No. 307. [*L.P. Co.*

30 p.m. Bournemouth and Weymouth express near Clapham Junction hauled by superheated "D15" 4-4-0 No. 467. [*Real Photos*

Bogie first class carriage of 1890–5 period.

Sleeping car of 1908, built for the Plymouth–Waterloo American boat specials.

Dining Car for the West of England services, built 1901.

[*All British Railwa*

"There have been many master strokes in the policy that has gone forth from Waterloo since March 1885, but none more momentous than that which led to the acquisition by the South Western Railway of the magnificent docks at Southampton."

The event could certainly have been hailed as momentous a mere five years later; but viewing in retrospect all that has happened at Southampton since 'momentous' seems to be an inadequate word. Not even Scotter, one would imagine, could have looked forward to the day when three lengthy boat trains would lie alongside the 83,000-ton Cunard liner *Queen Elizabeth*, or when the Southern Railway, as successor to the L.S.W.R. would construct the gigantic dry dock that can take these enormous liners. Southampton Docks provide, indeed, one of the greatest 'success-stories' of L.S.W.R. history, and of its originator, the man who learnt his job on the banks of the Humber.

While the more spectacular side of South Western maritime activities was concentrated upon the ocean traffic the company's own fleet was one of the finest sailing the narrow seas. I need not go into the early history of the packet services from Southampton, and of the rival companies engaged in the runs from Southampton and Weymouth to the Channel Islands. At first the railway company was not permitted to own and operate steamers, and so the South Western Steam Navigation Company was formed in 1845. This company immediately took over the mail service to the Channel Islands, and also ran to Havre and St. Malo. Three years later the railway company obtained authority to own, maintain, and operate steamships, for a period of 14 years; but in 1860 a further Act provided that authority to be given in perpetuity. Activities were gradually increasing, until at the turn of the century the L.S.W.R. owned no fewer than twenty vessels. The services worked some in the summer only, and some on no more than two or three days in the week, were then:

Southampton to Guernsey	104	nautical	miles
Southampton to Jersey (direct)	122½	"	"
Jersey to Guernsey	26½	"	"
Jersey to St. Malo	33½	"	"
Jersey to Granville	30	"	"
Southampton to St. Malo (direct)	151	"	"
Southampton to Havre	104	"	"
Southampton to Cherbourg	83	"	"
Guernsey to Cherbourg	45¾	"	"
Lymington to Yarmouth	4¼	"	"
Lymington to Totland Bay	8¼	"	"
Jersey to Cherbourg	57	"	"

Navigation in the seas immediately surrounding the Channel Islands can be exceedingly hazardous, especially in fog, and in the earlier days the annals of the L.S.W.R. fleet include several major disasters. The first of these tragedies befell one of the earliest ships of the fleet, the *Express*, built by Ditchburn & Marr, at Blackwall, in 1847. She earned fame a year later by conveying the fugitive King Louis Philippe of France from Havre to Southampton in 1848. She was a paddle steamer 160 ft. long, and her end came in September 1859 when she was wrecked off the Corbiere lighthouse, shortly after leaving Jersey, on the voyage to Southampton. Fog again led to a fatal collision in 1870 when the 550-ton *Normandy* was cut down and sunk by a larger steamer, with the loss of 33 lives. There is a memorial to the gallantry of the crew of the *Normandy*, at the entrance to St. Helier harbour.

At Southampton itself the usual working for the Channel Islands packet boats was to load up cargo at the docks, and then sail round to the Royal Pier to pick up the passengers. But from 1864 onwards the passengers joined the ship at the docks. Although it had been the practice to convey passengers by train to the landing stage the journey was apparently beset by a great many delays, and the new arrangement was welcomed by everyone except the Royal Pier authorities, who lost a good deal of money in the way of tolls and dues. The L.S.W.R. was by that time operating a large enough traffic to have some purely cargo boats in addition to the mail and packet steamers, and the business profited like so much in Great Britain at the time, from the incidence of the Franco-Prussian war of 1870–1. Trade was indeed such as to lead to the purchase of two additional vessels specially for conveying horses and other military supplies to France. Two large paddle steamers with clipper bows and heavily raked funnels were put on this work. They weie named *Fanny* and *Alice*. These two vessels were each ten years old at the time of their purchase by the L.S.W.R. They had already seen a good deal of war service of an exciting kind, having beeen engaged in blockade-running during the American Civil War. In L.S.W.R. service they had no further adventures, and both were in regular working from Southampton for nearly 30 years.

The year 1871 saw the last paddle steamers purchased for the cross-Channel run. After that only screw steamers were ordered, and by the speed demanded the design of the ships attracted particular attention. As a regular feat of mechanical engineering performance, the *Dora* of 1889 achieved something that in those days bordered on the phenomenal. She had a displacement of 1,114 tons and a speed of 16½ knots. But she was not what sailors call 'a good sea boat'. She rolled disconcertingly in rough sea, and despite her speed became most unpopular with travellers. She was sold in 1900 after only 11 years service. But the three larger vessels of 1890, the *Frederica*, the *Lydia* and the *Stella*, while still faster were very popular ships. They were of the twin-screw type, with a displacement of 1,630 tons, and the specification called for a guaranteed speed of 17 knots, with natural draught and 18 knots with a forced draught. When each of these three ships produced 19½ knots on trial they created much attention among marine engineers.

One of these fine vessels was lost in one of the greatest peacetime disasters to occur to British packet steamers. In March 1899, in dense fog, the *Stella* struck the Black Rock off the Casquets, Jersey, and sank with the loss of 104 lives; but even this tragedy was exceeded in November 1905, when one of the older ships, the *Hilda*, struck a rock at the entrance to St. Malo harbour during a snowstorm. She rolled off into deep water and sank with the great loss of life. No fewer than 128 persons were drowned—a terrible toll, with no more than a small packet steamer. Although it is inevitably these great misfortunes that stand out among the events of the L.S.W.R. maritime activities in the 19th century the steamer services of the company enjoyed a steadily increasing popularity even before the great reformation of the port of Southampton, following the appointment of Charles Scotter as General Manager. The ships *Frederica*, *Lydia*, and *Stella* were certainly a great credit to any steamship company.

But so far as ships were concerned the first result of Scotter's developments was a great improvement in the service between Southampton and Havre. On its transfer from Liverpool the Inman Line changed its name to the American Line, and its establishment at Southampton led to increased traffic between England and France. In 1894 two new vessels were put on to the Havre run, the *Alma*, and the *Columbia*. Although having a gross tonnage of no more than the *Frederica* and her two sisters—they were designed to have the appearance of an ocean-going liner. A first glance at a photograph of the *Columbia* could easily suggest a ship of 15,000 tons, or more. They had a guaranteed speed of 19 knots and were driven by two sets of four-cylinder triple expansion engines. The style of the *Alma* and of the *Columbia* became the standard for South Western vessels from that time onwards, and the *Victoria* and the *Vera*, introduced in 1896 and 1898 respectively followed the same general design. These ships, with their black hulls, and buff funnels without any black band at the top had a most distinctive and graceful appearance.

During the winter months around this period the Channel Islands mail service from Waterloo was run on three days a week, with a service on alternate days from Paddington and the Great Western route via Weymouth. During the summer the L.S.W.R. service was daily, with the boat train from Waterloo calling at Basingstoke, Winchester and Eastleigh. The actual running was not very fast by present standards as the overall time from Waterloo to the Channel Islands shed at Southampton Docks was 2 hr. 5 min. The Channel Islands boat train leaving Waterloo at 9.50 p.m. also provided the nightly service to France via Southampton and Havre, and connected with the North German Lloyd, Hamburg-America, and American Line steamers. The 9.50 p.m. departure from Waterloo ran daily throughout the year, but during the winter there was only the Havre steamer on three nights in the week.

The principal steamer services to the Isle of Wight were run jointly with the London Brighton & South Coast Railway, and worked from both Portsmouth Harbour and Stokes Bay to Ryde; but while on the Hampshire coast mention must also be made of the purely South Western services from Lymington to the western resorts of the Island. These were maintained by two pretty little paddle steamers, the *Lymington*, built by

Day, Summers & Co. of Southampton, in 1893, and the *Solent*, built by Mordey, Carney & Co. Ltd. of Southampton in 1902. The railways leading to the ferry terminals for the Isle of Wight services may also be mentioned. The extension of the Gosport branch to Stokes Bay was made in 1863, to provide railway connection to a convenient pier that would be available at all states of the tide. At that time the arrangements in Portsmouth were not particularly good. The Isle of Wight boats sailed from Clarence Pier, and railway traffic was worked through the streets over a tramway from Portsmouth Town station. The extension to the present Harbour station was made jointly by the L.S.W.R. and the L.B.S.C.R. in 1873.

The Lymington branch was the oldest of the three. The single line track from Brockenhurst was opened in 1858; it was at first an independent company which in 1859 purchased also the ferry between Lymington and the Island. The branch became the subject of an amusing 'inside' incident during the Second World War. Joint Anglo-American plans for the invasion of the European mainland were in full swing, and an American officer who was involved was appalled at what he considered was the inadequate nature of the Lymington branch; it was single-tracked, it was hilly, its course wandered about the country, there was very little siding accommodation at the ferry terminal, and in short it was quite useless for transporting troops and stores. The British railways, in his view, had got to do something about it, and do it quickly. A very old friend of mine, a railwayman of wide experience and then serving with the Royal Engineers, was attached to this American unit for liaison purposes, and he pointed out that it was hardly reasonable to expect money to be spent upon improving a branch line that would have very little chance of post-war developments. Being a railway enthusiast as well he told the Americans something of the past history of the branch.

The senior American officer listened, one fears with some impatience; then he addressed my friend and the other American officers thus: 'We're nart interested in the carst; we're nart interest in post-war development. We're gonna win this goddam war.' Then he rose imperiously, took a rule and strode to the map on the wall. 'Gentlemen', he said dramatically, 'we build a nu railroad.' He drew a thick straight line on the map from Brockenhurst to Lymington. 'That's the route. We start, Monday'! Despite this however the little branch line remained unaltered.

VII

Mechanical Engineering to 1900

Adams, and the First Phases of Drummond

W. G. Beattie did not survive his father for long at Nine Elms. As frequently happens when the head of an engineering department, locomotive or otherwise, is himself a designer of great individuality no steps are taken to build up a team to follow the chief, and when he is gone either the whole organisation, such as it is, falls to pieces, or a complete stranger has to be brought in to take over. Either process causes something of an upheaval, and on the L.S.W.R. when W. G. Beattie retired in 1877, due to ill health, the directors went outside for a successor. The choice fell upon William Adams then Locomotive Superintendent of the Great Eastern Railway. But Adams was very far removed from the kind of nineteenth century locomotive man who served his apprenticeship in one works, and then moved around from railway to railway gradually climbing the ladder. The early life and work of the new chief at Nine Elms had been connected entirely with ships; but that was perhaps not inappropriate for his new post carried with it responsibility for the mechanical engineering of the L.S.W.R. fleet of steamers.

His father was a marine engineer in the service of the East & West India Docks Company, and at a very early age young William was working at Limehouse under his father. When he was old enough he was apprenticed to another firm on Thames-side, and then, when he was a little more than 20 years of age, he went to the Mediterranean to a firm with shipyards at Marseilles and Genoa, where he was responsible for installing marine engines and carrying out trial trips. Then, in 1848, amid the many political upheavals in Europe that led, among other things, to the Kingdom of Sardinia incorporating the provinces of Lombardy and Venice, he became engineer to the Sardinian steam navy. He was then 25 years of age, and as a big hearty 'typical' Englishman—game for any adventure, or engineering experience,—his future might have seemed to have lain anywhere on earth. But in 1852 he was married, and soon afterwards he decided to return home, and make his career in England, and that came to mean with railways. Before he came to Nine Elms he had been locomotive superintendent of two other railways, the North London until 1873, and then the Great Eastern.

The career of William Adams was unusual in another respect. Many cases come to mind of men of strong personality with a record of success behind them coming to a new railway and then literally turning the place upside down. Adams did nothing of the kind at Nine Elms, instead taking the pulse of the place gradually, and so, as previously at Bow and

Stratford, getting the men solidly behind him. Wherever he had been Adams was a well-liked man; not only was his engineering practice essentially sound, but he had a very pleasant way of putting his ideas across to others. By a rather curious coincidence the way had been paved for him in the design of new locomotives by the changes W. G. Beattie had made from the practice of his father, and the outside cylinder 4-4-0s of 1876 could, in some aspects of their appearance, be regarded as having the Adams 'look' about them. The close correspondence between the time of their delivery on the L.S.W.R. and the retirement of Beattie has more than once been suggested as the reason for their appearance—namely that Adams had the task of finishing them off, so far as outward looks went.

Although he produced several other excellent designs for the L.S.W.R. the name of William Adams will always be associated with the 'family' of outside cylindered 4-4-0s put on the road from 1879 onwards, together with the associated 4-4-2 tanks. These latter were originally built as 4-4-0s after the style of his very successful North London engines of the same wheel arrangement. The suburban services of the South Western involved longer runs than those of the North London, and to provide increased bunker capacity these tank engines were altered from 4-4-0s to 4-4-2s. The four-coupled, bogie, outside-cylindered family can be summarised thus:

Date	Coupled wheel dia. ft.	in.	First engine Number	Cylinders in. dia.	stroke	No. in class	Type
1879	5	7	46	18	24	12	4-4-2T
1879	5	7	380	18	24	12	4-4-0
1880	6	7	135	18	24	33	4-4-0
1882	5	7	415	17½	24	71	4-4-2T
1883	7	1	445	18	24	12	4-4-0
1890	7	1	577	19	26	20	4-4-0
1892	6	7	557	19	26	20	4-4-0
1895	7	1	677	19	26	10	4-4-0
1895	6	7	657	19	26	10	4-4-0

Whatever deficiencies there may have been in Beattie's 4-4-0 passenger engines no such stigma could be attached to the early designs of William Adams. All his engines with 18 in. by 24 in. cylinders were uniformly excellent, and the '380' class of 5 ft. 7 in. 4-4-0, despite their relatively small numbers, had a way of turning up almost everywhere on the system. The 17½ in. 4-4-2 tanks were also universal favourites, and in quite recent years it would be interesting to know how much film, ciné and otherwise, has been exposed by countless railway enthusiasts in recording the going and comings of the two last survivors, on the Axminster–Lyme Regis branch. In their prime, in the London residential area these excellent engines were required for many fast services on the Aldershot and Farnham trains, while a batch of them had a monopoly of the Reading line, so far as the L.S.W.R. was concerned.

The express passenger 4-4-0s can be grouped in three distinct series: the 18 in. engines of 1880–3; the original 19 in. group of 1890–2, and the final 20, similar in general to the foregoing but with longer fireboxes. It is significant of the pressure of repair work at Nine Elms that for ten years after Adams had succeeded Beattie no new locomotives were built in the works. The first 12 of the new 6 ft. 7 in. 4-4-0s of 1880 were built by Beyer, Peacock & Co., and later engines of the class were built by both Neilsons, and Robert Stephenson & Co. With these 18 in. 4-4-0s Adams initiated the practice that both he and Dugald Drummond followed for nearly 30 years afterwards, in designing engines with large diameter driving wheels for the Salisbury and Bournemouth roads, and identical ones, with smaller wheels for the line west of Salisbury. Adams used 7 ft. 1 in., and 6 ft. 7 in. diameter wheels, and in later years Drummond used 6 ft. 7 in. and 6 ft. 0 in. The dimension of 6 ft. 7 in. for the driving wheel diameter remained standard for express passenger locomotives throughout the remainder of South Western history, and was used subsequently by R. E. L. Maunsell on the 'Lord Nelson' and 'Schools' classes on the Southern Railway.

It is a little strange that among locomotive enthusiasts of the 19th century, such as E. L. Ahrons and Charles Rous-Marten, there was considerably greater enthusiasm for the performance of the 18 in. 4-4-0s than for the later 19 in. engines. The latter, both of the 6 ft. 7 in., and of the 7 ft. 1 in. varieties, were among the most handsome locomotives running in all Britain, in the 'nineties'. They were not unduly embellished, but they had a magnificent symmetry and unity about their external design, in which the very plainness of their stove-pipe chimneys fitted perfectly. In later years, when Dugald Drummond fitted them with chimneys of his own pattern that looked so well on the 'T9' 4-4-0s, the appearance of the Adams engines descended from the outstanding to the commonplace. The schedules, even of the crack trains, were not fast, and at that time the average speed of the 12.30 p.m. from Waterloo to Bournemouth was only 47½ m.p.h. on the non-stop run to Southampton. The 12.15 p.m. from Waterloo ran non-stop to Christchurch, but averaged only 46 m.p.h.

Adams laid great emphasis on economical running, and what Joseph Beattie achieved with a plethora of gadgets hung around his engines, which increased the maintenance costs as much as they reduced the fuel costs, Adams achieved with simplicity in design, sound engineering principles and superb workmanship in construction. The slide valves had the conventional short lap of that period, only 1 in. with a travel in full gear of 3⅞ in., and there was nothing in the dimensions of the steam or exhaust ports to suggest that these 19 in. 4-4-0s would be anything out of the ordinary in running. It is sometimes assumed that any locomotive with short lap valves must of necessity be worked on a partly opened regulator and cut-offs of the order of 30 per cent.; but the big Adams 4-4-0s of both 6 ft. 7 in. and 7 ft. 1 in. classes were habitually run in 17 per cent., and they were very economical in consequence. They were fitted with screw reverse, which permitted of a much finer adjustment of cut-off than on the majority of contemporary engines having lever reverse; on the latter 'one-notch' usually meant a change of about 10 per cent. in cut-off.

The only design feature on these locomotives that could be regarded as unusual was the Adams Vortex blast pipe. The object of this device was to equalise the draught over all the tubes in the boiler, instead of creating the strongest draught in those tubes nearest in level to the top of the blast pipe. In the Adams arrangement instead of there being a solid cone of exhaust steam in the blastpipe the cross-section of the steam space is annular, as if a scientifically shaped 'dart' or 'jemmy' had been inserted in the centre. This was a well-known, though unofficial way of getting a bad engine to steam; but in the Adams design the cross-section of the annular space was proportioned to give a free exhaust, rather than to sharpen the blast. But the outer casing of the blastpipe was not continuous, and in the lower part there was an opening that faced the lower rows of tubes. The rush of exhaust steam up the blastpipe was thus exposed in this area, and had an entraining effect upon the smokebox gases, and created an additional draught upon the lower tubes. The reduction in velocity of the blast, at the point of issuing from the top of the blastpipe, accompanied by an equable action on the tubes, caused a more uniform flow of air through the firebox. It was found that no holes developed even with a thin fire, and there was a notable absence of spark throwing.

The thermodynamic performance of these engines was more fully documented for posterity than that of any other 19th century locomotives. In July 1891 one of the 7 ft. 1 in. class was put through a series of indicator trials as follows:

July 9, 1891: 5.50 a.m. Waterloo to Bournemouth
July 9, 1891: 1.55 p.m. Bournemouth to Waterloo
July 10, 1891: 11 a.m. Waterloo to Exeter
July 11, 1891: 12.45 p.m. Exeter to Woking
July 13, 1891: 2.40 p.m. Waterloo to Salisbury

These trials formed the subject of a very comprehensive paper presented to the Institution of Civil Engineers by Mr. Adams in collaboration with W. F. Pettigrew, who afterwards became Locomotive Engineer of the Furness Railway. In 1899 Pettigrew published his monumental book *A Manual of Locomotive Engineering*, to which A. F. Ravenshear of the Patent Office contributed an interesting section on American and Continental locomotives. In that book the trials of the Adams 7 ft. 4-4-0 are described and discussed at some length. The over-all results can be tabulated as follows:

Test No.	Average load tons tare	Number of Intermediate stops	Average running speed m.p.h.	Max. speed m.p.h.	Max. I.H.P.	Coal per mile lb.	Coal per I.H.P. hr.	Water per lb. of coal
1	179¾	11	37·2	68½	684	30·5	1·98	9·68
2	136	4	45·2	67	610	27·1	2·39	8·78
3	168	3	46·0	78	803½	28·4	2·14	8·84
4	199	5	42·3	81	804	33	2·20	7·91
5	137	3	46·7	75	626	28·1	2·12	9·34

The values of coal consumption per indicated horsepower hour are certainly remarkable. In 1925 a great stir was caused in locomotive engineering circles when the Great Western Railway published the test results from the 4-6-0 engine No. 4074 *Caldicot Castle*, and the value of coal per I.H.P. hour was given as 2·1 lb. It seems that William Adams was getting almost as good results from his 7 ft. 4-4-0s in 1891. The coal used in the L.S.W.R. trials was Welsh, with a calorific value of 13,903 B.Th.U. per lb. This was a little lower than the calorific value of coal used in the much publicised 'Castle' trials of 1924.

It is also very interesting to study the conditions in which the maximum indicated horsepower records were obtained, as follows:

MAXIMUM I.H.P. RECORDS

Test No.	Max. I.H.P.	Location	Speed m.p.h.	Cut-off per cent.	Conditions
1	684	Brookwood	40	29·5	Accelerating from Woking stop
2	610	Micheldever	43	26	Climbing on 1 in 249
3	803½	Honiton Bank	31	44	On 1 in 80, entrance to tunnel
4	804¼	Milepost 115	27½	48	Climbing from Sherborne
5	626	Grateley	50	20	Climbing from Andover

It is equally interesting to note some I.H.P. valves at short cut-offs and high speed, as follows:

Test No.	I.H.P.	Location	Speed m.p.h.	Cut-off per cent.	Remarks
1	480	Winchester Junction	68	17	Descending 1 in 251
2	571½	Woking	66	17	Descending 1 in 384
3	517	Hurstbourne	78	17	Descending 1 in 100
4	636	Axminster	80	17	Foot of Honiton bank
5	602	Andover	72½	17	Approaching Andover

All these can certainly be set down as most excellent results, and amply confirm that these engines were not only superb in appearance but were second to none in their performance. May I add two boyhood memories of them. The first was in 1912 when there was a coal strike on. The family was journeying from Reading to Southsea. We had to change at Eastleigh, and for what seemed an eternity we sat in a non-corridor train waiting for it to start. But that long wait was enlivened for me by the coming and going of many trains. I had never seen the Adams 4-4-0s before. At Reading in those days all the L.S.W.R. trains were hauled by the Drummond 0-4-4 tanks, and I can remember to this day how impressed—almost overawed—I was, with the sight of those seemingly huge engines, with their outside connecting rods and pistons plunging back and forth.

The second memory is of the following year when we were on holiday at Weymouth. We had made an expedition to Upwey, to see, among other things, the Wishing Well, and in the evening we made our way to Upwey Wishing Well Halt to catch the Great Western local back to Weymouth. While we were on the platform an up train was signalled and it proved to be a South Western. The gradient at that point, climbing to Bincombe Tunnel is 1 in 50, and this South Western train was coming up unassisted. The engine was one of the 6 ft. 7 in. Adams 4-4-0s, and I can't remember how many coaches she had on. What I *do* remember however is the positive cannonade of the exhaust, and the sight she made coming up that bank in the dusk. Whether she still had the Vortex blast pipe at that stage I cannot tell, but the sparks were going sky-high. If ever a British locomotive has given me the impression of really *fighting* a gradient I received it that evening at Upwey Wishing Well Halt.

In writing of the locomotives designed by William Adams it is natural that prominence should be given to his big outside-cylinder 4-4-0s. They were to the rest of the stud as Sir Nigel Gresley's streamlined 'A4's' were to the L.N.E.R. in the years just before World War II; but from 1887 onwards some very fine engines for less spectacular duties were built at Nine Elms. It was with the well-known 'Jubilee' 0-4-2s that new construction was resumed at the L.S.W.R. main works, after a period of 10 years; and a more appropriate design could not have been imagined. At the same time there was general surprise in railway circles that Adams should have abandoned outside cylinders; indeed except for the express passenger 4-4-0s he built no more outside cylindered engines at all. Furthermore, all of them, with the exception of some small 0-6-0 tanks for shunting were of the front-coupled type—0-4-2 for main line mixed-traffic, and 0-4-4 for local passenger trains. It is generally thought that Adams was influenced by the strong advocacy of Stroudley for the front-coupled type, and by the great success of the 'Gladstone' class. But he was not influenced sufficiently to adopt it for the heaviest express work.

Charles Rous-Marten discussed this matter at some length in an early issue of *The Railway Magazine*. In such matters he had the advantage of being on the friendliest personal terms with most of the leading railway mechanical engineers of the day, and in February 1903 he wrote:

"Mr. Adams was also a consistent advocate of outside cylinders for express work. All the 105 express engines he built for the London & South Western Railway had—indeed, I might say *have*, for all are still at work—outside cylinders. I had some most interesting talks with him on this subject. He always treated it very fairly and without prejudice, but declared that after full consideration he had come to the conclusion that the outside position for cylinders was preferable; firstly, on account of the cranked axle, with its inherent weakness of shape, being got rid of; and secondly, because of the superior accessibility of working parts which was obtained. He admitted frankly the drawbacks of exposure—with consequent liability to excessive condensation, and the 'punching' movement, and greater construction weight, also the advantage of a more central pull and middle line of motion possessed by inside cylinder engines; but stated that after weighing all advantages and disadvantages of each method his choice rested with outside-cylinders. In this decision he has, of course, the unanimous support of American engineers, and the almost unanimous concurrence of European and Continental engineers, excepting those of Belgium, Holland, and Northern France; but there is a virtual concensus of British, Belgian and Dutch engineers on the opposite side".

The three coupled types were the 'Jubilees', the big 0-4-4 tanks of Class 'T1', and the small 0-4-4s of Class 'O2'. The basic dimensions of these three classes were as follows:

ADAMS FRONT-COUPLED TYPES

Class Type	'A12' 0-4-2	'T1' 0-4-4T	'O2' 0-4-4T
Coupled wheel dia. ft. in.	6 1	5 7	4 10
Cylinders dia., stroke in.	18 × 26	18 × 26	17½ × 24
Total heating surface sq. ft.	1231·7	1231·7	987·5
Grate area sq. ft.	17	17·87	13·83
Boiler pressure p.s.i..	160	160	160
Total weight working order tons	75½	54	44½
total number of engines in class	90	50	60

In the first engines of the 'Jubilee' and 'T1' classes Adams followed Stroudley's practice in the 'Gladstones' by placing steam chests underneath the cylinders, with the two cylinders and their respective steam chests all in one single steel casting. The cylinders were inclined downwards towards the crank axle, and the port faces were inclined upwards. This feature was also used by James Holden on the Great Eastern, and William Dean followed it in his famous 7 ft. 8 in. singles on the G.W.R. When it became necessary to convert the first batches of the latter class from the 2-2-2 to the 4-2-2 wheel arrangement the presence of the steam chests beneath the cylinders led to the design of a special adaptation of the Dean carriage bogie in order to clear the steam chests. The underneath position had the disadvantage of requiring longer and less direct steam and exhaust ports, and in later batches of his front-coupled engines, both 0-4-2 and 0-4-4 tank, Adams placed the valves between the cylinders, with vertical port faces. The underneath position had, of course, the advantage of greater accessibility, but no doubt at the expense of reduced working efficiency.

The 0-4-2 and the large 0-4-4 tank had cylinders, motion and all working parts inter-changeable, and the same boilers too. The small 0-4-4 tanks had the valves between the cylinders from the outset. All three classes had the Adams Vortex blast pipe when originally built. The first batch of 'Jubilees', 30 strong, with the underslung valve chests, had screw reverse, like the 4-4-0 express engines, but in the later engines having the valves between the cylinders the reversing was by lever. All these front coupled engines had a conventional valve setting with short lap valves. Pettigrew states that the normal running cut-off was 28 per cent., as compared with 17 per cent. on the express engines. The big 0-4-4 tanks were primarily intended for the London area, and they worked the fast, outer residential trains as well as penetrating to the more complicated inner workings, like those over the Chatham line, to Ludgate Hill. They were long-lived engines. The first was not withdrawn until 1930, and at the time of nationalisation there were still 15 of them in service. Of the 'Jubilees' 4 passed into the stock of British Railways.

The small 0-4-4 tanks have a special place in the affection of railway enthusiasts. In their first years they were used all over the line as branch passenger engines, and a sturdier and more reliable little machine could hardly be imagined for the purpose. All 60 of them were built at Nine Elms between 1889 and 1895; but from 1923 onwards a number of them were transferred to the Isle of Wight. These engines, which eventually numbered 21 were fitted with the Westinghouse brake, and eventually also with increased bunker capacity. In the high-tide of publicity that accompanied the time when Sir John Elliot was Public Relations Officer at Waterloo the 'O2' tank engines transferred to the Isle of Wight were all named. In his booklet on L.S.W.R. locomotives F. Burtt stated:

> "The Island engines have always been excellently maintained at a degree of efficiency hardly surpassed in Adams' time."

At the time of writing, February 1965, 16 of them are still in service. Pettigrew's *Manual of Locomotive Engineering*' contained a magnificent working drawing of one of them in original conditions, complete with Vortex blast pipe.

Before leaving the Adams locomotives there are two curiosities to be mentioned—two of those odd items that delight the lovers of railway lore. The first is the one and only Adams compound. The intense publicity—for those days—that accompanied the introduction of the Webb 3-cylinder compounds on the L.N.W.R. attracted the attention of the South Western management, and Adams was authorised to borrow one of these engines for trial purposes. Some runs between Waterloo and Exeter were made in 1884, but the compound engine made a poor showing against the Adams 4-4-0s of the '445' class. Four years later however Adams converted engine No. 446 to a 2-cylinder compound on the Worsdell von Borries system, by fitting a new right hand cylinder, of no less than 26 in. diameter. That he could get such a cylinder within the loading gauge was due to the connecting rod being fitted next to the wheel-boss, with the coupling outside it. Had the arrangement of the rods been the more usual, with the coupling rod inside, it would have been impossible to get the low pressure cylinder in. Engine No. 446 ran for 3 years in this condition, but was converted back to the standard arrangement in February 1891.

The second curiosity was one of those fascinating 'might-have-beens', the drawings for which exist in so many locomotive offices. But no 'might-have-been' has been more superbly recorded than Adam's proposed eight-foot 4-2-2 single. It was a 'single' variant of the largest 7 ft. 4-4-0s, and would have been a true counterpart of the roughly contemporary 4-2-2s on the Great Western, on the Midland, the Great Eastern, and the North Eastern—not to mention of course the most celebrated 4-2-2s of all, those of Patrick Stirling, on the Great Northern. The boiler was pitched very high, to clear the large driving wheels, and this had the effect of shortening the stove pipe chimney, and making it look less impressive. A curious feature was the use of inside bearings for the rear pair of wheels when the 'Jubilees', very wisely, had outside bearings to keep them as far as possible from the firebox. The drawing, which is beautifully coloured, is preserved in the Eastleigh Museum. It is dated March 14, 1893. Adams has a far nobler memorial however in the 6 ft. 7 in. 4-4-0 No. 563 which has been so beautifully restored to its original condition and is now in the Transport Museum at Clapham.

After eighteen momentous and highly successful years at Nine Elms Adams retired. Although he was then 72 years of age it was not that his health was declining in the ordinary sense, but unhappily that his mind was giving way. And in that same year of 1895 Dugald Drummond's ill-starred excursion into the realms of engineering manufacture had reached such a state that he was glad enough to give it up and return to railways. On the South Western, indeed, he accepted a far lower salary than he had been receiving from the Caledonian when he left that railway in 1890. And so 'Dugald' came to Nine Elms, and before long the 'winds of change' were blowing through the establishment with hurricane force! But before passing on to the first five years of his administration some mention must be made of the day-to-day work of the Adams 4-4-0s. Considering the very high esteem in which these engines were held their daily work is no more than thinly documented, and some observers were not very enthusiastic either.

Nevertheless in the early issues of *The Railway Magazine* Rous-Marten gave outline details of a number of runs, and some of these are summarised in the accompanying tables.

ADAMS 4-4-0 PERFORMANCE

Route	Engine Number	Class	Load tons	Dist. miles	Time m.	s.	Average speed m.p.h.
Salisbury—Sherborne ..	452	1880 7-footer	190	34·5	42	19	49·0
Sherborne—Exeter ..	452	,,	190	53·5	62	28	51·4
Salisbury—Wimbledon ..	447	,,	240	76·5	89	54	51·2
Waterloo—Southampton ..	593	1890 7-footer	240	79·2	90	11	52·7
Salisbury—Wimbledon ..	596	,,	255	76·5	91	35	50·2
Bournemouth—Vauxhall ..	685	1895 7-footer	190	106·6	139	52	46·0
Salisbury—Vauxhall ..	686	,,	190	82·5	91	00	54·3
Southampton—Vauxhall ..	572	1892 6 ft. 7 in.	220	77·9	93	00	50·3
Exeter—Yeovil Jc. ..	557	,,	230	48·9	65	12	45·0
Exeter—Yeovil Jc. ..	564	,,	170	48·9	59	20	49·5
Yeovil Jc.—Exeter ..	558	,,	180	48·9	59	01	49·8

There are some excellent runs in this collection, and one only wishes that a little more detail of them was available. The work of the 18-inch engines 447 and 452 is particularly fine; No. 452 for example took her 190-ton train up to Honiton Tunnel at a minimum speed of 25½ m.p.h., and reached a maximum of 79 m.p.h. downhill. Another splendid effort was that of No. 593 in running a 240-ton train from Waterloo to Southampton at a start to stop average speed of 52·7 m.p.h.

So we come to the first years of Dugald Drummond, and one can say without much in the way of qualification that they were his finest years. In that period between 1895 and 1900 he produced two engine designs that may be fairly ranked among the immortals of the locomotive world—the 'M7' 0-4-4 tank, and the 'T9' class 4-4-0s. Superficially the 'M7' could be regarded as nothing more than a slight enlargement of the Adams 5 ft. 7 in. 0-4-4, with 18½ instead of 18-inch cylinders, and Drummond boiler mountings; but the new engines had the special design of Drummond cylinders, into which so much care had been put. They were designed to give a very free exhaust, and these little engines like their express passenger counterparts were extremely free running. Like most Drummond engines they needed handling on a light rein, and this characteristic led once to some comparisons between their merits and those of the 0-4-4s in recent years that were not to the advantage of the Drummonds. An old friend of mine was at one time shedmaster at Stewarts Lane, Battersea, and in addition to providing motive power for the boat trains and Kent Coast expresses he had many empty stock workings. On such duty those elegant little flyers that had run the South Western 'residentials' so efficiently in years gone by did not take too kindly to hauling 12-coach corridor trains in and out of Victoria. On such duties the tough little Wainwright 'H' class 0-4-4s could knock the proverbial spots off them. I could not imagine the latter engines skating out to Guildford, Aldershot, and Reading like the 'M7s' used to do.

The 'M7s' were introduced on the L.S.W.R. in 1897, and the class eventually became 105 strong. In the same year Drummond put to work what might be termed the South Western version of the standard 'family' 0-6-0 goods engines. The following gives the basic dimensions, and show how they compare with the 'Caley Jumbos', and the Highland 'Barneys', of Peter Drummond.

DRUMMOND 0-6-0 GOODS ENGINES

Railway Brother First built	Caledonian Dugald 1883	Highland Peter 1900	L.S.W.R. Dugald 1897
Cylinders dia. × stroke in.	18 × 26	18¼ × 26	18½ × 26
Wheel dia. ft. in.	5 0	5 0	5 0
Total heating surface sq. ft.	1,202	1,175	1,191·6
Grate area sq. ft.	19·5	20·3	20·36
Boiler pressure p.s.i.	150	175	175
Total weight, engine only, tons	41·3	43	42¾

Then in that same year of 1897 Nine Elms works completed the first Drummond express locomotive for the South Western, and in this celebrated engine, No. 720, were to be seen the first signs of that unorthodoxy that was to become so marked a feature of Drummond's later work. It is difficult to imagine just what this engine was supposed to achieve. One would have thought there had been enough trials and tribulations with the Webb 3-cylinder compound to put off anyone with thoughts of uncoupled driving wheels; but then Drummond fitted this engine with *four* cylinders of the colossal size of 16½ in. diameter by 26 in. stroke—a greater cylinder volume than a Great Western 'Castle' class 4-6-0! The absence of coupling rods enabled the driving axles to be spaced no less than 11 ft. apart, and this in turn permitted of a very long firebox, with a grate area of 27½ sq. ft.; indeed the total heating surface was 1,664 sq. ft. Nevertheless this boiler proved inadequate and the cylinders were lined up to 14 in. Engine No. 720 saw the introduction of another novel Drummond feature, the cross water tubes in the firebox. The principle behind this device was that by carrying these tubes athwartships across the firebox, and bringing columns of water across the hottest part, the circulation of water would be accelerated, and the steaming improved. For two years however No. 720 remained the only engine so fitted.

In 1898 from Nine Elms there appeared what I always considered to be Drummond's masterpiece in locomotive design, the 'T9' 4-4-0. The earliest engines of the series, Nos. 290-299 had 18½ in. by 26 in. cylinders, and having boilers interchangeable with the 0-4-4 tanks and the 0-6-0s were classified 'C8'; but the next twenty, Nos. 280–289 and 113–122 while also having 18½ in. cylinders, had much larger boilers and were classified 'T9'. Although not so large as that of No. 720 the boiler was generous in its proportions, with a total heating surface of 1335 sq. ft. and a grate area of 24 sq. ft. The coupling rods were 10 ft. long. None of the first 30 of the class had cross-water tubes. These were incorporated first on 30 engines built by Dübs & Co. in 1899, and they increased the total heating surface to 1,500 sq. ft. The final batch of these engines built in 1899–1901, had, for the first time, the double bogie tenders with inside bearings to all wheels. Ahrons hated these tenders, which he stigmatised as ugly and unprepossessing; but today one rather cherishes their memory, as another example of the delightful individuality of the old railway companies. So by the end of 1901 the L.S.W.R. had a stud of magnificent new express locomotives—the 66 'T9' 4-4-0s, to add to the 105 Adams 4-4-0s and the 10 Drummond intermediate 'C8s'.

VIII

Waterloo

Waterloo is one of the really great stations of the world. Its present form originates from Parliamentary powers granted to the L.S.W.R. in 1899–1900; but the original station—or more correctly the group of old stations—had grown up piece-meal, group by group, to meet the ever-increasing passenger traffic. By the end of the nineteenth century it had expanded to become a sprawling heterogeneous collection of platforms of all lengths and widths—a signal engineer's Valhalla, in the sense that the multiplicity of crossings, alternative routes and such like afforded him unlimited scope on which to exercise his skill in interlocking, but nevertheless it was an operator's nightmare. It was this latter that led the enterprising South Western management of the 'nineties' to take the decision to rebuild the station completely. While at that time the South Eastern and the Brighton railways may have taken the palm for chaotic working of their traffic out on the line, Waterloo, by common consent, was one of the worst examples of terminal working to be found anywhere. When Euston was enlarged in 1892, and the temporary arrangements outside the station led to much confusion among passengers arriving by cab, or private carriage, an enraged director said to an operating man: 'You've turned Euston into a Waterloo'!

At the beginning of the twentieth century the L.S.W.R. was carrying a greater intensity of passenger traffic at Waterloo than could be seen anywhere else in Great Britain, even at Liverpool Street. But what the station lacked in the way of passenger convenience and simplicity of working it gained in its signalling arrangements. It is, in fact, no exaggeration to say that Waterloo represented what was probably the highest development of the signalling art, with purely mechanical apparatus, that the world has even seen. Nevertheless, despite the traffic working facilities, and the safety features provided by the great new interlocking installed in 1892, the station itself was considered inadequate. And towards the close of the century the South Western became one of the very few British railways to grasp the nettle of a huge, inconvenient terminal station, and to take the decision to rebuild it completely. What the British Railways Board is now doing at Euston the L.S.W.R. did at Waterloo from 1900 onwards. But I am writing of the climax of the story before the fascinating chain of events that led up to it.

Historically, the successive stages in the great build-up at Waterloo may be summarised thus:

1848: Original station opened: 4 platform lines.
1860: North station (Windsor lines) opened, 4 additional platform lines.
1864: Connection to Waterloo Junction, South Eastern Railway made.

1869: S.E.R. opens station at Waterloo Junction.
1878: South station opened: 2 platform lines.
1884–5: Windsor lines of North station added: 6 platform lines.

In the above summary I have used the term 'platform line' rather than 'platform', because the numbering in old Waterloo was somewhat confusing. There were some platforms, for example numbers 6 to 9, which had running lines on both faces, but with no apparent distinction; and there were others, like two of those in the original station of 1848, which had platform faces on both sides of a running line. When arriving at the latter one could, apparently, alight at whichever face one chose. This was not so bad, but if a train was advertised to leave from platform 6, and there were two sitting there, one on either face, all ready to go, how was a stranger to decide which was which! Furthermore, the South Station was quite separate, so far as passenger working was concerned, and its platforms had their own series of numbers. The offices were all scattered about, and there were no fewer than *four* approach roads!

The plan facing page 88 shows the layout as it was in 1900, at the time when the connection to the South Eastern still existed; this shows the situation that prevailed when complete reconstruction was decided upon. But the plan really gives no idea of the higgledy-piggledy state of affairs that prevailed within the precincts. The original station of 1848 is represented by the platforms 1, 2, 3 and 4, and these had remained the main line arrival and departure lines. The buffer stops of numbers 2 and 3 lines came quite near to the station frontage in Waterloo Road, and the small circulating area around them was complicated by the slope-down of the platform level necessary to provide a level crossing of the connecting line to the South Eastern. Outside, what had originally been designed as a classical frontage, crowned by a handsome portico looked most odd with the covered way of the single-tracked bridge to the South Eastern Railway emerging from that impressive frontage—like a horizontal jet of water from the mouth of a gargoyle. On the portico itself were the words 'South Western Railway' in huge letters, while at road level, beneath the S.E.R. connection was the full name 'London & South-Western Railway' in equally large letters. The broad space between platforms 4 and 5 was used as a cab rank for arriving long distance trains, and was frequently the scene of intense animation and confusion.

Particular reference will be made to the main line signalling later; but at the time of the reconstruction there still remained a relic of much earlier days in the old 'Crow's Nest' signal box, perched up high beneath the valance of the old station roof, above No. 4 platform line. In the 20th century it acted as a subsidiary to the great 'A' box at the entrance to the station and controlled a few local movements in the main line station, and the connection to the South Eastern line. But its original function was much more important. In the days when four-wheeled carriages were the rule, Waterloo like many other terminal stations had a series of one-carriage turntables on the platform lines with a cross-connection extending at right angles from platform to platform. At one time this turntable cross-connection extended from No. 1 to No. 7 road, and it was used to transfer horseboxes and carriage trucks, and also to do a certain amount of remarshalling. A regular job was to turn the travelling post office van round after its arrival in the morning, because it had doors on one side only. The turntables had bolt locks which were controlled from the 'Crow's Nest', and many are the tales told of acrimonious exchanges between the signalman on duty and the platform inspectors who used to demand the unlocking of the turntables *before* a train came in, so that exchange traffic could be cleared instantly. The locking of the turntables was a safety measure added later; but to the platform inspectors it was just a hampering nuisance, which in their view gave the signalman a chance to delay the station working!

In an earlier chapter I have referred to the very infrequent use made of the connection to the South Eastern Railway. It had one very important function which is not generally known, and that was in the working of Royal Trains. The stories of the railway journeys of Queen Victoria, largely through the vivid reminiscences of G. P. Neale, are mainly associated with her annual trip from Windsor to Balmoral, in which the Great Western, the London and North Western and the Caledonian were mainly involved. But in Victorian times it was the South Western, and not the Great Western that was known as 'The Royal Road', and when the Queen paid her occasional visits to the Continent it was from the L.S.W.R. station at Windsor that she travelled. Then the Royal Train went through Waterloo and over the connecting bridge to the South Eastern on her way to Dover. This route was also used on occasions by special trains conveying foreign royalty, who would be visiting Queen Victoria at Windsor. There was also a certain amount of transfer traffic in single vehicles, such as horseboxes and milk vans, and in addition the occasional wealthy passenger travelling in a family saloon.

It is however by the developments in signalling that the growth of Waterloo from its primitive early stages can most readily be traced. Even in the year 1864, when the connection to the South Eastern Railway was opened, there was very little signalling. The points were worked by hand levers and there was a small hut outside where a man was stationed to work a signal used to stop incoming trains at the Westminster Bridge Road when they could not be accommodated in the station. But even while there was no more elaborate control than this the station was dealing with some 220 trains a day. The installation of the first semaphore signalling, in 1867, with interlocking between points and signals provides one of the earliest known photographs of what Waterloo looked like in mid-Victorian times. The signalbox was erected on a gantry spanning all four tracks just at the points where they began to spread out to serve the various platforms and sidings. It was known as 'A' box, and contained two separate locking frames. Contrary to what might have been expected these frames were each parallel to the direction of running of the trains;

one frame of 24 levers dealt with the main line traffic, and the other, of 23 levers, with the Windsor lines.

In those early days of interlocking it was customary to mount the semaphore arms on posts integral with the signal cabin structure, often passing through the roof; but at Waterloo 'A' box the two masts—one for Main, and one for Windsor lines,—were at each end of the gantry carrying the signal box. Each mast carried six semaphore arms—three for incoming and three for outgoing trains,—and in keeping with a very common practice of the day the arms were arranged in pairs, with one down and one up arm on the same pivot. The lamps were separate, and below the arms to which they referred. The installation was built by the oldest of all railway signalling firms, Stevens & Sons, and the masts carrying the semaphore signals were of the very distinctive 'inconspicuous lattice' iron type. Judging from the layout of the signals on that pioneer gantry trains arriving on either the main or the Windsor lines could be terminated in the station on any one of three routes. At that time there were only four running lines in the approach. As usual at that time the ballasting of the track was carried almost up to the tops of the rails. Immediately beyond the south end of the gantry carrying 'A' box was another of the curiosities of old Waterloo, the Necropolis station; this was a small private station for funeral trains running to Brookwood cemetery.

The original 'A' box did not last long, and a new one was built in 1874, containing a locking frame of 109 levers, in one continuous row. The contractors this time were Saxby & Farmer Ltd. and they put in their well-known 'rocker- and grid' type of frame. This apparatus became very common on the Brighton line in later years, though Saxby and Farmer did not do a great deal of other work on the South Western. The second 'A' box, in its original form, lasted an even shorter time than its predecessor; for in 1878 the new South Station was opened, and a considerable number of additional signals and points were involved. Stevens & Sons secured the contract for the enlargement, and it was done in a most ingenious and far-sighted way. On the gantry spanning the tracks they built an enlarged signalbox completely encasing the old one. When it was finished the walls of the old box were removed, and there was space outside to instal an additional section of locking frames—35 levers in a row parallel to that of the 109-lever Saxby frame of 1874. By this form of construction there was ample room for enlargement. How far-sighted this arrangement was is shown later, when it was necessary to add 20 or more levers in 1880, and another 65 in 1885 when the big enlargement of the North Station was made.

Up to this time it will be appreciated that the additions had been made piecemeal, though the rapid increase in the number of levers in the 'A' box was in itself enough to show how the volume of traffic handled was growing. Some of the inconveniences of working, both from the traffic and from the passenger point of view have already been mentioned.

Another awkward thing was the continued existence of an engine shed sandwiched in between the main and the south stations. This was something akin to the little locomotive yard that used to exist at Kings Cross immediately to the west of No. 10 departure platform. There was also one at Euston beyond No. 15 platform, though neither of these included an actual shed. They were small yards where engines making a quick turnround could be turned and watered. But at Waterloo quite apart from such things as the Necropolis station, the engine shed, and the rarely-used connection to the South Eastern, the connections from the platforms to the running lines outside were not ideal, and among the numerous great reforms initiated by Charles Scotter was a plan for a complete rearrangement of the approach tracks. This was going to involve a vast amount of change to the signalling and interlocking, with facilities for many additional movements, and after all aspects had been most carefully studied it was realised that the simplest way to make the change was to have an entirely new interlocking, to accompany the changes in track layout programmed to be completed by the spring of 1892.

So plans were made for yet another 'A' Box. The problem was, where to put it! It was not merely a question of designing and building it, but of changing over from the old to the new when the time came for bringing it into service. The existing 'A' box, like its predecessor of 1867, was mounted on a gantry athwart the tracks. Its southern end abutted upon the wall of the Necropolis station, but with successive widenings of the approach lines on the northern side there was a considerable space on the gantry that was not then occupied. So the decision was taken to build the new box also on the gantry, end-on to the old one. There the new interlocking apparatus could be built completely, and the connections to the outside apparatus made when the time came for the transfer of the control. Before describing the new work in detail however something must be said of the men who were mainly responsible for it. Throughout London and South Western history the Civil Engineer had responsibility for signalling, and this practice was continued for the 25 years of the Southern Railway. Although the South Western had some very able and distinguished Signal Engineers, the over-riding responsibility of the Civil Engineer was no mere formality.

Pre-eminent among those responsible for signalling on the L.S.W.R. was the great personality of Alfred Weeks Szlumper, who was Divisional Engineer, London, until 1904, and then Chief Engineer. He was in fact the first man to carry the latter title. His predecessor was J. W. Jacomb-Hood, but he had the title of Resident Engineer. This title can be traced back to the time when Joseph Locke was consulting engineer to the line, and the man in charge on the spot was titled Resident Engineer. Jacomb-Hood was the 'architect' of new Waterloo. During his term of office plans were made for the new station, and the Parliamentary powers obtained; while a very important part of the work, construction of the new South Station, had been completed before his untimely death in 1914. The

Signal Engineer at that time was A. H. Johnson, a very able man who fathered the introduction of power signalling on the L.S.W.R., in the form of the low-pressure pneumatic system to be described in a later chapter of this book. He also had the task of adapting the signalling, where necessary, to suit the needs of electric traction on the riverside lines.

But so far as Waterloo was concerned, and particularly the great new interlocking of 1892, it was Szlumper who took the most prominent part, and it was he who presented to the Institution of Civil Engineers in that same year a most comprehensive paper on the subject. Even after he had succeeded to the still higher office of Chief Engineer of the Southern Railway he continued to take a very active interest in signalling matters. In 1925, when the Westinghouse Brake and Saxby Signal Company—as it was known—was entrusted with the supply of material for the huge task of re-signalling at Charing Cross and Cannon Street, it was Szlumper who personally signed the authority to proceed with the work, and it was he who personally settled questions of priority so far as the installations of the new interlocking frames were concerned. At Waterloo, in the reconstruction work of 1892, he was naturally in the thick of the detailed execution of the job, as London Divisional Engineer.

Even though there was a vacant space on the gantry spanning the tracks that space was nevertheless limited, and there would not have been sufficient room for an interlocking frame of the conventional type. The rearrangement of the tracks and the improved traffic working facilities proposed would have required far more levers than were included in the existing frame in the 'A' box, as finally enlarged in 1885, namely 209. A total of more than 400 levers would have been required. A means of lever saving had however been invented by Mr. J. P. O'Donnell, and study of the conditions in the new layout at Waterloo showed that in no fewer than 72 cases one lever could, in different conditions, be made to work three signals. Applying to each of the platform lines there were three signals mutually related, namely the passenger train starter, the outgoing shunt signal, and the incoming shunt signal. The clearing of any one of these must necessarily lock the other two at danger. In more recent years with miniature-lever power interlocking frames levers have been saved by making one lever stand normally in the mid-position, and actuate two conflicting signals by a push action for one, and a pull for the other; but in Waterloo 'A' box of 1892 72 levers were arranged for *triple* working—thus effecting a saving of 144 levers in the frame. In all these cases the first position (shortest stroke) worked the passenger train departure signals; the second position worked the outgoing shunt signals, and the third the incoming shunt signals.

The working was safeguarded by use of what were termed 'gear' levers. These also had three positions corresponding to the three different signal movements controlled by the triple working levers. These gear levers controlled groups of platform signal levers according to the destination of the train outside the station. There were six gear levers in all, one for each of the six running lines in the station approach. As it was not possible to have an ingoing or an outgoing shunt movement at the same time, or yet a passenger train movement, the gear lever for the Road B, for example, could be set for the kind of movement required—say outgoing shunt—and this would set all the interlocks on every signal concerned so that it would be possible to clear only the outgoing shunting signals. If the signalman inadvertently pulled his triple lever to the wrong position nothing would happen. The actual layout of the signals, and the numbering of the lines is shown in the plan facing page 76, which is reproduced by courtesy of the Council of the Institution of Civil Engineers. As a result of this use of triple working only 102 levers were necessary to work 247 signals. Of these levers only 30 worked no more than a single semaphore arm

The firm of Stevens & Sons was once again entrusted with the construction and installation of the locking frame, and the work was a lasting monument to the genius of their engineer, W. F. Burleigh. Behind any great engineering project, backing up the broad conception of top management, and the plans of chief engineers, there must inevitably be the technicians—the men with year upon year of solid experience in working out details and getting it done. The vast majority of such men concerned in the building and modernising of railways remain completely unknown; but in the case of Waterloo it was my privilege and pleasure to have as very senior and elderly colleague for more than 10 years the remarkable man who interlocked the great 'A' box of 1892. Bill Burleigh—what a character he was! At over 80 years of age he was still a first class draughtsman, and somewhat naturally one with a host of memories. As engineer to Stevens & Sons he had been concerned in several stages in the development of Waterloo. The firm was later absorbed by McKenzie & Holland Ltd. and it was as a servant of the latter company that Burleigh eventually came into Westinghouse. He liked nothing better than to yarn about the old days—for so long and so fascinatingly at times that it was hard to get away once he started. It was perhaps appropriate that Burleigh's retirement took place soon after the famous 'A' box had been replaced, in 1936, by the present power interlocking. But to the very last he always went up the back stairs to the drawing office three at a time!

Quite apart from the ingenuity of the interlocking contained in the new 'A' box of 1892, the gantry that carried the box also carried one of the most picturesque gantries of mechanical semaphore signals ever installed anywhere in the world. There were six triple bracket signals, each relating to the six running lines A, B, C, D, E and F in the approach to the station. These were carried at a tremendous height above rail level, and one modern commentator has wondered how anyone ever managed to see them in a dense fog, while another writer of our own times, in more whimsical vein, said that when the gantry was taken down, in 1936, a landmark ranking with the Shot Tower, and the Lion Brewery was removed from the prospect of Lambeth seen across the river from Adelphi

Terrace! Technically this 67-arm signal assembly had two top arms, namely down Windsor through and down Windsor local indicating arms, working in connection with the row of Windsor-line signals, informing the engine driver which of the two down-Windsor lines the lower signal is given for; the upper row had twenty arms referring to the main lines and the lower row 27 arms referring to the Windsor line passenger train movements to and from the 18 platform bays and the six running lines, A, B, C, D, E, and F. The lowest row had twelve arms referring to shunting movements, these 12 arms being repeated on the opposite side of the signal box, and partially so on Westminster Road signal-bridge.

Each of the bracket signals at the outer end of the platforms had three arms, relating to passenger train 'starting', shunt 'out' on right road, and shunt 'out' on wrong road; these latter signals were distinguished by a scissors-shaped semaphore—or bow tie—and by a purple light at night. These posts at the platform ends had also an arm for ingoing movements, and were distinctive in that they worked to three positions. These signals were operated from what Szlumper described as the Yard Boxes, which in the case of the main line platforms of course meant that celebrated 'Crows Nest'. If these signals were in the clear position it meant that the line was clear up to the buffer stops, but if in the caution position then the line was already partly occupied by a train. The aspect displayed was controlled automatically by electric treadle bars—indeed it is remarkable to find how much auxilliary electrical equipment was used at Waterloo in 1892 to provide additional operating safeguards.

As in the case of all signal reconstruction work, or indeed, of any reconstruction works on the railway that have to be carried out while normal traffic is flowing, the arrangements for transfer of the connections from the old to the new signal box had to be planned with very great care. It was not merely a question of signalling: a great deal of alteration to the permanent way had to be made, and temporary working instituted. The work of relaying was timed to be completed at approximately the same time as the interlocking in the new box was complete, tested, and approved by the Board of Trade Inspector, and then the work of transfer could be commenced. This was done in two stages. On May 1st, 1892, the main line connections were removed from the old signal box and connected to the new one. A fortnight then elapsed, during which period preparations were made for the final move. During that fortnight the main line traffic was worked from the new box and the Windsor line traffic from the old one. Although these two parts of the station and its train services have always been quite distinct from each other, there is, nevertheless, a certain amount of interchange and shunting between the two, and to provide for this during the transition period a special temporary ground frame was installed, electrically controlled from both the old and the new signal box.

Then on Sunday May 15th, the final move was made, when all the Windsor line connections were removed from the old box and connected to the new one. Even when this operation was completed the work of reconstructing the station approaches was not quite finished. Certain alterations to the track layout required the removal of some stanchions supporting the old signal box. Before this could be done the signalbox itself had to be dismantled and removed, and all the old signals taken down. This work could be done while normal traffic was flowing, and so, no more than a single week was allowed between the complete commissioning of the new box and the complete disappearance of the old one. Dismantling gangs worked night and day, and by Sunday May 22, all was removed, and it was safe to remove the stanchions. Then the final change to the permanent way could be made.

This very complicated change, which involved working to a very tight schedule on every stage, was carried through with remarkably little dislocation to traffic. For the first three days after the final move, it was necessary to discontinue a few local trains, and extra men were stationed in the yard to assist traffic movements. Apart from that the new installation worked with perfect smoothness from the outset and by the summer of 1892 was handling an unprecedented volume of traffic. The record, up to that time, was reached on Saturday July 16, when the number of train movements recorded reached a total of 879, made up as follows:

WATERLOO: NUMBER OF TRAINS ETC.

Line	Down Main	Up Main	Down Windsor	Up Windsor
Regular Passenger trains ..	118	128	132	127
Light engines	40	53	30	27
Empty stock trains	21	50	63	22
Special trains	23	30	8	7
Totals	202	261	233	183

This is an amazing record. Even taken as an average over the entire 24 hours this indicates an average of nearly 11 movements an hour on the up main line. But one can safely assume that the bulk of this activity took place during 18 hours of the day at most, which suggests that at the height of the traffic movements were taking place at 4 min. intervals, or less.

Some 20 years later a South Western veteran, Ness Wilson, wrote some reminiscences in *The Railway Magazine*, and as nearly all his service with the company had been spent at Waterloo he had some vivid recollections of the various changes in signalling. By the time they came to the 1892 metamorphosis the Signal Department had acquired a vast amount of experience in carrying out changes, and it was generally known that they regarded 1892 as 'child's play' compared with some previous openings, because it was possible to get the new box completely erected, interlocked, and tested before any disturbance was made to the old one. In the earlier operations everything had to be done 'on the ground' as it were, and there was, for example, one monumental occasion in 1878, when one girder for the new 'A' box of that period got wedged across the line on a Sunday morning, and literally shut up the entire station. The overnight mail from the west had to be terminated on Westminster Road bridge, and the passengers conducted down the grim stone staircase of the Necropolis station to the street below.

Although the older men of the Signal Department were apt to deprecate their efforts in the 1892 operation it was generally recognised as an outstanding piece of work. Great personal interest in it was taken by several of the directors, and Archibald Scott, the former General Manager wrote the following letter of commendation to Inspector Maynard, who had been in charge.

> "Waterloo Station, S.E., May 4th 1892.
> Dear Sir,—I congratulate you on having been so successful in carrying out the change to the new 'A' box. I know that in accomplishing so well a work so difficult you have undergone a very severe strain, and fear that you may suffer for a time from such an overstrain upon your strength. However, you, and all assisting you, can congratulate themselves on having successfully got through a very tough job without the slightest accident. Of course, delays to trains were certain to occur during the progress of the change, and we all should be very thankful that detention was the only occurrence. The only thing to be wondered at is that matters were so soon got into fairly good working order, and that the signalmen so soon mastered their new work, and made no mistakes. I feel that we ought to thank you and all your assistant signalmen for the exertions made—regardless of self-consideration—to cope with the unavoidable difficulties, and for the great care exercised whereby the work was so successfully accomplished. Too much credit cannot be given to all concerned in the change.
>
> I am, yours truly,
> (Signed) Arch. Scott."

From the date of the letter it will be seen that it was written when no more than half the change had been completed.

A curious accident took place in the station four years after the opening of the new signalling, and although slight in its results, it is interesting as an example of the intense working that was necessary even in those days. It took place on August 21, 1896, and centred round the departure of the 5 p.m. express to Portsmouth Harbour. It shows also, that however intricately and comprehensively the working of signals and points may be interlocked in a large station, a great deal still depended, as now, upon the human element. On that day an Adams 5 ft. 7 in. 0-4-4 tank locomotive, No. 20, was in the engine shed on the long pit siding, and was being prepared ready to take a train to Hampton Court. This engine was signalled out by hand along the siding in order to be ready to go into the South Station to be attached to its train. Unfortunately the driver, in obeying the hand signal given him in the yard overran the clearance point just as the 5 o'clock train was starting out of No. 1 Platform road. The two locomotives came into sidelong collision, and although this collision was a very slight one it was enough to derail the engine of the express. The driver of the latter immediately applied his brakes and stopped the train within a few yards.

Unfortunately this sudden stop had repercussions at the rear end of the train. The empty stock had been drawn into the platform by an Adams 4-4-0 locomotive No. 664, which was to work a succeeding passenger train, and was due to follow the loaded Portsmouth train out of the platform. The regulations concerning such movements were quite clear, as follows:

> "*Light engines following Trains.*—It is very important that when a light engine follows a train from any platform it should do so very slowly and cautiously, under perfect control, in order that it may be at once stopped should the train it is following have to stop or slacken speed from any cause."

Unfortunately the driver of Engine No. 664 was over anxious to draw up to the starting signal, and when the Portsmouth express left he started away, and without really observing what was happening ahead of him, followed it at such a speed that when it came to a sudden stop he could not avoid colliding with it. The collision was so violent, indeed, that five passengers were injured in the train, and some vehicles became buffer-locked. Although both collisions were caused by want of care on the part of the drivers of the light engines 20 and 664 the Inspecting Officer of the Board of Trade found the L.S.W.R. to blame in one respect, that no catch points were provided on the outlet from the engine siding. If these had been installed the light engine coming from the shed would have been derailed instead of colliding with the engine of the express.

Other than this the safety record in working at Waterloo was a very fine one. So far as traffic working was concerned things were never allowed to remain static for long, and so to become out of date. It seemed as though the management had no sooner completed one great improvement before it was looking ahead to the next; and so far as the new signalling of 1892 was concerned only 7 years were to elapse before Parliamentary powers were obtained for the reconstruction of the entire station. This chapter is primarily concerned with events in the nineteenth century, and so with this passing reference to the great work that lay ahead I will close it.

IX

The Race from the West

The transfer of the European terminus of the American Line Steamers from Liverpool to Southampton proved the first shot in one of the most exciting pieces of railway rivalry that ever blazed up in Great Britain. Having established their terminus on the English Channel, and put into service a fleet of considerably larger and faster liners to make the Atlantic Crossing, the fever of acceleration led to a further step in the speeding up of communications between London and New York. It was realised that if the inward-bound liners set down their passengers by tender at Plymouth instead of conveying them up-channel to the steamship terminus at Southampton, a day could be saved on the journey from New York to London. But while it was due to the enterprise of the London & South Western Railway that the American Line had transferred its terminus from Liverpool to Southampton that railway company might well have been caught unprepared for the developments at Plymouth.

At the end of the nineteenth century the Great Western was the only railway equipped to deal with ocean traffic on any scale at Plymouth. Passengers and mail from various parts of the world had been landed at Millbay Docks for many years, and the organisation for dealing with traffic, both at the port and in handling it forward to London and the Midlands was already well established. Against the installation at Millbay the London & South Western could well have been at a strong disadvantage. Fortunately however, the close cooperation and cordial relations between the American Line and the L.S.W.R. were such that the railway had prior warning of the proposed change of arrangements by the steamship company, and they had time to prepare for the change and to be able to compete with the Great Western on more or less equal terms. The L.S.W.R. laid plans to deal with ocean traffic at Stonehouse Pool Quay. They owned a short branch line, less than a mile long, leading to this quay from their own line at a junction near Devenport Station. The map on page 50 of Plymouth district shows that this line joined into the main line from Tavistock and Exeter in a direction facing Plymouth, and the only disadvantage was that a boat train coming up from Stonehouse Pool would have to reverse direction once it entered upon the main line. This was no very great handicap, as in any case the branch line with its sharp curves was not suitable for use by main line express locomotives.

At Stonehouse Pool excellent accommodation was built to deal with the ocean traffic in all its various ramifications: passenger waiting rooms and lounges; buffets; facilities for customs examination; and a Post Office.

Although it was not expected that incoming passengers would have to wait very long between disembarking and entering the waiting train, it was not only the passengers themselves that were given ample consideration. When people are travelling across the Atlantic it is frequently the case that friends and relations journey to the port to meet them off the steamer, rather than wait until they reach their final destination at home; and with the inevitable uncertainty of timing on long sea voyages, waiting friends, or others, might find themselves with an hour or more to spend on the quayside before the tender put out to meet the steamer. The L.S.W.R. took good care to see that any such sojourn was made as pleasant as possible.

Needless to say the Great Western Railway were not slow in realising the implications of this South Western enterprise at Plymouth, nor the possibilities of additional traffic for themselves; and early in the present century a tacit understanding grew up between the two companies that in the case of inward-bound ocean liners calling at Plymouth, the L.S.W.R. would convey the passengers and the G.W.R. the mails. Stonehouse Pool and Millbay Docks were relatively close to each other on the northern shores of Plymouth Sound, and the tenders returning from alongside the liners would each berth within a very few minutes of each other. Although the two railway companies were very much intermingled in their interests and in their joint establishments in Plymouth, the routes of the respective boat trains did not at any time converge—at any rate in the Plymouth district. The South Western had the disadvantage of having to cross the Great Western line at Exeter, by virtue of the running powers they possessed between Cowley Bridge and St. Davids, and this state of affairs was in due course to lead to a certain amount of difficulty, and acrimony.

It was perhaps inevitable that in the working of services which from the very first were regarded as prestige runs, a keen rivalry should have grown up between the two companies. The Great Western as the established line for the ocean services from Plymouth could, to some extent, afford to rest on previous laurels. But from the very outset it was evident that the London & South Western Railway was making a very special effort to secure the best results from this potential traffic. A new set of particularly luxurious carriages was buit specially for the boat trains, and all officers concerned made the working of these trains a matter for their own personal attention. Because of the varied times at which liners might drop anchor in Plymouth Sound it could well happen that the boat trains to London would have to be run at night; and so eventually the L.S.W.R. built a sleeping car specially for the job. Restuarant cars were also set aside for use when boat trains were running in the daytime.

The locomotive workings on the South Western were arranged so that only one stop was needed between Devonport and Waterloo. The South Western would undoubtedly have run non-stop, just as the Great Western were doing, if their line had been equipped with water troughs; but these latter were not required in the working of any of the normal services of the company, and although the American specials were given very high priority among all activities of the company it was hardly thought worth while putting in water troughs specially for these services. In order to make the two stages of the run as equally distanced as possible the one intermediate stop, purely for the purpose of changing engines, was made at Templecombe—117·8 miles from Devonport Junction and 112·2 miles from Waterloo. When the Ocean service was first introduced in 1904, the Drummond 'T9' 4-4-os with double-bogie tenders were used at the London end, and at the western end the new 'S.11' class of 6 ft. 4-4-os, with larger boilers, were allocated to this duty. These had originally been intended for the Salisbury–Exeter section; but with their huge tenders they were very suitable for the through boat train workings between Devonport and Templecombe. Some interesting technical features of these fine engines will be discussed in a later chapter.

The inauguration of the new arrangements took place in the early hours of Saturday April 9, 1904 with the arrival of the S.S. *St. Louis* at Plymouth. It was typical of the vagaries of ocean boat train workings that on the previous evening it had been expected that the tender would go out at about 6 a.m. Unfortunately for those who were hoping to have something of a night's sleep the *St. Louis* had made a record crossing from New York, and arrived some 4 hr. earlier than she had originally been expected. G. A. Sekon, the Founder, and first Editor of *The Railway Magazine* was a privileged observer on that occasion, and in these days it is rather amusing to read those passages of his account in which he dilates upon the advantages of that new tool of management, the telephone, when it came to improvising arrangements at short notice. Whereas all had been planned for the Saturday morning personnel ranging in status from the Superintendent of the Line, and the Chief Mechanical Engineer, to barmaids and porters had to be summoned before midnight, and by 1.30 a.m. Stonehouse Pool station was a scene of great animation—all ready to begin its career as an Ocean Terminal.

On this inaugural occasion there was a very full turnout of senior officers, and in addition to Henry Holmes, the Superintendent of the Line, and Dugald Drummond, there were the District Superintendents, and engineers, representatives of the American Line, and the Plymouth Medical Officer of Health. With fires blazing in the refreshment and waiting rooms, all spick and span, and a full quota of porters on duty, the passengers landing from the *St. Louis* must have gained an excellent impression of British railway efficiency. The tender, which left the Ocean Quay around 2 a.m. carried a number of passengers bound for Cherbourg who were joining the liner. The tender was alongside the *St. Louis* by 3.25 a.m., and at 3.44, having embarked 57 passengers and their luggage, she started back for Stonehouse Pool. It is interesting to record also the times at which the various operations took place after the tender made fast once again at the quayside:

4.15 a.m. Tender alongside
4.40 a.m. Customs examinations started
5.3 a.m. Special train left for Waterloo

The train consisted of four coaches, and from Devonport Junction which was left at 5.12 a.m., the engine was a large-boilered Drummond 4-4-0, No. 399. The possibilities of securing a non-stop run to Templecombe were rather remote, because the Great Western Railway had the right to stop all South Western trains in St. David's station. It was hoped that sporting instincts might have prevailed on this occasion, to waive that right for once and give their rivals a clear road. As it turned out there were two other intermediate stops—one, the reason for which was not explained, took place near Whimple, and another rather curiously at Dugald Drummond's behest, for him to give an instruction to his inspector who was riding on the footplate. Seeing that this was the first venture of the L.S.W.R. into this kind of special running the performance was a very good one. Details are given in the accompanying log, and it may be added that the overall time from Stonehouse Pool to Waterloo turned out to be 4 hr. 24½ min. The last stage, from the 'Drummond stop' at the 91st milepost to Waterloo took only 88 min.

Before going into any details of the running as detailed in the accompanying log it is evident that on that very first occasion it was a close 'race' between the L.S.W.R. and the Great Western. While Sekon was travelling with the passenger special the Rev. W. J. Scott was riding with the mails, and the comparative times between the two runs were:

OCEAN SPECIALS: APRIL 9, 1904

L.S.W.R.		a.m.	G.W.R.		a.m.
Stonehouse Pool	dep.	5 3	Millbay Crossing	dep.	4 59
Stonehouse Junc.	dep.	5 12	North Road	pass	5 2½
Exeter St. Davids	arr.	6 21¾	Exeter St. Davids	arr.	6 10¾
Exeter St. Davids	dep.	6 22¼	Exeter St. Davids	dep.	6 14½
Templecombe	arr.	7 43¾	Bristol Temple Meads	arr.	7 21
Templecombe	dep.	7 46	Bristol Temple Meads	dep.	7 28½
Waterloo	arr.	9 36½	Paddington	arr.	9 17¼

The South Western lost 7 min. on the Great Western time to Exeter St. Davids, where the latter special stopped to exchange a 'Camel' class 4-4-0 for a 'City'. The Great Western changed engines a second time, at Bristol, where a 7 ft. 8 in. single, the *Duchess of Albany* replaced the *City of Exeter*. A very fast run was made from Bristol to Paddington albeit with no more than 3 vans; but against such practised runners the South Western made a splendid first try. And although the 6 ft. engine No. 399 had been most restrained on the downhill sections the 'T9' that took over at Templecombe made some very fast running over certain sections, notably from Basingstoke to Surbiton at an average speed of exactly 70 m.p.h. for 36 miles on end.

Even on this very first participation in the working of ocean specials from Plymouth the authorities of the L.S.W.R. fully expected to win the race. During the trip Henry Holmes stressed the point with Sekon that they had 18 less miles to go. But in their anxiety to ensure that all was safe for this fast running time was consumed in taking careful precautions. There was the examination during the reversal of direction at Stonehouse Pool Junction; the unexplained stop of 7 min. near Whimple, and the stop asked for by Dugald Drummond. Against this the Rev. W. J. Scott claims that 10 min. were lost by the Great Western special by out-of-course slacks, apart from the stops at Exeter and Bristol. The South Western were certainly running at standards well below those achieved in later years between Exeter and Templecombe, though the performance between Salisbury and Waterloo, 78 min. 19 sec., for 83·8 miles was very fine. One point of some significance is the time of only 3 min. for the 2·5 miles from Wilton to Salisbury. A speed restriction was imposed round the curve at Wilton, and at Salisbury there is of course an extremely bad curve at the east end of the station.

The next special working was on April 18. How the South Western fared on this occasion is not recorded, but the Great Western did not do notably better than on April 9, seeing that on this later run, by working the 'City' class engine through from Millbay to Bristol, they avoided the Exeter stop. They cut their time from 4 hr. 18¼ min. to 4 hr. 13 min. But the next ocean special occasion was on April 23. By this time the South Western were thoroughly warming up to the task, and Charles Rous-Marten journeyed to Plymouth to record the running. The same train formation and the same engines as on the inaugural trip of April 9 were used, and he was able to record a truly magnificent performance. The time of departure from the quay is not given, but from Stonehouse Pool Junction to Waterloo the time was 4 hr. 2¾ min. On that same day the Great Western time from Millbay Crossing to Paddington was 4 hr. 12 min. Despite all the South Western had done however, intrinsically the honours were still with the Great Western. The South Western advantage of 9¼ min. was not enough to offset the Great Western disadvantage in mileage. Nevertheless a race it was in very truth, with both sides beginning to take risks that would not have been tolerated in ordinary passenger working.

At that period in railway history there is no doubt that many curves were taken at far higher speeds than would be run today. Locomotives were lighter, and with smaller boilers and lower boiler pressures the centre lines of the boilers were not only lower, but the lower working pressures required lighter plates and consequently a lower centre of gravity on any account. I was never more aware of the difference in running conditions between those of today and those of 60 years ago than when I was privileged to ride on the footplate of an Ocean Mail special from Plymouth to Paddington in 1954. The inspector and crew were out to lower the record for the run, which had recently been cut to 217 min. for the 226·4 miles from Millbay Crossing to Paddington. With a load of only 7 coaches and a 'Castle' in superb condition the circumstances were certainly favourable. At the same time careful observance had to be made of all the prescribed speed limits. Between these restricted sections the engine was put to it hard; yet with a modern engine and a light load we took 46¾ min. to pass Newton Abbot from the start, whereas on the Great Western record run of May 9, 1904, the *City of Truro* took a mere 36¾ min. The difference is amply explained by very much faster running downhill and on curved sections of the line, which in turn enabled the two principal banks to be rushed.

The enginemen of the L.S.W.R. were not so venturesome on the western part of the line; but in describing the run of April 23, Rous-Marten wrote:

> "At Templecombe West, No. 335, already referred to, replaced No. 399, and the driver (F. Gare) from the first evidently had set his heart upon record-making. We ran through Salisbury station at full speed, and after attaining a very high maximum down the descent at 1 in 165 near Porton . . ."

I repeat, and underline one phrase *we ran through Salisbury station at full speed.* Rous-Marten did not specify what that speed was at the time, and his reference to a high speed afterwards, near Porton, is of course a mistake for the descent from Grateley to Andover. On the up journey one is climbing, not descending at Porton. But his log shows a time of only 28 min. for the 28·8 miles from Templecombe to Salisbury, and of 17 min. for the 17·2 miles from Salisbury to Andover. It was not until two years later that the actual circumstances surrounding that fast run through Salisbury were to some extent revealed.

So far as I can trace however the run of April 23, was the last L.S.W.R. ocean special to be logged in detail; and while this might appear strange, after all the laudatory comments passed upon their entering upon the traffic, it must not be forgotten that in just over a fortnight from that much praised run the Great Western, on May 9, made the run 'to end all runs' on the Ocean Mail service, when the *City of Truro* and the *Duke of Connaught* between them made the wonderful record time of 3 hr. 46¾ min. from Millbay Crossing to Paddington. In the face of such running the South Western more or less *had* to accept second place. Nevertheless the running of the passenger specials from Stonehouse Pool remained very much a prestige job, and all concerned took an immense pride in the task. Then two years later, at 1.57 a.m. on July 1, 1906, came tragedy. An American special was derailed on the curve immediately east of Salisbury station, with great destruction of stock, and 28 persons were killed.

By a melancholy coincidence there were in that same year of 1906 no fewer than three other accidents in which trains ran through junctions at such excessive speed as to cause derailment and loss of life, and in every case the enginemen were killed. The other instances were the wrecking of an express goods train at Goswick, North Eastern Railway; the Grantham disaster, in which a down night Scotch express was involved, and the tremendous smash-up outside Shrewsbury when the L.N.W.R. West of England night mail approached the station at greatly excessive speed. But there was one very important difference in the case of Salisbury. Previous to the accident no one had ever tried running through Grantham at full speed, turning on to the Nottingham branch, and rounding the curve without any check. Equally no one had ever tried taking the final curve into Shrewsbury at 60 m.p.h.! But at Salisbury there is strong evidence to suggest that it was quite usual for the American specials to run through the station and round the curve at the east end with very little slackening of speed. That it was a very risky thing to do will not be denied. The first curve after the station was of no more than 8 chains radius, and even though this had some super-elevation it was followed up by an even sharper double curve of 7½ chains radius through a scissors crossing, and having no cant, nor check rail.

Incredible though it may seem the regular route of the boat trains was not in a normal continuation of the 8-chain curve, albeit on a slightly sharper radius and over the points of the scissors crossing, but through the middle of the scissors, with a reversal of curvature from left-hand to right-hand half way through. There were two up lines through the station, the 'up main' and the 'up through' and the latter terminated beyond the scissors crossing in an engine siding used by engines waiting to take over expresses from the west and haul them on to Waterloo. A train on the 'up through' line proceeding towards London had therefore to cross over from 'up through' to 'up main' via the scissors, with the 7½-chain curves.

After the accident Rous-Marten immediately referred to his own experience on April 23, 1904, and he revealed some astonishing facts. Approaching Salisbury station from the west the speed was sustained at 75 m.p.h.; the last two quarter-miles before the station itself were covered in 12 sec. apiece. He then went on to say that there was no appreciable slowing, and that after the train had rounded the curve, passed through the yards and threaded Fisherton Tunnel his next reading was one of exactly 60 m.p.h. At this point, he is quite emphatic that the speed was *decreasing* and there is every probability that the curve immediately east of Salisbury station was taken at about 65 m.p.h. He asserted, though more than two years after the event, that the negotiation of the curve was perfectly smooth and comfortable; but then he added: 'Most assuredly I should have not felt quite comfortable had I been aware of those small radii at the time I rounded the curve at such high speed. Fortunately for my peace of mind I was not, and we got round in safety by what must, I suppose, be regarded as a special dispensation of Providence!'

Rous-Marten was travelling behind a 'T9', whereas the train of July 1, 1906, was hauled by one of the large-boilered 'L12' 4-4-0s, No. 421. The centre line of the boiler on the latter engine was 8 ft. 6 in. above rail level against 7 ft. 9 in. in the 'T9'. With a higher centre of gravity there would be some slightly greater tendency to overturn, but I feel sure that factors other than this combined to cause the disaster of 1906. Although there was wholesale destruction of coaching stock the Board of Trade Inspector found strangely little damage on the track leading to the point of overturning. The engine did not 'burst the road', and go off at a tangent, galloping across the metals, still upright, like the L.N.W.R. 'Jumbos' did in the Preston accident of 1896. The South Western 4-4-0 No. 421 appears to have held the road, and began rounding the curve until turning over towards its right-hand side, and colliding violently with a milk train on the down line. This overturning took place on the 8-chain curve—not on the far more dangerous 7½-chain curves included in the scissors crossing. The results were terrible, all the more so for coming upon the passengers in the dead of night. There were 43 passengers aboard together with the guard, the travelling ticket collector, and two waiters, and of those 43 passengers 24 were killed. The dead also included the driver and fireman of engine No. 421, and the fireman and guard of the milk train on the adjoining line.

My guess—and it is no more than a guess!—as to why the train of April 23, 1904, got safely round, and why that of July 1, 1906 came so terribly to grief, lies with the individual engines. Both were obviously being driven at a speed that was highly dangerous on such a curve; but the 'T9' with its massive frame-structure and relatively small and low-pitched boiler would undoubtedly stand a better chance of holding the road than the 'L12'. In a situation that was in any case on a razor-edge that difference in design could easily have made all the difference between safety and disaster. The 'L12' appears to have *entered* upon the curve satisfactorily; there was no initial lurch as she came off the tangent track. But a roll of the engine itself might easily have been the fatal factor. From my experience of many thousands of miles on the footplate, on all sorts and conditions of engines, I know only too well how some individual engines of a class can develop a wild, swinging roll. It is probably due to some maladjustment of the springs, but there are times, even on straight track, when it feels horribly unsafe. As the driver and fireman of No. 421 perished in the wreck of the train, there was no evidence to show if anything unusual occurred in the running of the engine. But so far as speed was concerned it does seem as though they were not travelling so very differently from what had previously been done with the American special. One point that did come out in the Enquiry however was that it was the first time the particular driver had ever worked one of these boat trains.

The log of the running of the ill-fated train from the time engine No. 421 took over the haulage was as follows:

Dist. Miles		Sch. min.	Actual min.	Av. Speed m.p.h.
0·0	TEMPLECOMBE WEST	0	0	—
6·75	Gillingham	—	9½	42·7
10·9	Semley	—	15	45·4
15·8	Tisbury	—	20	59·3
20·1	Dinton..	20	24	64·4
25·9	Wilton	25½	29	70·0
28·2	*Salisbury West Box*	29	31	69·4
28·6	*Salisbury East Box*	30	—	—

Considering that the load was one of only four coaches the start was poor, and it was evident that the engine was not being extended at all on the uphill sections, to Buckhorn West Tunnel, and then up to Semley. Although the initial point-to-point allowance from Templecombe to Dinton was admittedly a sharp one it will be seen that this driver, working the train for the first time, lost no less than 4 min. over this section. While making full allowance for the probability of the times as recorded above being no more than approximate it does seem that the driver was making little or no reduction of speed as he neared Salisbury station.

One cannot unfortunately make direct comparison between the run on April 9—the inaugural trip—and April 23, because the former included the momentary stop at the 91st milepost, for Dugald Drummond to give an instruction to his inspector on the footplate of No. 336. The times from the Templecombe start to passing Andover were 48 min. 55 sec. and 45 min. 9 sec. But the difference of only 3 min. 46 sec. between the two trips, which included 52 sec. standing, could be very well accounted for by the time consumed in slowing down for the stop and re-accelerating. Rous-Marten stated that the speed on the Porton incline fell from 60 m.p.h. at the east end of Fisherton Tunnel to a minimum of 55·8 m.p.h. On the inaugural run Sekon's careful timing gives an *average* speed of 55·8 m.p.h. from Salisbury to Porton, and this certainly suggests that the speed through Salisbury itself cannot have been much less that on April 23. Furthermore, on the inaugural trip there was a galaxy of senior officers on the train, and if the run through Salisbury had been considered dangerous very good care would surely have been taken to see that such speeds were not repeated on subsequent trips. These American specials were, after all, the only passenger trains to pass Salisbury without stopping, and one can well imagine that on such prestige runs every precaution would be taken.

Even if one is bound to accept that some difference in design or riding qualities between engines 336 and 421 accounted for the safe passage in the one case and disaster in the other there still remains the safe, but inexplicable passage of No. 336 through the scissors crossover at a speed that was probably at least 60 m.p.h. The only parallel, and equally alarming case was that of the Press trip of the Coronation Scot on June 29, 1937, when we were doing 114 m.p.h. 2 miles from Crewe station and entered the latter over three crossover roads in succession. We struck the first of these at 57 m.p.h., and went through with such amazing smoothness that I for one never realised anything untoward was happening. It was only when we entered the *third* crossover at much reduced speed that the coaches were rocking in a somewhat disconcerting manner. If the L.S.W.R. boat train of April 23 ran through that one crossover as smoothly as we did on the Coronation Scot I can quite imagine that Rous-Marten, nor anyone else on that train realised how dangerous their going had been.

When the time came for the Board of Trade enquiry into the smash of July 1, 1906, it was stated that the speed limit round the curve was 30 m.p.h. After learning of the actual radii, and admittedly being very

L.S.W.R. AMERICAN SPECIAL: 9 APRIL 1904
PLYMOUTH–TEMPLECOMBE

Load: 4 coaches. 105 tons full
Engine: 6 ft. 4-4-0 No. 399

Dist. Miles			Actual m.	Actual s.	Av. Speed m.p.h.
0·0	STONEHOUSE POOL JUNC.		0	00	—
0·3	DEVONPORT		1	35	—
2·8	St. Budeaux		5	35	37·5
5·1	Tamerton		7	53	60·0
9·8	Bere Alston		14	31	42·5
16·2	TAVISTOCK		21	57	51·8
21·3	Brentor		28	27	47·1
32·5	OKEHAMPTON		42	33	51·9
50·6	Crediton		60	27	60·7
53·2	Newton St. Cyres		63	16	55·5
57·6	EXETER (ST. DAVIDS)	arr.	69	50	—
		dep.	70	15	—
58·3	EXETER (QUEEN ST.)		72	44	—
65·0	*Milepost* 165		80	28	52·0
66·0	*Milepost* 164	arr.	81	45	—
		dep.	88	46	—
70·4	SIDMOUTH JUNC.		96	30	—
75·0	Honiton		101	58	50·6
82·0	Seaton Junc.		110	26	49·7
85·2	Axminster		113	49	56·8
90·3	Chard Junc.		119	33	53·3
98·3	Crewkerne		128	45	52·2
107·1	YEOVIL JUNC.		138	16	55·6
111·7	Sherborne		143	18	54·9
115·4	Milborne Port		148	02	46·9
117·8	TEMPLECOMBE		151	53	

wise after the event, Rous-Marten said he thought it ought to be 15 m.p.h. But whatever it was that actually tipped the scales on July 1, and caused engine No. 421 to turn completely over, there is no doubt that her crew were not doing anything very far from the usual with those trains. The accident, coming in the same year as those at Grantham, and Shrewsbury, had a deplorable effect on public opinion. The daily newspapers indulged in a vast amount of scare-mongering; the railways generally were blamed for having faulty equipment, and of demanding too much of their servants, and the effect was soon to be seen in the deceleration of some schedules, and a general disinclination on the part of some drivers to run at high speeds, even on the straightest and best maintained sections of line. But so far as the main subject of this chapter is concerned it ended, once and for all, the Race from the West between the Great Western and the

L.S.W.R. AMERICAN SPECIAL: 9 APRIL 1904
TEMPLECOMBE–WATERLOO

Load: 4 coaches, 105 tons full
Engine: 'T9' class 4-4-0 No. 336

Dist. Miles		Actual m.	Actual s.	Av. Speed m.p.h.
0·0	TEMPLECOMBE	0	00	—
21·1	*Milepost* 91	21	06	—
		21	56	—
25·9	Wilton	29	06	39·4
28·4	SALISBURY	32	06	50·0
33·9	Porton	37	48	57·9
39·4	Grateley	43	24	58·9
45·8	ANDOVER	48	55	69·7
51·1	Hurstbourne	53	12	74·2
53·0	Whitchurch	55	22	53·8
59·8	Oakley	61	24	67·8
61·9	*Worting Junc.*	63	13	69·3
64·4	BASINGSTOKE	65	18	72·0
70·0	Hook	70	22	66·5
72·5	Winchfield	72	30	70·3
79·0	Farnborough	78	23	66·3
84·2	Brookwood	83	05	66·4
87·8	WOKING	85	59	74·5
91·2	*Milepost* 21	89	01	67·4
100·2	Surbiton	96	04	76·5
104·9	Wimbledon	101	19	53·8
108·3	Clapham Junc.	104	28	
112·2	WATERLOO	110	25	

L.S.W.R. AMERICAN SPECIAL: 23 APRIL 1904
TEMPLECOMBE–WATERLOO

Engine: 'T9' 4-4-0 No. 336

Dist. Miles		Actual m.	Actual s.	Av. Speed m.p.h.
0·0	Templecombe	0	00	—
28·4	Salisbury	28	03	60·8
45·8	Andover	45	09	61·1
64·4	Basingstoke	62	00	66·2
79·0	Farnborough	74	13	71·8
87·8	Woking	81	49	70·0
100·2	Surbiton	92	30	69·7
108·3	Clapham Junc.	99	39	68·0
112·2	Waterloo	104	33	47·8

L.S.W.R. Shortly after the accident the boat train workings were revised to include stops at Exeter and Salisbury, instead of the one stop at Templecombe; and running to normal express passenger schedules the overall times then became 4 hr. 28 min. But in May 1910, following an agreement between the G.W.R. and the L.S.W.R. to pool all competitive traffic, in a proportion based on the returns for the year 1908, the running of ocean specials by the South Western route ceased altogether.

X

The years of evolution

Apart from the tragedy of July 1, 1906, the first decade of the twentieth century was a great period for the London & South Western Railway. It saw numerous improvements to the line itself, in the way of better junction layouts, new stations and yard facilities; there was the introduction of power signalling; there was the removal of the locomotive works, from Nine Elms to the splendid new plant at Eastleigh—perhaps the most abiding monument to the career of Dugald Drummond; and in 1907 the Nelson Centenary was aptly marked by the opening of the enormous new graving dock, the Trafalgar, at Southampton. Above all, the great work of rebuilding Waterloo had reached its first phase by the end of 1910. Throughout this momentous 10 years the management and engineering of the company remained largely in the same hands. Sir Charles Owens was General Manager; J. W. Jacomb-Hood was Resident Engineer, Dugald Drummond, Chief Mechanical Engineer, and A. H. Johnson, Signal and Telegraph Engineer. Furthermore, the L.S.W.R. was fortunate in having on the Board a railwayman of such experience and reputation as Sir Charles Scotter, and from March 1904 he became Chairman.

There were two changes of personnel of some significance. At the end of 1905 the Carriage and Wagon Superintendent, W. Panter, retired. He had come from the North Western in 1885, and had been responsible for a complete modernisation of the L.S.W.R. carriage stock. The North Western had also set great store upon the smooth riding of its passenger trains, and Panter brought something of that tradition to the South Western. It was in his time that the carriage livery was eventually finalised. At one time the trains of the L.S.W.R. could have something of a harlequin appearance; but by the turn of the century the handsome, pleasing chocolate and orange yellow livery was almost ubiquitous. I have seen the colour of the upper panels described as 'salmon-coloured', and there have been coloured representations in which the lower panels were rendered as almost black. But the actual 'two-tone' scheme of the South Western was a very pleasing one, and harmonised beautifully with the pale olive green of the Drummond engines, and what is more important, with the smiling rural countryside through which the line ran.

Mentioning locomotive colours there was a marked distinction between the styles of Adams and Drummond, both in the basic colour and in the lining out, and the change marks one of the very few instances where a more elaborate turnout was adopted. The South Eastern & Chatham was another, though that, like the change from the Manchester, Sheffield & Lincolnshire to the Great Central was one aimed at publicity and prestige rather than the work of an individual locomotive superintendent. When Adams retired the locomotives of the L.S.W.R. stood ace-high in engineering and popular esteem; they needed no new and more colourful livery to boost their status. Besides using a different shade of green Drummond added a purple-brown border to the tenders, cab side-sheets, and splashers, and at the same time added broad bands of the same colour on either side of the usual black and white lining out of the boiler bands. A change regretted by many connoisseurs of the minutiae of locomotive adornment was the replacement of the fine cast number plates of Adams days, eventually, by nothing more elaborate than transfer figures. But the locomotive stock, whether of Drummond or Adams design was maintained in magnificent condition, and a later chapter will show what these engines could do in ordinary traffic.

Even before Charles Scotter came to Waterloo a series of important improvements to the line had been put in hand. The value of the flying junction had been amply demonstrated on the London & North Western Railway, and the first one to be constructed on the South Western was opened at Twickenham in 1882; it carried the up Kingston line over the Windsor lines. Another followed in 1884, at Raynes Park, where the up Leatherhead line was carried under all four tracks of the main line, which at the same time was in course of widening from two to four tracks throughout from Clapham Junction to Surbiton. It was no less significant of the tremendous growth of suburban traffic that the Windsor lines were also being widened to four tracks between Clapham Junction and Barnes. By November 1885 the main line widening had been extended to Hampton Court Junction, though the 'fly-over' carrying the down branch line over all tracks of the main line was not put in until 1915. The provision of four tracks throughout from Hampton Court Junction to the point of divergence of the Salisbury and Southampton lines was accompanied by the construction of yet another 'fly-over', this time carrying the up Southampton line over the up and down Salisbury lines. The actual junction points are about a mile east of the fly-over, at Worting; but originally there was an intermediate signal box at the flyover itself, named Battledown. As a boy I always remember being greatly intrigued by a coloured picture of Battledown Junction, that included three trains at speed; up and down expresses were passing on the Salisbury Lines, while an up train from Bournemouth was running on the high embankment east of the 'fly-over'. The automatic signalling installed on the widened lines east of Basingstoke is described later in this chapter.

The period from 1900 to 1910 was also marked by some outstanding developments at Southampton. When it was opened, in 1895, the Prince of Wales Dock was considered one of the wonders of the world; but it had not been in use for very long before the increasing size of passenger liners demanded something still larger, and the Trafalgar Dock was constructed: 875 ft. long, 90 ft. wide at sill, and 125 ft. wide at cope level. This vast graving dock, then the largest in the world, was opened in 1907;

but in a very short time came the news that the White Star Line had ordered two great liners in what was then frequently called the 'Palace Hotel' category—the *Olympic* and the *Titanic*. These were not intended to compete for the Blue Riband of speed on the North Atlantic. The Cunard 'flyers' *Mauretania* and *Lusitania* held that honour, and the White Star policy was to provide luxury ships travelling at a more moderate speed. But so far as the L.S.W.R. was concerned the Trafalgar Dock would not take the new White Star liners, and the first proposal was to build an entirely new dry dock on the eastern side of the river Itchen, at Woolston. This proposal however caused great concern in Southampton itself, and urgent representations were made to the railway company on the undesirability of having part of the dock estate on one side of the river, and part on the other. And so, after further consideration, the L.S.W.R. decided upon an enlargement of the Trafalgar Dock.

Work was commenced in 1910, and when finished the principal dimensions of the dock were:

Extreme inside length of dock from caisson to head	897 ft.
Width at entrance	100 ft.
Working width inside	102 ft.

A sliding caisson was fitted instead of the original dock gates, and this change required a lengthening of the dock by 15 ft. at the upper end, where a recess was provided for ships bows. Furthermore, to allow vessels to dock in the quickest possible time pumping plant was installed sufficient to keep a full head of water inside the dock. This allowed shoring operations to be carried out at leisure. It was not possible to do this previously, and with such saving in time to be had the dock was more extensively used, particularly by vessels with which the time available for examination and repair was small.

Further preparations for accommodation of the *Olympic* and the *Titanic* led to an amusing 'breeze' between the local authorities and the White Star Line. The L.S.W.R. put in hand the construction of new Ocean Quays, and a new open dock to take the largest liners afloat. To provide for adequate access to these quays and dock continual dredging would be required to maintain the requisite depth of water. The town of Southampton had benefited enormously from the very enterprising action of the L.S.W.R. in developing the dock estate on such a colossal scale; but when there was a prospect of extra dredging being required the local authorities coolly suggested that the cost of this should be borne entirely by the White Star Line and the L.S.W.R.! The White Star, which also had strong associations at Liverpool, somewhat naturally refused to bear any of the cost, whereupon the local authorities agreed to go shares with the L.S.W.R. in paying for the work to be done.

It was a time of intense competition on the North Atlantic Route, and the leading dimensions of the new White Star liners had no sooner been announced when the North German Lloyd stated that they had ordered a ship that was even larger. The length would be 879 ft. 3 in. and the width 95 ft. 2 in. This would have been a very tight fit in the enlarged Trafalgar Dock, but this great ship was barely finished before the outbreak of war, in 1914, and up to that time it is unlikely that the occasion would have arisen for her to go into dry dock. Quite apart from docking facilities however, the L.S.W.R. took advantage of the comings and goings of the White Star liners at Southampton to institute a most audacious service—in hot competition with the Great Western—to and from Southern Ireland above all places! This was in some way a reply to the Great Western steamship service from Plymouth to Brittany. The South Western took advantage of the calling of the White Star liners at Queenstown, and arranged special rail and steamer tickets, at 91s. first class and 67s. second class from Waterloo to Queenstown. Tourists making use of these facilities, which were available every Wednesday, had the fascinating experience of travelling by an ocean liner. At that time the ships on the New York run were the *Adriatic*, *Majestic*, *Oceanic*, and *Teutonic*—ships incidentally after which certain famous London & North Western engines were named. The journey from Waterloo to Queenstown took about 24 hrs., landing at the Irish port by tender.

At the turn of the century another powerful railway personality—Sam Fay—made a brief but lasting impression upon the affairs of the L.S.W.R. He had been on the South Western from 1872 to 1892; but after a spell as General Manager of the Midland & South Western Junction Railway he returned to Waterloo in 1899, as Superintendent of the Line. In the short time during which he held that office he paid two visits to the U.S.A., one to study operating methods, and a second, in company with Jacomb-Hood, to study the layout and working of large stations, in connection with the planned rebuilding of Waterloo. It was no doubt due, in no small measure, to his strong influence that power signalling was adopted so early on the L.S.W.R. At that time the American railways were installing it on a wide scale, and Fay was extremely impressed with its possibilities. His influence in this respect was seen later, after he had become General Manager of the Great Central Railway, and that company put into commission a considerable number of installations on the same system that had been adopted earlier on the L.S.W.R.

At the end of the 19th century a variety of systems was being developed in this country, in America, and on the continent of Europe. These included the electro-pneumatic and all-electric systems—the latter being of several different designs. But the system chosen by the London & South Western Railway was the low-pressure pneumatic, sometimes referred to as the 'all-air' system. It involved a network of pipes, and was slower in its response to the movement of control switches than with electricity; but it was claimed to be cheaper. On the recommendation of J. W. Jacomb-Hood the management of the London & South Western Railway decided to standardise on this system. It used a pressure of not more than 15 lb. per square inch, while the valves of the point and signal motors

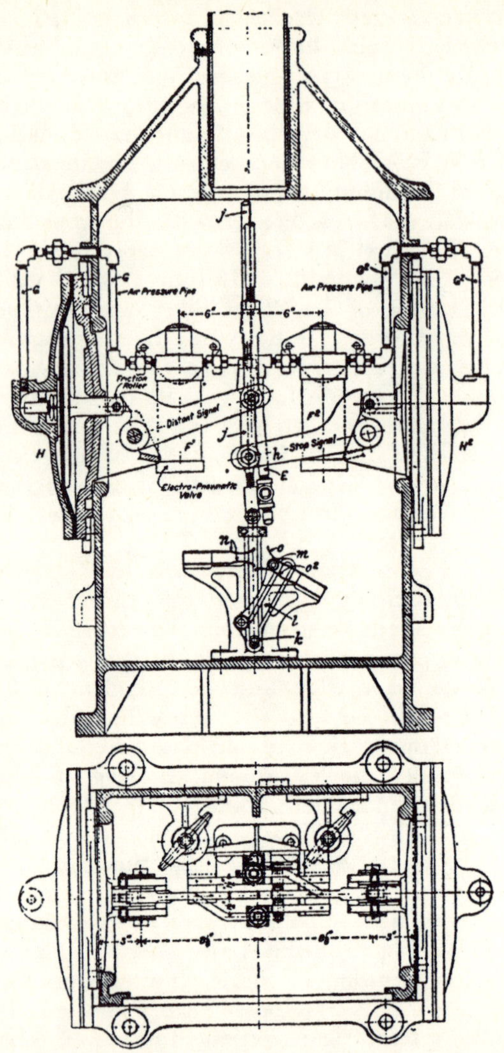

Low pressure pneumatic signal operating valves and controls.

were operated at a pressure of no more than 7 lb. per square inch. The amount of piping was complicated by the fact that the return indications were also given by air; for example, each signal lever required a pipe for lowering the signal, a second for restoring the signal to danger, and a third for the return indication to show the signal had gone to danger. No indication was given to show that the signal had been pulled off.

The first installation of this system on the London & South Western Railway, and indeed anywhere in Great Britain was at Grateley, and with this interlocking were associated the automatic signals installed at the same time between Grateley and Andover. It was brought into service in the summer of 1901, and in the following year a larger installation was completed at Salisbury which included two signal boxes each having 64 levers and a ground frame with 8 levers. The apparatus at Grateley consisted of a single interlocking frame of 72 levers. By the use of this system a considerable reduction in size of the signal cabin was obtained.

Name of Station	Levers							Automatic		
	Signal	Points	Control	Spaces	Total	Signals	Points	Station Distants	Sections	Signals
Grateley..	36	17	—	19	72	46	31	1		
Grateley Ground Frame ..	—	2	—	6	8	—	4	—		
Grateley–Andover	—	—	—	—	—	—	—	—	12	22
Salisbury East	26	17	3	18	64	33	30	2		
Salisbury West	22	20	7	15	64	34	30	2		
Salisbury Ground Frame ..	2	1	1	4	8	2	2	—		
Basingstoke East	24	20	—	16	60	32	36	4		
Basingstoke West	31	23	1	13	68	37	40	4		
Basingstoke Ground Frame ..	1	1	1	1	4	1	2	—		
Barton Mill	12	8	1	11	32	19	14	4		
Barton Mill to Hook	—	—	—	—	—	—	—	—	16	28
Hook	16	11	2	11	40	23	22	4		
Hook to Winchfield	21	—	—	—	—	—	—	—	4	4
Winchfield	2	14	1	12	48	34	28	4		
Newnham sidings	—	1	1	4	8	2	2	—		
Winchfield to Fleet	—	—	—	—	—	—	—	—	8	12
Fleet	16	10	1	5	32	24	2	4		
Fleet to Farnborough	—	—	—	—	—	—	—	—	8	12
Farnborough	19	11	1	9	40	23	22	5		
Sturt Lane	10	4	1	5	20	12	4	7		
Sturt Lane to Pirbright ..	—	—	—	—	—	—	—	6	4	4
Pirbright	6	2	1	3	12	7	2	5		
Brookwood	18	15	2	5	40	26	28	—		
Brookwood to Woking ..	—	—	—	—	—	—	—	—	10	4
Staines East	15	10	1	6	32	20	19	3		
Staines West	22	13	1	4	40	25	21	3		
Staines Ground Frame ..	2	1	2	3	8	—	—	—		
Clapham Junc. W. Main ..	5	3	—	4	12	8	5	5		
Clapham West Windsor ..	18	13	—	5	36	21	22	12		
Clapham E. Windsor & Main	43	28	—	13	84	56	46	13		
West London Junc.	23	15	2	8	48	33	26	14		
West Ground Frame	3	4	2	3	12	5	5	4		

The levers were pitched at 3 in. centres as against the 5 in. centres normal on the London & South Western Railway in mechanical frames; and by an economy of levers in the interlocking itself, by combining the actuation of facing point locks by the same lever as their associated points, and by the working of more than one signal by the same lever through selection methods, only 72 levers were required in the frame against 87 that would normally have been required had traditional methods then current been used. The comparative lengths of the 72-lever frame actually installed, and an 87-lever mechanical frame with levers at 5 in. pitch were 24 ft. and 36 ft. 3 in. Of course, the use of such a low pressure meant that the operating cylinders for the points were relatively large; but on the other hand, a low pressure system is less susceptible to troubles from leakage than a high pressure one.

The actual form of the interlocking frame was looked at somewhat askance by those who adhered to the traditional idea of an interlocking frame. The 'levers' consisted of a series of handles mounted vertically on horizontal slides, and these were pulled out horizontally towards the signalman. Shortly before that time the Great Eastern Railway had introduced the very first power interlocking frame ever to be used in Great Britain, at Granary Junction, Bishopsgate, and had used an interlocking machine that was not only of American design, but was actually manufactured by the Union Switch & Signal Company in Pittsburgh. In this interlocking machine the levers again took the form of handles, but they were rotated instead of being pulled out. So strong was the prejudice in Great Britain against anything but a direct pull, that when the electro-pneumatic system of interlocking was put on to the British market by the Westinghouse Brake Company insistence was placed upon having a lever of conventional form, albeit a greatly miniaturised one. The distinguished signal engineering designer, Walter Allan Pearce, under whom I myself worked for several years, often spoke of the difficulties he had in adapting the American interlocking frame in order to give British railway engineers the traditional lever pull they demanded. On the London & South Western Railway the strong advocacy of Jacomb-Hood and his signal engineer A. H. Johnson for the low-pressure pneumatic system, in its entirety, overcame this prejudice, and quite a number of additional locking frames of the low pressure type were installed. The complete list of them, and the number of levers involved makes a most impressive record.

In addition to the interlocking at various junctions and larger centres, special mention must be made of the instances of automatic signals on the London & South Western main line. Between Woking and Basingstoke a considerable number of three-aspect signals were installed on gantries spanning all four tracks. I have used the modern term 'aspect' in connection with these signals rather than the word 'position', because the great majority of them were two-arm signals showing three aspects, namely, 'stop' with both arms in the horizontal position, 'Caution' with the upper (home arm) lowered, and the distant arm horizontal, and 'clear' with both arms lowered. The signal sections were arranged so that the gantries spanning all the tracks supported signals for all four roads. The signal sections were about 1,500 yards long, and the control valves were opened and closed by relays connected with the track circuits. The movement of the arms was regulated by a combined operating mechanism contained in a large cast iron case which formed the foot of the posts on which the

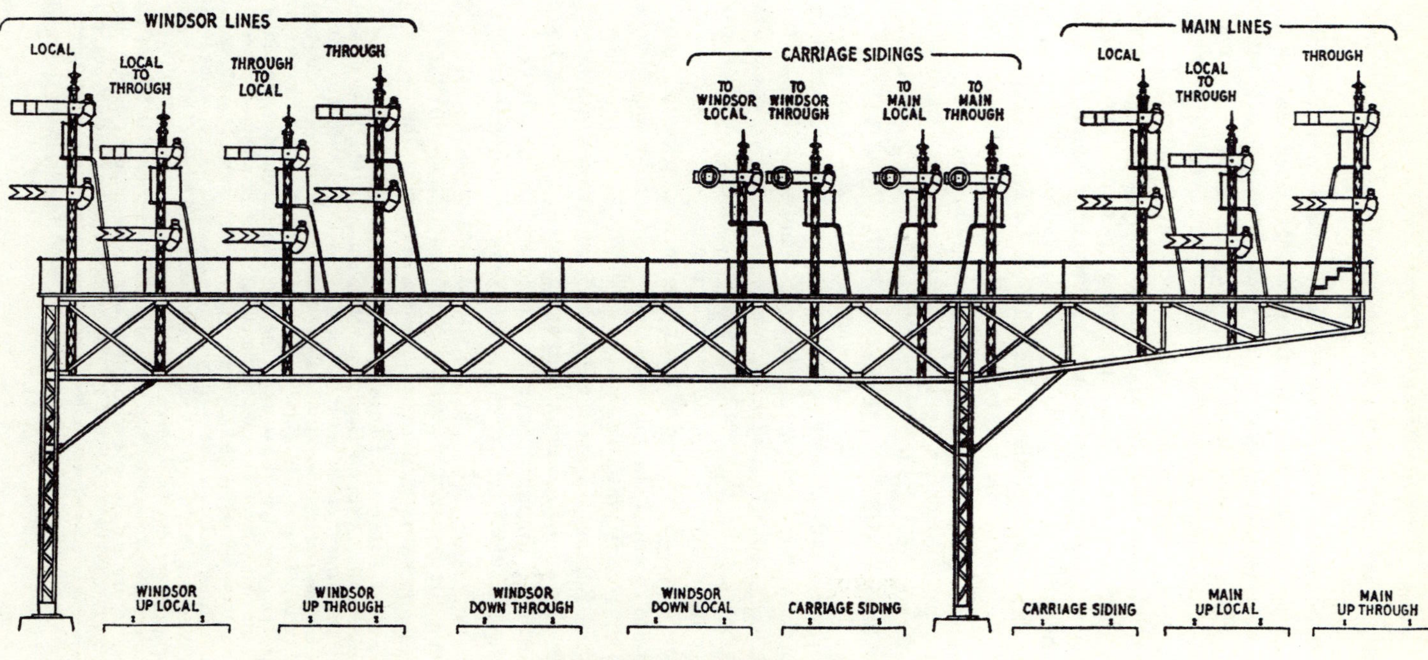

Signal bridge near Clapham Junction.

signal arms themselves were mounted. These boxes could be mounted either on a concrete base at ground level, or carried on a signal bridge. The posts were tubular, and by having the operating rods inside the posts an extremely neat and tidy arrangement was obtained. As will be seen from the cross-sectional view of the mechanism case, the actual movement of the arms in these signals was initiated not by pneumatic cylinders, but by diaphrams. The controls were extremely simple, and interlocking was, of course, provided between the 'stop' and the 'distant' arm mechanism to ensure that the 'distant' arm could not be lowered unless the 'stop' arm was also in the 'clear' position. The introduction of power worked signals and so many automatic sections in the early years of the 20th century was a notable feather in the cap of the engineering department of the London & South Western Railway. Extensive use of track circuiting was made at other parts of the line, while so far as manual block working was concerned, the company was one of the largest users of the Sykes 'Lock and Block' system. It will be described in a later chapter how the track circuited lines in the London area were adapted to meet the requirements of d.c. electric traction.

So far as the signals themselves were concerned, the South Western was at one time a railway very prolific in its use of semaphore arms; and on the multiple track sections particularly, between Clapham Junction and Waterloo, there were some very spectacular signal configurations. Elsewhere bracket signals were extensively used, of a handsome design, with lattice main masts and doll posts, and many of these bracket posts again carried a large number of arms. There was, however, nothing on the line quite to equal the famous signal gantry that was carried high above the 'A' box at Waterloo.

The Signal Engineer of the London & South Western Railway, A. H. Johnson, took a very prominent part in the founding of The Institution of Railway Signal Engineers, and the records of his participation in some of the early discussions are extremely interesting as showing something of his strong personality and his genial wit. At one of the earliest meetings, in discussing the position of signalling in general, and in particular in regard to the operating department, he spoke thus:

"We have in the past, and I have said so in the Railway Press and other places, been obsessed by the Operating Department. I do not think it has been the fault of the Operating Department at all, but it is a position which has been forced upon them. The old engineers were followed by a state of things in which construction and design stagnated, because the roads together with signals etc., had to a large extent, been constructed, and it was quite natural that the importance of improvements in operation should, for a time, dwarf the constructional and engineering part of the business. Perhaps it was quite natural, and my view is that the Operating Department has been unintentionally forced into a false position; so much so, that you get young men writing to the papers saying that we, and the Loco. Engineers, and others of our Constructional Departments are merely the servants of the Traffic Department.

"Well Sir, I venture to state that we will not allow ourselves to become the helots of another department, for under such a condition, we cannot perform those great functions that should be expected of us. There is no Department which ever performed a great function in a great way unless it had free initiative to a great extent. Well I think we are in a fair way to overcome this domination by the Operating Department."

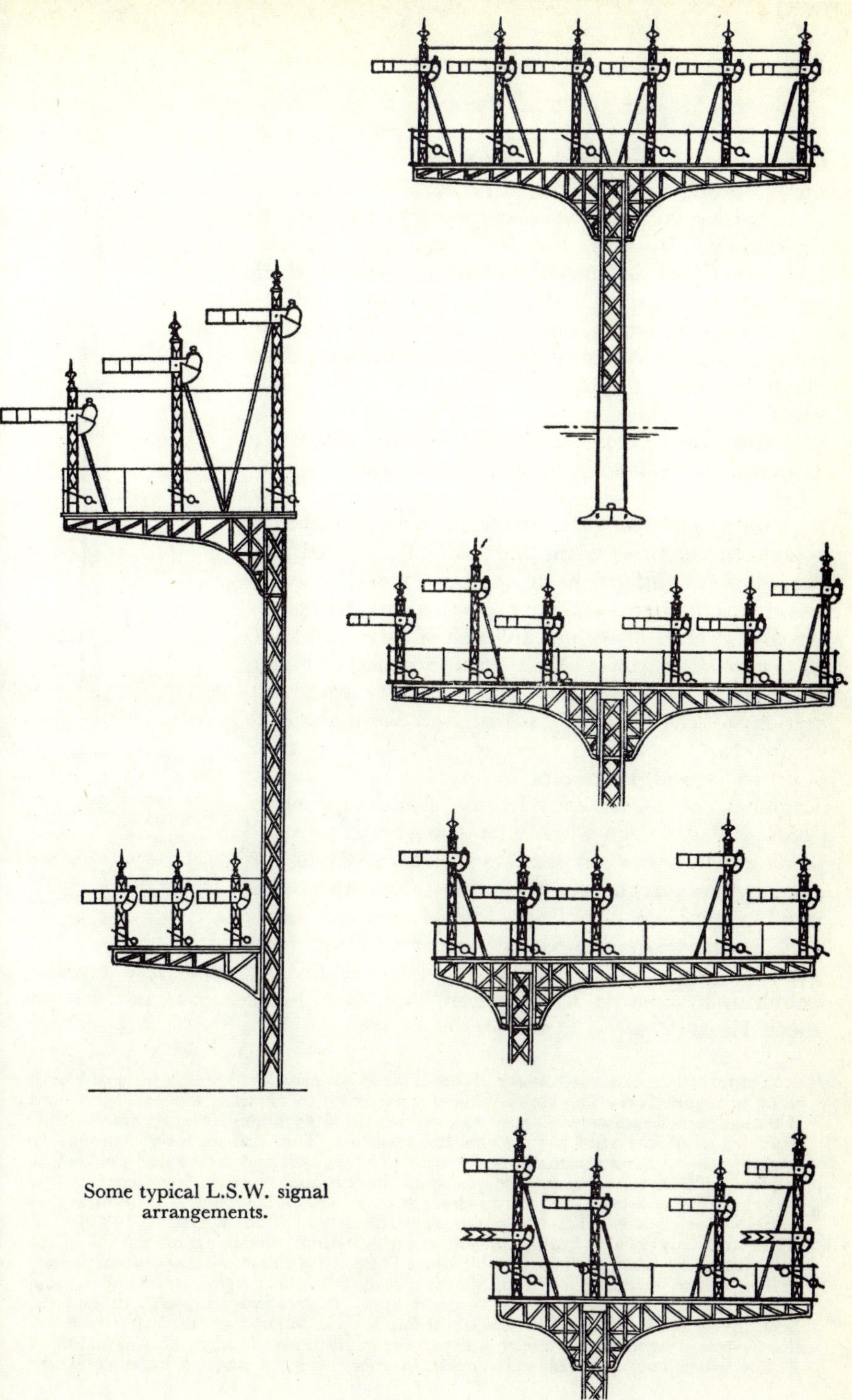

Some typical L.S.W. signal arrangements.

One could interject that there must have been many times when signal engineers of modern times felt they were completely under the domination of the operating department, so far as the preparation of signalling layouts was concerned. But reverting to the early years of the century one can find no better example of Johnson's precepts than the way in which the engineers of the London & South Western Railway had introduced, and virtually standardised in many instances, the unconventional low-pressure type of interlocking frame, and evidently over-ridden, either by persuasion or sheer will power, any prejudice there may have been in the Operating Department in favour of the conventional type of lever.

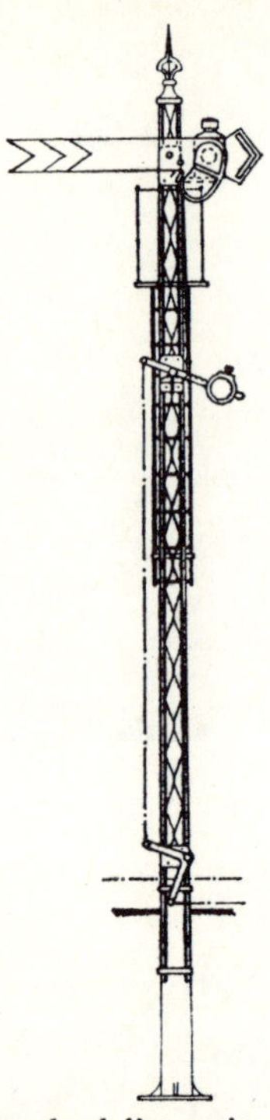

Standard distant signal with Welch distinguishing fish-tail lamp to right of main lamp used before the adoption of yellow as a caution indication at night.

Johnson was also very outspoken on the subject of 3-position signalling when this was first discussed, and suggested for adoption in this country. By three-position signalling I am here referring to semaphore signals which can assume any one of three positions, as distinct from the 3-aspect semaphore signal giving three indications with two arms, as on the automatic sections of line between Woking and Basingstoke. A Paper had been presented to The Institution of Railway Signal Engineers by A. H. Rudd, Signal Engineer of the Pennsylvania Railroad, whom Johnson had known when he was a young man and serving in America on the Pennsylvania. Rudd was stressing the advantages, as he saw it, of the three-position upper-quadrant signal which was then being very extensively adopted in America. There were some engineers on the railways of Great Britain who were equally enthusiastic towards its adoption here, but Johnson was not one of them. He said:

"I think the idea of the three-position signal is basically wrong. It is a very difficult thing to argue about. The idea is basically wrong for this reason: the use of the word 'Caution' is misleading; it is very easy to be misled by names. The meaning of the word 'caution' is a vital thing to an engine driver. They use the word 'caution' as applying to the Distant signal when it is in what we call, and very aptly too, I think the 'on' or 'Danger' position. They call that the 'caution' position. Now what are the actual facts? Say a train is speeding along at 60 m.p.h. on a declivity. It perhaps goes round a sharp bend and the driver suddenly finds the Distant signal 'on'. Well now, if you study any reliable brake diagram you will find that a train running at this speed will take a very long distance in which to pull up, with either ordinary or emergency brakes, and to let the driver think that is merely a 'caution' signal is, in my opinion, entirely wrong. What it actually means is 'stop'. It does not necessarily mean 'stop here', but it really means to a very fast train, 'Stop as soon as you can'; but with this three position signal you are letting the driver get into his mind the idea of 'caution'. I know what 'caution' means: it means, in effect, shut off steam a little, apply the brake a little. These are wrong terms and from wrong terms you get wrong practice. I can, however, see their mode of thought. I knew them very well as a young man, and I can follow their reasoning. They made their Distant signal in the 'on' position at 45°, and so doing they made that signal of secondary importance because they made it in an inclined position. I notice the yellow light is referred to. I was responsible for first suggesting that in America. But as regards the Distant Signal they have given it secondary importance, and that is my quarrel with them. Whereas I say the Distant signal is of the first importance. It is 'on' when in the horizontal position just as much as the Home is 'on' when in a similar position, for the Distant is simply a reflection of the Home.

"A moment ago I referred to the yellow light. They bring in the yellow light to make three signals at night. The yellow light is usually safe, but in some conditions of atmosphere it is not. There is not that vital distinction that you have between red and green, and under some atmospheric conditions such a light may take on a greenish hue.

"Then they say that one great feature of the one arm signal is simplicity. You have first got to find simplicity. What it is you are principally concerned about is simplicity in the engine-driver's understanding, not simplicity in the apparatus. It is true that the three-position signal has got only one arm, but it has got many arms to the driver's mind. You can draw a rough simile between a one-armed clock and a two-armed clock. You can make a one-armed clock—it would be a very simple thing—but you won't read the time by it near as well as you would by a two-armed clock!"

Although the London & South Western Railway had been in the forefront of signalling development in the first decade of the 20th century, and had been in advance of many in its adoption of track circuiting and power signalling there was never any consideration towards the following of what was then the popular trend in America, and which influenced such a conservative line as the Great Western to the extent of installing three-position upper-quadrant signal at Paddington, and many more on the Ealing–Shepherds Bush line. When the time came for Johnson's successor on the London & South Western Railway, W. J. Thorrowgood, to recommend a system of multi-aspect signalling for the Southern Railway he went straight to colour lights.

Before closing this account of developments during the period 1900–1910 reference must be made to the completion of the first stage in the rebuilding of Waterloo. This enabled the new 'South' platforms to be brought into service during the year 1910, and so smoothly was the change effected, and so handsome the new concourse and buildings associated with the new platforms, 1–5, that the development immediately won the warm appreciation of the public. The plan on page 110 shows this very interesting intermediate stage in the reconstruction of the station. The Parliamentary powers obtained in 1899 involved the removal of a church in the street named Lower Marsh, and many dwelling houses. In exchange the L.S.W.R. built several blocks of houses on a site in the Westminster Bridge Road that provided accommodation for considerably more persons than were displaced, while a cordial arrangement with the ecclesiastical authorities resulted in the incorporation of the former parish of All Saints, in the Lower Marsh, with that of St. John's church, in Waterloo Road. Very great care was taken to ensure that the inevitable disruption caused by such a vast constructional programme should be carried through with goodwill on all sides. The L.S.W.R. was conspicuously successful in this.

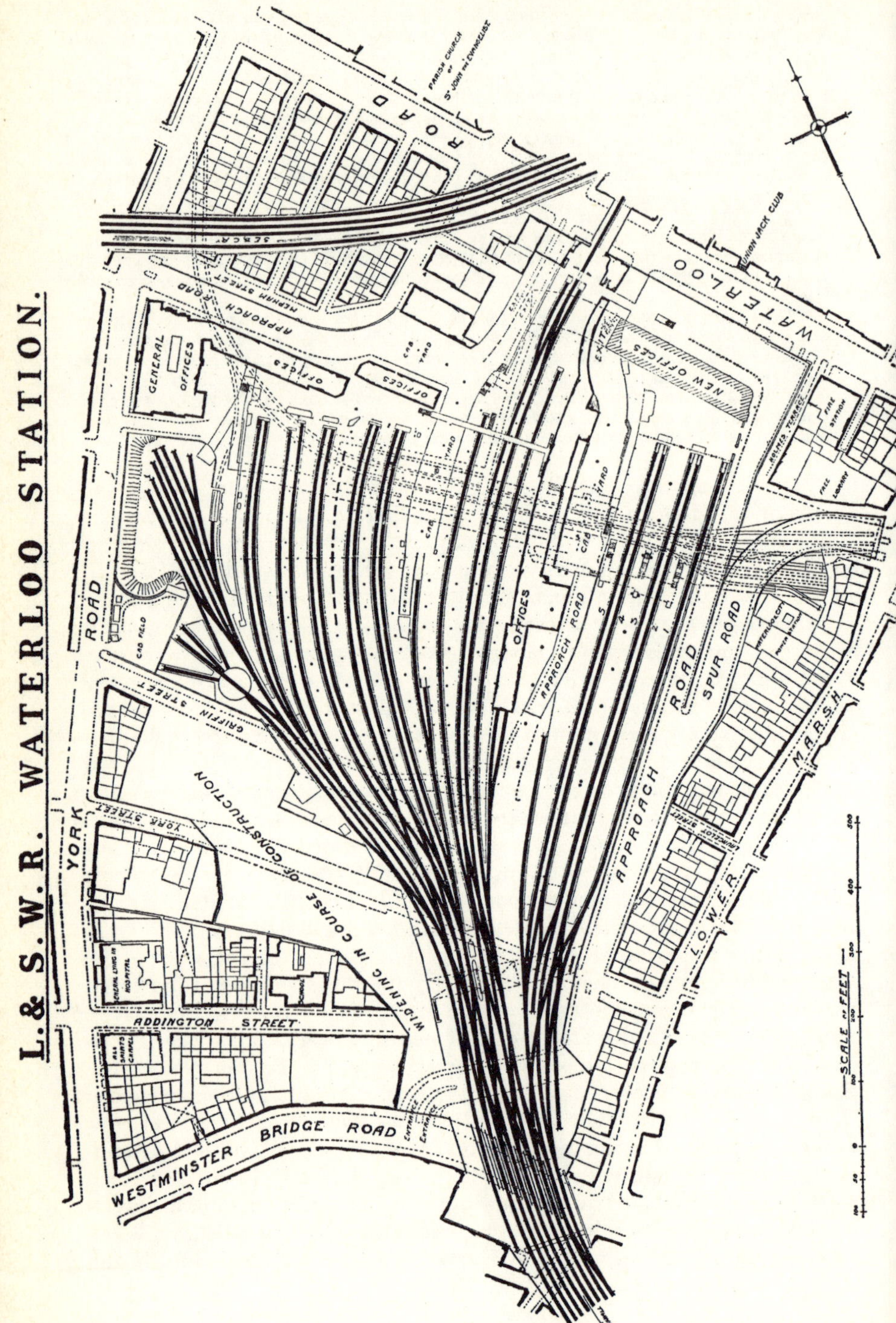
L. & S. W. R. WATERLOO STATION.
WATERLOO ROAD
PARISH CHURCH OF St. JOHN THE EVANGELIST
UNION JACK CLUB
S.E. & C. R.
HENHAM STREET
APPROACH ROAD
GENERAL OFFICES
OFFICES
CAB YARD
NEW OFFICES
EXIT
FIRE STATION
HOLMES TERRACE
FREE LIBRARY
CAB FIELD
GRIFFIN STREET
YORK ROAD
YORK STREET
WIDENING IN COURSE OF CONSTRUCTION
APPROACH ROAD
SPUR ROAD
LOWER MARSH
ADDINGTON STREET
WESTMINSTER BRIDGE ROAD
ENTRANCE
SCALE OF FEET

In this phase of the work the familiar approach road of today was built, and the first section of the fine concourse, and headquarters buildings. But in 1910 the old main line platforms remained, and also the connection to the S.E. & C.R. By the summer of 1910 therefore the south side of the station had assumed the aspect that is so familiar today; and in readiness for the next stage of the reconstruction some main line trains were diverted to the new platforms 4 and 5. At the time the new platforms were opened to the public Parliamentary powers had not yet been obtained for the alterations in the approaches from the north side, but these were readily obtained in time for the gradual evolution of the present station to be carried out smoothly. A feature of the new station which was greatly appreciated from the outset was its spacious air, resulting from the lofty glass roof, and the generous amount of glazing in the end wall. That atmosphere was to continue, and even in its busiest steam days Waterloo never seemed to get dingy and dirty like some other great London Termini one could name.

XI

Dugald Drummond

1900–1912

Around Dugald Drummond, one of the greatest characters of British railway history, it is only natural that a host of stories and legends have grown up. One feels that many of these were apochryphal and others wildly exaggerated. He has been described as a 'cantankerous old Clydesider'; but it is not my intention to repeat any of these well-worn legends, or to retail any new ones. That he was a very strong personality there is no doubt; and some of the stories associated with him stem from his incisive and resolute handling of one of the most difficult problems of personnel that existed on the railways of this country at the turn of the century—that of insobriety. Drunkenness among footplate men was in its way as great a problem at that time as the present day drunken driver in charge of a motor car. Adams, genial soul that he was had, in his later years, not given the matter the attention it needed, and Drummond set about the situation he found on the L.S.W.R. with a vigour and severity as to let it be known from end to end of the line that a positive firebrand had come to Nine Elms.

The drivers and firemen knew that any irregularities in working would be dealt with personally by the chief, and woebetide those who were summonded to what Drummond himself called the 'leevees' held in his office every Monday morning. His invariable rule in dealing with drunkenness on the footplate was a terrific reprimand and an order to sign the pledge, at the first offence. The second time there was no redress; it was the sack. And in a very short time he had virtually stamped out drunkenness in the locomotive running department. But no resentment towards him was borne by the great majority of the men. He was always respected, and in course of time a genuine affection was formed towards him. Enginemen liked working for Dugald Drummond. Men who had known him in Scotland joined the L.S.W.R., and at one time quite a number of the express drivers were Scotsmen. It was the same in the Drawing Office and in the Works, and the Scottish influence at Eastleigh lasted well into Southern Railway days.

On the Caledonian Railway Drummond's reputation as an engine designer and as a works administrator had soared to great heights, and when he brought his basic 4-4-0 express passenger locomotive to the South Western, in the form of the 'T9' class, he produced one of the best and most long-lived small-powered engines of all time. Splendid though the work of these engines was, attention on the L.S.W.R. became centred upon the series of large 4-6-0s that he introduced from 1905 onwards.

It was a time when engineers all over the world were designing progressively larger locomotives. Some were urgently needed to handle increasing traffic; some, like those of the Great Central were built largely for prestige purposes; while some lines like the London & North Western, which had perhaps the greatest need of any, seemed to accept the need for larger locomotives grudgingly and built the smallest machines that would handle the traffic. It is however a little difficult to determine the category into which the first of Dugald Drummond's 4-6-0s should be placed.

In November 1905 *The Railway Magazine* published a photograph which it entitled 'The Locomotive Giant of 1905'. This was Dugald Drummond's first 4-6-0, the huge No. 330, with four cylinders 16 in. diameter by 24 in. stroke; 6 ft. diameter coupled wheels, and a boiler having the unprecedented total heating surface of 2,727 sq. ft. The idea behind the construction of these great engines was to provide power for hauling a load of 350 tons up Honiton bank without assistance. The story goes that Drummond paid a visit to J. F. McIntosh, at St. Rollox, and on visiting the scene of previous labours was shown one of the two 6 ft. 6 in. express 4-6-0s, Nos. 49 and 50, which were then the most powerful locomotives in Great Britain. Drummond, always outspoken, is said to have upbraided McIntosh for building such unnecessarily large engines; but having heard what they were doing on the Beattock bank he returned south with some ideas of how heavier trains might be taken over Honiton.

The failure of many engineers who had built excellent small locomotives, when they came to try something much larger, has frequently been discussed. Some got into trouble with the frames, others provided inadequate boilers and fire-boxes, while in some cases there were structural defects, such as the method of attachment of cylinders to frames, or the design of the slide bars. Drummond seems to have avoided all these pitfalls in his gigantic '330' class, and it is thus all the more inexplicable that a man who had previously set such store upon all the factors that go to make up a free running engine should have contrived the layout of cylinders and valve gear that completely hamstrung the 330's from the outset.

Drummond used a divided drive, which so far as four-cylinder locomotives were concerned was then confined to the de Glehn compound Atlantics on the Great Western. The inside cylinders were fed through slide valves with vertical faces mounted between the cylinders and actuated by Stephenson's link motion. With cylinders only 15 in. diameter there was plenty of room for the eccentrics and no need to skimp the main bearings. So far so good. It might then have seemed that all that was necessary was to put in a simple arrangement of rocking levers to actuate the valves of the outside cylinders from the inside motion. The fact that the outside cylinders had piston valves while the inside had slide valves should have made no difference. But rather than put in a rocking lever mechanism Drummond actuated the outside valves by separate sets of *Walschaerts* gear, mounted outside.

The result was to strangle the engine, as an express passenger unit. The inside and outside valve gears had different characteristics. When notching up, the outside gear maintained a constant lead on the valves, while with the inside gear the inherent characteristic of the Stephenson link motion increased the lead as the engine was notched up. The inside and outside cylinders were receiving an uneven distribution of steam, and the effect was to make the locomotive extraordinarily sluggish. In consequence these grandly impressive machines were a complete failure in the traffic for which they were designed, and from a very early date in their career they were relegated to goods working. Drummond seems to have been conscious enough of their shortcomings, and in December 1907 a sixth engine was built, with the same huge boiler but even larger cylinders—16½ in. by 26 in. against 16 in. by 24 in. In this engine, No. 335, the valve chests for the outside cylinders were placed above, rather than below the cylinders as in Nos. 330–334. But No. 335 seems to have been even less successful than the earlier ones, and she made no impression in express passenger traffic.

The results obtained with No. 335 disappointing as they were in themselves, seemed to have finally given Nine Elms the clue as to where the shortcomings of the '330' class really lay; and it was remarkable that in the next essay towards meeting the haulage problem of Honiton bank an engine that was dimensionally *smaller* in every respect was produced. It was still a four-cylinder 4-6-0, but one in which the total heating surface was reduced from 2,727 to 1,920 sq. ft., and the cylinders changed to 15 in. diameter by 26 in. stroke. The drive was still divided, and there were still four sets of valve gear; but the inside gear like the outside was Walschaerts, and thus the inside and outside 'engines' could at least work in harmony. The 'G14' class, as they were known, were in fact vastly better in express traffic than the giant 330s, and from their first introduction, in 1908, they had a virtual monopoly of the Salisbury–Exeter road, until the construction of the Urie 'N15' class, in 1918–9. It is true that many trains west of Salisbury continued to be worked by 4-4-0 engines; but the 'G14' 4-6-0s formed the first-line power, and to the first five built at Nine Elms there were added five more in 1910–11. These latter were the first express passenger engines to be built at Eastleigh after the transfer of the locomotive works from Nine Elms.

The first engine of the new class was numbered 453, followed by 454-457. Those who care to attach significance to numbers may feel that it is not without significance that Drummond's No. 453 was the first reasonably successful 4-6-0 to work in express traffic on the L.S.W.R., and that it was taken later for the first of the incomparable 'King Arthur' class 4-6-0s of the Southern. The later 453, *King Arthur* himself, was stationed at Salisbury, and worked regularly on the routes previously run by the earlier 453 and her sisters. The second five of Drummond's 6 ft. 4-6-0s were numbered 448-452. In the following chapter some runs with these engines are recalled. They seemed to run freely enough up to

75 m.p.h. or so; but the drivers were reluctant to allow them really to have their heads downhill. At the time this was attributed to the relative smallness of their coupled wheels imparting a degree of sluggishness; but in his copious records of performance over the Salisbury–Exeter road R. E. Charlewood has frequently noted that steam was shut off downhill after attaining 70 m.p.h. or so, whereas the 4-4-0s were taken down pell-mell to reach 80 or 85 as a regular thing.

When drivers so addicted to hard running as the top link men at Salisbury and Exmouth Junction have always been, to shut off steam downhill suggests to me that the engines were not riding well. There is of course a clear distinction between rough and bad riding. The 'King Arthurs', in later years, could be unconscionably harsh and rough; but at their worst they never developed that dangerous hunting roll that can strike apprehension into the hearts of the toughest and most experienced enginemen, and certain slowings in the records of the work of the Drummond 'G14' class suggest that they may have been prone to that kind of behaviour. Be that as it may they stayed on the Salisbury and Exeter top link workings for many years. Some time ago it was suggested that Drummond introduced his 6 ft. 7 in. 4-6-0s of the 'T14' class because the 'G14s' were not fast enough for the competitive services to the West of England. This cannot really have been the case, because the later engines with larger wheels were employed almost entirely at the London end, and on the Bournemouth services.

The first of the 'T14' class four-cylinder 4-6-0s were built at Eastleigh in 1911, and they were without question the most successful of Drummonds 4-6-0 designs. Apart from the use of 6 ft. 7 in. coupled wheels there were certain important changes from ordinary practice. The boilers were the same as those of the 'G14s', but carrying a pressure of 200 lb. per sq. in., instead of 175 lb. The dimensions of both classes were:

	Heating Surface in sq. ft.
Tubes	1580
Cross water tubes ..	200
Firebox	140
Total	1920
Grate Area	31·5

The later 'T14s', built in 1912 managed to acquire an additional 56 sq. ft. of tube heating surface; for although they had the same number and the same size of tubes as previously the heating surface was given as 1,636 sq. ft. The length between the tube plates may have been slightly increased.

Mechanically the most important change was the placing of all four cylinders in line, under the smokebox, and thus arose the need for a long connecting rod for the outside cylinders. Walschaerts gear was retained with the inside valves actuated by a rocking shaft mechanism. An excellent feature of these engines was the use of piston valves of no less than 9 in. diameter, for 15 in. cylinders. The front end arrangements were skilfully contained in an outward spread of the smokebox sides that recalled the old Allan engines on the Caledonian with which Drummond would have been very familiar in his younger days. The coupled-wheel splashers were made very wide to contain the outside valve gear, with a single inspection cover, originally of glass. It was these splashers that gave rise to the well-known nickname of the class, though in later years the nickname itself has undergone something of a change. Older South-Western men, in using the term 'paddle-box' meant only the splashers themselves. The engines were known as the 'paddle-boats'—the paddlebox being an integral part of the whole, but in later years it has become usual to refer to the engines as the 'paddleboxes'.

The first five of these engines, built at Eastleigh in 1911, were numbered 443 to 447. The second batch, completed in 1912 and numbered 458 to 462 differed from the original one in having the Drummond steam-dryer, contained in the smokebox. This device provided for a moderate degree of superheat, and it consisted of a number of 2 in. diameter tubes, which were in line with the flue tubes of the boiler, in such a way that the hot gases of combustion were drawn through both sets of tubes. The steam entered the chamber containing these tubes through a tee-pipe, and was directed by three baffle plates to the bottom, and thence upward to the cylinder steam pipe connection at the top. In this device a steam temperature of about 400 degrees Fah. was obtained, which Drummond considered adequate. No special arrangement of dampers, or forced lubrication was required, and the device required no alteration to the design of the boiler. It could be removed easily for cleaning, or other attention to the boiler.

The 'T14' class from the very beginning proved very fast and free running engines, and on the Bournemouth expresses speeds of more than 80 m.p.h. with them were frequent on the long descent from Litchfield Tunnel towards Eastleigh. But recorders of locomotive performance were not generally enthusiastic about their work. On up expresses in particular one rarely could note those long-sustained spells of high speed running between Basingstoke and Clapham Junction with which the 4-4-0 engines so often delighted the compiler of logs. Some commentators have suggested that they were prone to heating, others that they were shy steamers, both of which points may to some extent have been re-inforced by the alterations to these engines subsequently made, first by R. W. Urie, and later by R. E. L. Maunsell. But I do not think that either of these assumptions get at the true reason for the difficulties sometimes experienced in running the 'T14s'. I think the explanation is to be found in the design of the firebox.

Many years later I made the acquaintance of that inimitable character Dan Knight, who was senior locomotive running inspector on the Western section of the Southern Region. From our mutual love of locomotives that acquaintance ripened into friendship, and with a man whose footplate experience went back to the days of Dugald Drummond there were many occasions when he talked of the older engines. From his reminiscences, and his tales of the troubles he had in firing the 'T14s' I studied the fireboxes of those engines afresh. The floor of the grate is almost horizontal and only a few inches below footplate level. The brick-arch is low down, and I could then well appreciate how difficult it was to keep an even firebed over the 31½ square feet of grate-area when the coal had to be shot at a very shallow angle in order to reach the front, and avoid putting at least some of the coal on top of the brick arch. The North-Western men had similar difficulties in firing George Whale's 'Experiment' class, 4-6-0s in the early days; but as these latter became greatly multiplied, and were developed into the very numerous 'Prince of Wales' class with identical boilers, the technique for success became widely known. On the South Western there were only 10 of the 'G14' class and 10 of the 'T14s', and the special technique needed in firing did not render them general service engines.

Among lovers of locomotives, as distinct from the enthusiasts who worked amongst them, the 'T14s' had their very ardent admirers, among them I would add, your humble servant. Many years ago my friend Henry Maxwell wrote to me of them:

> "Those engines possessed a dignity and a distinction, and above all a balanced plastic symmetry which no other design, to my mind, has equalled. They are the high aristocrats in every line."

Drummond, despite his rugged temperament was one of the great artists of the locomotive world, and although his most fervent admirer would have to admit that his 4-6-0s generally could not be counted among his most successful designs they possessed great individuality of character in appearance, and in the 'T14' class, no less than the original '330s' he achieved a marked degree of grace and line. In that greatly cherished series of coloured picture postcards of locomotives and trains published by F. Moore, there was a very pleasing broadside picture of No. 330. She had not the 'greyhound' appearance of the 'T14s', which gave the impression that they were inherently very fast engines; but whatever her shortcomings, if the like of No. 330 were to ride the rails again today, in original livery, I would not like to guess what acreage of film would be exposed in capturing her tremendous individuality among engines.

In writing of the 'G14' 6 ft. 4-6-0s I mentioned the transfer of the locomotive works from Nine Elms to Eastleigh. This took place in 1909, and the actual removal was carried out with the clock-like precision that one expected from any operation directed by Dugald Drummond. At the half-yearly meeting of the Company in February 1910, Sir Charles Scotter read to the shareholders a report from Drummond, thus:

"The locomotive works at Nine Elms are now closed and the men and machinery are removed to Eastleigh. The works are designed to reduce to the minimum the handling of material, and the process of manufacture and the machinery are the finest that can be procured for our requirements. This transfer has been accomplished without an employee of the department being one hour out of work or the output of the work interfered with. I have no hesitation in saying that the company possess the most complete and up-to-date works owned by any railway company."

It was from this time onwards that Dugald Drummond's picturesque little 'Cab' began to amass some mileage. When he came to the L.S.W.R. Drummond took up residence at Surbiton, and in 1899 he built for himself a private engine and saloon—a single-driven locomotive and an inspection cab on a 4-2-4 chassis. It was somewhat irreverently known as 'The Bug', and Drummond used it daily between Nine Elms and Surbiton. One certainly looks back with some curiosity to the days when a chief mechanical engineer could ride about the line, almost at will, in his own private 'car'. After the removal of the works to Eastleigh Drummond used 'The Bug' daily, and the little unit thereafter covered at least 120 miles a day. It had a regular 'path' in the timetable, morning and evening, and ran at something very near to express passenger train speed. The driving wheels were 5 ft. 7 in. diameter, and the cylinders 11½ in. dia. by 18 in. stroke. In L.S.W.R. days it was a very pretty little ensemble, with the engine in the standard light green and the saloon in the passenger carriage livery. Drummond seems to have had quite an affection for tiny engines, and his motor-train locomotives—2-2-0s of Class C14, and the 0-4-0s of Class S.14—were very pretty little things.

It so happened that the very last engines to be built at Nine Elms were three 0-4-0 Dock shunting tank engines, Nos. 82, 83 and 84, completed in June 1908. Moreover the very first engines turned out of Eastleigh Works were two 0-4-0 Motor-Train engines, the 'S.14' Nos. 101 and 147, in September 1910. While the record of new construction at Nine Elms, totalling no more than 817 locomotives, including 17 rail motor cars, does not seem very large for a line of the importance of the L.S.W.R. the traditions of the works, for turning out locomotives of superb workmanship, were of the highest. With the transfer of the works there eventually disappeared Joseph Beattie's picturesque old drawing office, which was just as much a landmark of locomotive history as the carved stone broad gauge engines on the G.W.R. locomotive headquarters at Swindon, the 'classical' water tower at Inverness, or the old timber-roofed roundhouse at Derby. As for Eastleigh, Drummond was not unduly blowing his own trumpet in his report to Sir Charles Scotter. It was a grand works.

Drummond's last locomotive design, the 'D15' 4-4-0, was one of his very best. It was no mere enlargement of the '415' class of 1904, but a synthesis of some of the best practice from his career. Basically these engines originally had 19½ in. by 26 in. cylinders; 6 ft. 7 in. coupled wheels, and a boiler providing a total heating surface of 1,724 sq. ft. The grate area was 27 sq. ft. and the working pressure 200 lb. per sq. in. They had Walschaerts valve gear, the steam dryer, and firebox water tubes. The tube plates were interchangeable with those of the 'G14' and 'T14' four-cylinder 4-6-0s, with 247 tubes of 1¾ in. outside diameter. Although they had the same bogie and coupled wheelbase as the 'T9' and 'L12' classes, namely 6 ft. 6 in. and 10 ft. the distance between the rear bogie wheels and the leading coupled wheels was 8 ft. 3 in. against 6 ft. 9 in. and this made a very long and graceful engine. From the time of their introduction they worked from Nine Elms, on both the West of England and the Bournemouth trains, but it was after R. W. Urie had fitted them with superheaters that they did their finest work. Most of them were then stationed at Bournemouth, and I have the liveliest recollections of their running in the years from 1922 onwards.

Dugald Drummond's end was tragic. At the age of 72 he was still in office, and still acting as vigorously as ever. But in November 1912 he suffered the same misfortune as David Jones on the Highland; he sustained a very severe scald in the leg, while on the footplate. But Dugald Drummond was not so fortunate as Jones. The leg had to be amputated, and at his age the shock to him was too great. He died on the following day, November 8, 1912. He was buried at Brookwood, and his funeral train was drawn by the first of the new 'D15' 4-4-0s, No. 463. His life and work could be summed up in the laconic phrases of one of his Scottish express drivers:

> "He's a gr-r-reat mon is Mr. Dr-r-rummond, and I've a guid opeenion of his engines too."

XII

Locomotive Performance

1900–1914

The work of the Drummond locomotives of the L.S.W.R. is very fully documented so far as the London–Exeter service is concerned. The late R. E. Charlewood made a great many journeys on almost every train on the service. By the kindness of Mr. G. J. Aston, I have had the opportunity of studying the logs of these journeys, and taken as a whole Charlewood is not over-enthusiastic about the results. Signal checks were fairly frequent, and many of the drivers seemed to do little to make up lost time. Nevertheless it must be appreciated that the Salisbury accident of 1906 had put a very severe damper upon the South Western running. No one in authority was likely to criticise a driver for not making up time, and it was only the more enterprising of the men who really went for it, when the occasion demanded it. Another interesting group of records are those compiled by Cecil J. Allen, in 1912 and 1913. In the former year he enjoyed the privilege of an all-line footplate pass for a month in the summer; but while he experienced some very good running the published details of his journeys unfortunately contain little or no information as to how the locomotives were being worked.

Another point brought out from a study of these old records is the extent to which the various engine classes were used, indiscriminately it would appear, on the principal expresses. For example, on a certain day in the summer of 1913 the three mid-morning expresses from Waterloo to the West of England were hauled as follows:

10.50 a.m. Plymouth	4-2-2-0	Class 'E10'
11.00 a.m. Padstow	4-4-0	'D15'
11.10 a.m. Ilfracombe	4-6-0	'T14'

The four-cylinder 4-2-2-0s were regularly used turn and turn about with the larger and later engines, and on the whole they did remarkably well. Unfortunately I have not been able to turn up a record of a pre-war run with the one large-boilered engine of this series, No. 720, which I always thought was one of the most handsome engines Dugald Drummond ever produced; but there is a fine one in a subsequent chapter. But quite apart from the facts and figures of running in those interesting years, and the incidents that led Allen and Charlewood to be critical on many occasions, it would be fascinating indeed if the conditions of 50 and 55 years ago could be reproduced today, and one could travel once again behind 'L12' and 'D15' 4-4-0s in their original condition; could ride on the footplate of 'G14' and 'T14' 4-cylinder 4-6-0s, and witness all the colourful pageantry of railway travel before World War I. Just imagine the glittering array of spotless locomotives that would be on show for the passing traveller to see outside sheds like Basingstoke and Salisbury!

In a more critical vein one can indeed question whether any serious thought was given to the operating implications of the summer timetable so far as it concerned the morning expresses to the West of England. Here one had three trains leaving Waterloo at 10 min. intervals, and yet their point-to-point bookings west of Salisbury were such as to involve a gradual shortening of the headway. On the Exeter run the first of the three trains made an intermediate stop at Sidmouth Junction; the second ran non-stop to Exeter in 98 min., and the third was the fastest of all, with a non-stop run in 96 min. All three trains were liable to load up to 300 tons, or more, and with the apparently indiscriminate use of locomotives it was not surprising that the third and fastest of those trains rarely got a clear road. Drivers waiting for their trains at Salisbury could not fail to note the loading and engine power on preceding trains, and very often they would run more easily than the schedule demanded knowing only too well that they would be checked later in the run, or if nothing worse be stopped outside Exeter while the preceeding train was still in the platform. On one occasion noted by Cecil J. Allen the 11 a.m. ex-Waterloo with a 320-ton train was taken forward from Salisbury by and 'L12' 4-4-0, while the similarly loaded 11.10 a.m. had a 'T14' 4-6-0. This was logical enough so far as the scheduling of the two trains was concerned; but with the 11 a.m. itself delayed outside Salisbury, and getting away late it meant that the 11.10 a.m. was on its tail from the very beginning. In such circumstances the driver of engine No. 445 did very well to reach Exeter Queen Street home signals—a dead stop—in 99½ min. from Salisbury. This run is described in detail later in this chapter.

In the years before World War I by far the best running on the West of England road used to be made on the 3.30 p.m. from Waterloo, which also had the crack 96-min. booking from Salisbury to Exeter, but had the great advantage of having the line to itself, as it were. Some of the finest runs of the period were made on this train. At the same time it is interesting to see that while the run of 88 miles from Salisbury to Exeter was allowed only 96 min. the eastern part of the run, over the 83·8 miles from Waterloo to Salisbury was allowed 94 min. The fastest of the morning trains from Waterloo was then allowed 91 min. The two-hour Bournemouth trains naturally received preferential treatment; but taken all-round the records that have been preserved of their running are inclined to be patchy. Despite their big tenders both 4-4-0 and 4-6-0 locomotives seemed to be frequently in trouble for water, and for this of course Dugald Drummond's rather parsimonious policy regarding superheating can be held largely to blame. In their original condition with steam dryers, the 'D15' 4-4-0s, for example, were very fast and efficient engines, but as all-round motive power units they were transformed when

R. W. Urie substituted a proper superheater. However this chapter is a record of Drummond days, and it can be commenced with a series of runs from Waterloo to Salisbury on West of England expresses. In the table, reproduced below, every type of locomotive in regular use on the eastern part of the line is represented.

Before discussing the actual runs some reference is needed to the road itself. Although it includes some stretches of dead level track, and a few favourable lengths—as from Surbiton down to Esher, and from Oatlands

L.S.W.R. WATERLOO—SALISBURY

Miles		1	2	3	4	5	6	7	8	9	1
	Run No.	1	2	3	4	5	6	7	8	9	1
	Year	1909	1907	1909	1912	1912	1912	1912	1912	1912	19
	Engine No.	287	425	371	464	460	461	453	472	457	45
	Engine Type	4-4-0	4-4-0	4-2-2-0	4-4-0	4-6-0	4-6-0	4-6-0	4-4-0	4-6-0	4-6
	Engine Class	'T9'	'L.12'	'E.10'	'D15'	'T.14'	'T.14'	G14	D15	G14	G
	Load, tons full	195	210	240	240	240	290	315	320	330	34
Miles		m. s.	m. s.	m. s.	m. s.	m. s.	m. s.	m. s.	m. s.	m. s.	m.
0·0	WATERLOO	0 00	0 00	0 00	0 00	0 00	0 00	0 00	0 00	0 00	0
3·9	Clapham Junc.	6 22	6 55	7 22	6 56	7 05	6 54	6 50	7 05	8 00	7
—		—	—	—	sigs	—	—	—	—	—	—
7·3	Winbledon	10 17	10 57	11 45	11 10	10 55	10 55	10 46	11 25	12 20	11
—		—	—	—	—	—	—	—	—	—	sig
12·0	Surbiton	15 14	16 01	17 03	17 00	15 50	15 59	15 52	16 35	17 50	17
—		—	—	—	p.w.s.	—	—	—	—	sigs	—
14·4	Esher	—	18 21	19 28	—	18 05	18 21	18 22	—	20 20	20
19·1	Weybridge	22 18	23 07	24 23	24 20	22 50	23 04	23 08	23 55	25 45	25
24·4	WOKING	27 36	28 29	29 58	29 36	28 15	28 16	28 35	29 30	31 20	31
31·0	*Milepost* 31	35 15	36 10	38 10	37 13	—	36 08	36 28	—	—	39
33·2	Farnborough	37 33	38 31	40 43	39 40	38 35	38 41	39 05	40 35	41 55	41
47·8	BASINGSTOKE	52 00	53 03	56 12	54 13	53 15	53 09	53 59	56 15	57 10	57
50·3	*Worting Junc.*	54 42	55 57	59 18	57 04	56 10	56 04	56 57	—	60 15	60
—		—	—	—	—	—	—	sigs	—	—	—
59·2	Whitchurch	64 08	64 57	68 52	66 08	65 20	65 17	66 59	—	70 00	70
—		—	—	p.w.s.	—	—	—	—	—	—	—
66·4	ANDOVER	70 29	71 21	75 30	72 04	71 25	71 24	74 54	75 45	76 25	76
—		—	—	—	—	—	p.w.s.	—	—	—	—
72·8	Grateley	77 29	78 25	83 58	77 57	78 05	79 49	82 45	85 05	83 00	83
78·3	Porton	83 32	84 22	90 33	83 28	84 00	85 59	88 57	92 10	89 05	89
—		—	—	—	—	—	—	—	sig stop	—	—
83·8	SALISBURY	89 26	90 07	96 04	89 05	89 45	91 14	94 46	—	94 30	94
	Schedule time min.	94	91	94	91	91	91	94	94	94	94
	Net time min.	89½	90	94	87¼	89¾	89¾	92½	—	94	9
	Speeds : m.p.h.										
	max. to Weybridge	63	61	60	64	66	63	—	64½	60½	6
	Milepost 31	50½	51	46½	50	47½	48	48	46	48½	4
	Max. to Basingstoke	64	61	57	63	64	63	62	60	60	5
	Battledown	49	49	46	49	47	48	46	45	44¾	4
	Andover	68½	70	—	78	75	73	—	72½	75	7
	Grateley	44½	45	—	51½	45	42	42½	34	43	4
	Porton	68	65	67	76½	76½	68	66	75	79	68

cutting to Byfleet—there is in effect a long upward 'grind' the whole way from Clapham Junction to Oakley; and the prevailing wind is adverse. In view of this the schedules of 47 min. and 49 min. for the 43·9 miles from Clapham Junction to Basingstoke required very good work, seeing that they had often to be worked with loads of more than 300 tons. The worst stretches are the 10½-mile climb between Mileposts 20½ and 31 on gradients gradually steepening from 1 in 387 to 1 in 300, and the 5 miles at 1 in 249 from Milepost 46 to Battledown 'flyover'. The steepest gradient of all, from Andover up to Grateley, with nearly

A "T9" 4-4-0 No. 313 rebuilt with superheater.

One of the Feltham hump shunting 4-8-0s, No. 494.

Heavy goods tank 4-6-2 No. 519, for freight workings to and from Feltham.

[*All the late W. J. Reynolds*

Bournemouth Pullman car express near Swaythling, double-headed with two "T9" 4-4-0s. [L.P. Co.

Bournemouth Express near Surbiton, hauled by "L12" Class 4-4-0 No. 421. This train, like that in the upper photograph is carrying the old head code. [L.G.R.P.

Local train leaving Weymouth, and starting up the ascent to Bincombe Tunnel, hauled by an Adams 7 ft. 4-4-0 No. 684. [*L.G.R.P.*

Up Bournemouth express near Earlsfield hauled by "T9" 4-4-0 No. 716. [*L.P. Co.*

Top. "T9" class 4–4–0 No. 282: one of the series built without cross-water tubes in 1899. [*The late W. J. Reynolds*

Centre. 4-cylinder 4–2–2–0 No. 369, at Nine Elms, built 1901. [*Real Photographs*

Bottom. 0–6–0 Goods engine of 1897, No. 459, later renumbered 316 [*L.P. Co.*

One of the handsome Drummond "L12" Class 4-4-0s No. 434 as originally built with cross-water tubes. [*L.P. Co.*

An "L12", No. 430, as rebuilt and superheated by R. W. Urie. [*L.G.R.P.*

Exeter Queen Street (now Central) *circa* 1910. The locomotives waiting for up expresses are No. 727 a "T9" 4–4–0, and No. 576, an Adams 6 ft. 7 in. 4–4–0 of Class "T3". [*L.G.R.P.*

. W. Jacomb-Hood, Resident Engineer until 1914.

Dugald Drummond, Chief Mechanical Engineer 1895–1912.

A. W. Szlumper, Chief Engineer 1914–1922.

R. W. Urie, Chief Mechanical Engineer 1912–1922. [*British Railways*

A Drummond "T14", No. 447 as originally built in 1911.
[*Real Photographs*

A "T14" rebuilt and superheated by R. W. Urie in 1915, No. 445.
[*The late W. J. Reynolds*

A Urie 2-cylinder "N15" 4–6–0 of 1918—forerunner of the "King Arthur" class.
[*L.G.R.P.*

3 miles at 1 in 165 could usually be rushed, from the high speed at which it was customary to attain through Andover itself. The summit of the line, between Waterloo and Salisbury is adjacent to Milepost 53½, a mile west of Oakley. There is however a stretch of 1¾ miles of level between Battledown, and the ¾ mile of 1 in 287 that leads to the summit.

I have tabulated 10 runs on various West of England expresses, with loads ranging from 195 to 345 tons, and the collection is appropriately opened by one of those splendid little engines, the 'T9' 4-4-0s. The actual locomotive concerned, No. 287, was one of the first group of engines in the class, built between 1899 and 1900, before Drummond had introduced his cross water tubes in the fireboxes. These engines also had six-wheeled tenders. Engine No. 287 was working the Sunday 4 p.m. express from Waterloo, which was allowed 94 min. to Salisbury. Although not heavily loaded No. 287 made a beautifully even run, going hard uphill, and not needing to indulge in anything very fast on the downhill sections. This run was indeed fully up to the standards required on the fastest of the weekday bookings. Speed had not exceeded 63 m.p.h. by the time the long climb to milepost 31 was commenced; but on this the minimum speed was 50½ m.p.h., and with a maximum of 64 m.p.h. on the level beyond, and a minimum of 49 m.p.h. at Battledown, Oakley was passed in the excellent time of 57 min. 24 sec., and nearly 55 miles were covered in the first hour from Waterloo.

The 'L.12' class engines in their non-superheater days never seemed to be much better than the 'T9s'; their large boiler and cross water tubes did not give them the advantage hoped for, and details are given later in this chapter of a run on one of the up Bournemouth two-hour trains when the driver had to run easily over a critical section in order to spin out his water supply. No such conditions applied of course to runs between Waterloo and Salisbury, and the work of No. 425, tabulated herewith, shows an entirely adequate performance—albeit with no more than a moderate load—on the 91-min. schedule. The start was slower than that of the 'T9', in column 1, but once again the hill-climbing was excellent and the train reached Salisbury almost a minute early.

Next come three runs with 240-ton trains. This was a very common loading on the principal expresses at midweek, but the interest of the journeys tabulated in columns 3, 4, and 5 lies in the locomotives that were employed—an 'E10' 4-cylinder 4-2-2-0; a 'D15' in original condition, and a 'Paddleboat'. In the ordinary way the last mentioned engine should have had a relatively easy task; but the weather conditions were very bad, with a strong westerly wind and heavy rain throughout. On this occasion Cecil J. Allen was riding on the footplate, but other than a note that the boiler pressure was well maintained he gives no details of the engine working. One can appreciate however that work very much harder than normal would have been required in such weather conditions—the equivalent, probably, of two extra coaches on the train.

The small-boilered 4-cylinder 4-2-2-0 was working to a schedule of

94 min., and seemed to have nothing whatever in hand. This run was clocked by R. E. Charlewood, in 1909, and by that time these engines would have had their cylinders lined up from the original 16½ in. to 14 in. But even so, the drivers would have little chance of using the nominal tractive effort of the engines—even if their adhesion weight would have enabled the power to be transmitted to the drawbar. Nevertheless on this run the uphill speeds were not at all bad, with minima of 46½ m.p.h. at Milepost 31 and 46 m.p.h. at Battledown. But the start had been slow, and the going was poor on the easy stretch from Farnborough to Basingstoke. One gathers that this particular driver was not a very enterprising character, or he would have come down Porton bank much harder. Although the net time showed no loss of time to engine—there was in fact a gain of ¾ min. on schedule to passing Basingstoke—a minute could have been saved by a normally fast finish into Salisbury.

In column 4 is shown the work of a 'D15', in 1912 when brand new, and it was an excellent performance. The train was checked in the early stages by both signals and engineering work; and the ascent to Milepost 31 was commenced at lower speed than usual, with Woking passed 1½ min. late. But some very good work followed. Speed did not drop below 50 m.p.h. at Milepost 31; Basingstoke was passed practically on time, and some really brisk running followed. A maximum speed of 78 m.p.h. was obtained at Andover; Grateley summit was cleared at 51½ m.p.h., and with a top speed of 76½ m.p.h. below Porton the train clocked into Salisbury nearly 2 min. early. In column 5 of the table, the 'Paddleboat', No. 460, with Cecil J. Allen on the footplate, was running ahead of time all the way from Woking, though the speeds were lower than those of the 'D15' just mentioned. Owing to the weather conditions prevailing one cannot assess the merit of this run on times and speeds alone; but it was evidently a fine performance. Mr. Allen mentions that on the same day the two trains on either side of this express—the 10.50 a.m. and the 11.10—took 96 and 100 min. respectively to reach Salisbury—both hauled by 4-4-0 engines.

The next run in the table, No. 6, shows a 'Paddleboat' more heavily loaded, and putting up a thoroughly sound performance, with good hillclimbing, but perhaps the most interesting runs of all are on the four with loads of over 300 tons. The 3.30 p.m. from Waterloo was a Salisbury turn; it normally had one of the 6 ft. four-cylinder 4-6-0s of the 'G14' class, and one must agree that the engines concerned did well with their heavy trains. At the same time it should be emphasised that the runs chosen for mention in this chapter represent the cream of London & South Western running in the period before 1914. There are very many in which it was evident that drivers were not attempting to make up time, or to put forth any extra effort when weather conditions were adverse. Nevertheless the runs tabulated show clearly what the Drummond *engines* could do. On the three runs with 'G14' class engines the minimum speeds at Milepost 31 were 48, 48¼, and 46 m.p.h. and 46, 45, and 48 m.p.h. at

Battledown. The last mentioned was an especially good piece of work. Note should also be taken of the free running of No. 457 down from Grateley, with the highest speed of any run attained near Porton, namely 79 m.p.h.

The remaining run with a load of over 300 tons, No. 8, was also made on a 94-min. schedule, on the summer 11 a.m. to Padstow, in 1913. On this occasion the 10.50 a.m. Plymouth had been taken by an 'E10', and the driver of the 'D15', No. 472, was evidently expecting delays. He did well to Basingstoke; passing through ¾ min. ahead of time, after speeds of 65 m.p.h. at Esher, 46 m.p.h. at Milepost 31, and 60 m.p.h. near Hook. After that there was a pronounced falling off in the effort, which in other circumstances might have been construed as due to shortage of steam; but the driver knew it would be useless to 'push' the engine unduly, realising that any time he gained would be thrown away waiting outside Salisbury station. And even with his very slow ascent to Grateley (minimum speed 33¾ m.p.h.) and leisurely running afterwards he was still stopped at the home signals. Nevertheless, the work out to Basingstoke was enough to show what *could* be done.

L.S.W.R. 2 p.m. WATERLOO—BOURNEMOUTH

Load: 10 non-corridors, 270 tons full
Engine: Class 'T14' 4-6-0 No. 459

Dist. miles		Sch. min.	Actual m. s.	Speeds m.p.h.
0·0	WATERLOO	0	0 00	—
3·9	Clapham Junction	7	7 25	—
7·3	Wimbledon		11 35	—
12·0	Surbiton		16 40	60
			sigs.	
14·4	Esher		19 05	—
19·1	Weybridge		24 25	
24·4	WOKING	28	29 55	
28·0	Brookwood		34 05	48½*
33·2	Farnborough		40 25	61½
47·8	BASINGSTOKE	54	55 10	—
50·3	*Worting Junc.*		58 05	53
58·2	Micheldever		66 55	—
66·7	Winchester		73 50	83½
—			sigs.	
73·6	EASTLEIGH	79	80 15	68 (max)
79·3	SOUTHAMPTON WEST	87½	86 45	15 (slack)
82·0	Redbridge		90 10	30 (slack)
85·4	Lyndhurst Road		94 35	—
92·8	Brockenhurst		102 15	—
98·6	New Milton		108 25	74 (max)
104·3	Christchurch	116	114 10	
2·5	Boscombe		6 30	
3·7	BOURNEMOUTH	8	8 50	

Net time to Christchurch 111 min.

* at Milepost 31

Before continuing over the exciting section of line west of Salisbury there are two interesting runs on the Bournemouth trains logged in 1912 by Cecil J. Allen. At that time the crack 2 p.m. down made an intermediate stop at Christchurch, in 116 min. from Waterloo, and the overall time to Bournemouth Central was 125 min. It is however strange to recall that even by that time this important train was still composed entirely of non-corridor stock! On this train the engine was almost invariably a Nine Elms 'T14', and the performance of No. 459 as tabulated herewith shows some interesting and significant features. Weather conditions were good, and the load was not too heavy, but an early hindrance took place in a slack through Esher, which was apparently enforced on days when there was racing at Sandown Park. The minimum speed at Milepost 31 was 48½ m.p.h. and nothing higher than 61½ m.p.h. was reached on the easy stretch to Basingstoke. But then the driver began to pile it on, and although the 1 in 249 ascent from Basingstoke extends for a full mile further on the Southampton line than on the West of England the speed there did not fall below 53 m.p.h. Then came some very fast running down the long descent towards Eastleigh, with a long sustained spell at 80 to 83½ m.p.h. between Wallers Ash and Shawford Junction.

This fine burst of speed was cut short by a signal check before Eastleigh, but it was enough to show the vast improvement Drummond had effected in his 4-6-0 locomotives since the days of the impressive but inept '330' class of 1905. Proportionately to the diameter of the driving wheels however this 80–83 m.p.h. spurt by No. 459 did not involve such high piston speeds as those on No. 457 of the 'G14' class, descending Porton bank at 79 m.p.h. An equivalent piston speed would have given a maximum of 86 m.p.h. from a 'Paddleboat'. I shall always remember with much pleasure a run I had with one of the latter as recently as July 1939 on the 11.22 a.m. from Waterloo to Swanage, when No. 443 took me over the 11·7 miles from Wallers Ash to Eastleigh in exactly 9 min., at an average speed of 78 m.p.h. The engine was, of course, then in its Maunsellised condition; but the 'Paddleboats' have always been flyers, and on that 1939 occasion she made a net time of 86¾ min. from Waterloo to Southampton with a load of 315 tons.

But to revert to Mr. Allen's run of 1912, Southampton West—as it was then—was passed just inside the schedule time of 87½ min., and some pleasantly brisk work was done through the New Forest. No maximum and minimum speeds are quoted other than the final effort of 74 m.p.h. down Hinton Admiral bank, and Christchurch was reached 1¾ min. early. The net time was no more than 111 min. There was good reason for getting to Christchurch a minute or so ahead of time, for the concluding point to point booking of only 8 min. for the 3·7 miles from Christchurch to Bournemouth, was exceedingly sharp with any sort of a train. After a short stretch of level there came the 1¼ miles of 1 in 99 up to Pokesdown; and even with so good an engine and so keen a driver as on Mr. Allen's footplate trip the time was 8 min. 50 sec. Nevertheless because of the early arrival at Christchurch it was possible to get away again slightly ahead of time and the actual arrival in Bournemouth Central was 124 min. 35 sec. from Waterloo—a most satisfying run.

In those days one could not take the best trains on the service in a single round trip from London. In addition to the 125-min. 2 p.m. down the non-stop 2-hour trains were the 4-10 p.m. down, and the 9.8 a.m. and 2 p.m. up. Another interesting trip was logged by Mr. Allen on the last

L.S.W.R. 2 p.m. BOURNEMOUTH–WATERLOO

Load: 10 non-corridors, 270 tons full
Engine: Class 'L12' 4-4-0 No. 419

Dist. Miles		Sch. min.	Actual m.	s.	Speeds m.p.h.
0·0	BOURNEMOUTH CENTRAL	0	0	00	—
1·2	Boscombe		3	15	—
3·7	Christchurch		6	15	64½
9·4	New Milton		13	55	38½ (min)
15·2	Brockenhurst		20	35	68
22·6	Lyndhurst Road		28	15	—
26·0	Redbridge		31	55	64½/30*
28·7	SOUTHAMPTON WEST	34	35	15	—
34·4	EASTLEIGH	43	42	35	
41·3	Winchester		51	40	44½
49·8	Micheldever		63	20	43½
57·7	*Worting Junc.*		72	25	
60·2	BASINGSTOKE	71	74	40	74
74·8	Farnborough		87	35	62½ (min)
80·0	Brookwood		92	35	
83·6	WOKING	93	95	35	76½
88·9	Weybridge		99	55	
93·6	Esher		104	10	
96·0	Surbiton		106	25	63½
100·7	Wimbledon		111	00	
104·1	Clapham Junc.	113	114	15	
			p.w.s.		
106·6	Vauxhall		117	35	
108·0	WATERLOO	120	120	30	

* Speed restriction

mentioned train, with an 'L12' class engine and a load of 270 tons. Apart for a slight check for underline bridge repairs at Vauxhall this run was entirely unchecked. This slack accounted for the odd half-minute by which schedule time was exceeded; but with this class of engine, and a load of 270 tons there was nothing in hand. There was some smart initial running through the New Forest, with a maximum speed of 68 m.p.h. at Lymington Junction, and although strict time was not kept to Southampton the train was slightly ahead on passing Eastleigh. Then to conserve his water supply the driver was reluctant to extend the engine as hard as he would have wished to do on the long climb to Litchfield, and speed was sustained at 43½ to 44½ m.p.h. on the 1 in 250. This was not at all a bad climb in itself, for a non-superheater 4-4-0 engine of moderate cylinder dimensions; but it was not good enough for timekeeping, and Basingstoke was passed 3¾ min. late.

Some fine running followed in which the 44 miles from Basingstoke to Clapham Junction were covered in 39 min. 35 sec. The maximum speeds on this stretch were 74 m.p.h. below Basingstoke and 76½ m.p.h. at Byfleet. It is a great pity that details of the footplate working were not taken because it would have been most interesting, as on all these runs, to see to what extent the drivers were putting into practice the theories expounded to them by Drummond in the lectures he gave to the men. He certainly 'preached the gospel' of full-regulator working, with the gear notched up to work at short cut-offs; though in actual practice, with

L.S.W.R.—SALISBURY—EXETER

	Run No.	1	2	3	4	5	6	7	8
	Year	1907	1908	1912	1912	1912	1911	1908	191[illegible]
	Engine No.	431	398	456	289	113	719	335	445
	Engine Type	4-4-0	4-4-0	4-6-0	4-4-0	4-4-0	4-4-0	4-6-0	4-6-
	Engine Class	'L.12'	'S.11'	'G.14'	'T9'	'T9'	'T9'	'E14'	'T.1
	Load, tons full	210	210	210	240	240	265	295	325
Miles		m. s.	m. s.	m. s.	m. s.	m. s.	m. s.	m. s.	m.
0·0	SALISBURY	0 00	0 00	0 00	0 00	0 00	0 00	0 00	0
—		—	—	—	—	—	—	—	sig
2·5	Wilton	5 04	5 10	5 18	5 36	5 40	5 34	5 29	—
8·2	Dinton	11 46	12 05	11 32	12 35	12 30	12 34	12 23	12
12·5	Tisbury	16 37	16 43	15 58	17 29	17 45	17 38	17 40	—
17·5	Semley	22 40	22 37	21 52	23 32	24 00	23 57	24 21	24
21·6	GILLINGHAM	26 34	26 44	25 43	27 19	27 45	27 44	28 28	—
28·4	TEMPLECOMBE	32 48	32 41	31 59	33 08	33 40	33 30	34 52	34
29·9	*Milepost* 113½	34 40	—	33 47	34 58	—	35 15	37 03	—
34·5	Sherborne	39 10	38 44	38 22	39 23	40 10	39 44	41 51	41
		p.w.s.	—	—	—	—	—	p.w.s.	—
39·1	YEOVIL JUNC.	43 26	42 21	42 41	43 06	43 50	43 33	46 05	45
41·3	Sutton Bingham	46 53	44 23	44 56	45 11	46 00	45 38	49 34	—
42·7	*Milepost* 126½	48 58	—	46 40	46 45	—	47 18	51 46	—
47·9	Crewkerne	54 27	50 55	51 41	51 51	52 40	52 27	57 31	—
49·7	*Milepost* 133¼	57 24	53 53	54 10	54 41	—	55 34	60 34	—
55·9	Chard Junc.	63 36	60 20	60 20	60 50	61 30	61 36	66 44	—
61·0	AXMINSTER	67 50	64 46	64 37	64 45	65 30	65 36	70 54	68
64·3	Seaton Junc.	70 40	68 01	67 33	67 24	68 10	68 23	73 41	71
67·0	*Milepost* 150½	73 41	73 00	71 26	—	71 55	72 26	77 20	—
69·0	,, 152½	78 44	77 48	75 02	76 04	76 10	77 07	81 13	80
70·0	,, 153½	80 36	—	76 42	78 24	78 15	79 17	83 12	—
—		p.w.s.	—	—	—	—	—	—	—
71·2	Honiton	82 15	81 26	78 01	79 54	79 45	80 44	84 49	84
75·8	SIDMOUTH JUNC.	86 40	85 28	82 05	83 43	83 30	84 36	88 43	88
79·5	Whimple	90 06	88 49	85 22	86 49	86 25	87 44	92 02	—
—		—	—	—	sigs	—	—	—	—
83·2	Broad Clyst	92 56	91 42	88 22	90 20	89 15	90 29	94 58	—
86·9	*Exmouth Jc.*	96 19	95 15	92 08	98 29	92 35	93 46	98 35	97
—		—	—	—	—	—	—	—	sig st
88·0	EXETER (QUEEN ST.)	98 15	97 16	93 56	100 36	94 40	95 31	100 25	—
Schedule	min.	98	96	96	96	96	96	98	96
Net time	min.	97¼	97¼	94	94½	94¾	95½	100½	—
Speeds m.p.h.									
	Semley	45	46	—	—	43	40	38	43
	Gillingham	75	68	65	78½	77½	—	72	75
	Milepost 113½	45	—	45	45	44	44	36	42
	Sherborne	76	—	70	78½	80½	77	75	79
	Milepost 133¼	32	30	36	32½	34½	30	30	31
	Axminster	69	—	69	80	80½	80	75	75
	Honiton Summit	28	22½	32½	21½	26	24½	30	22
	Broad Clyst	80	—	76½	—	86½	82	78½	82

non-superheater engines, a certain amount of wire-drawing can be advantageous in high speed running. All these engines were fitted with the Drummond steam reverser, which permitted a considerably finer adjustment of cut-off than with the conventional form of reversing gear. From my own footplate experience I would not think that within certain limits, the actual technique of driving would have a great deal of effect, either on the freedom of running, or on the economy. The main point was that all these Drummond engines (save the '330' class!) had a good front-end, and they ran accordingly.

On the Exeter road an equally great variety of locomotives was to be seen working the fast express trains. The 'Paddleboats' and the 'D15' 4-4-0s did not often penetrate west of Salisbury, though Cecil J. Allen clocked a run with one of the former in 1913. Among Charlewood's records there are runs with the 'S11' 4-4-0s—the small-wheeled variant of the 'L12' class—and there is one run with the Drummond 'behemoth' No. 335. Again it is the little 'T9s' that absolutely steal the show, and in the accompanying table the three runs on the 5.9 p.m. from Salisbury (the 3.30 p.m. ex-Waterloo) are unquestionably the finest of the whole collection. In relation to the severity of the intermediate gradients the scheduled speeds over this line were quite remarkable. No less remarkable were the loads taken unassisted by the 'T9' 4-4-0s. But the switchback nature of the route, and the splendid alignment that enables the principal banks to be charged from speeds of 80 m.p.h. or so, makes things easier than would otherwise be the case. The schedules of 96 min. non-stop over the 88 miles from Salisbury to Exeter Queen Street would have been quite impracticable with 4-4-0 engines had not the drivers been prepared to go pell-mell downhill from Semley to Gillingham; from Buckhorn Weston tunnel towards Templecombe, through Sherborne, and above all on the long racing descent from Hewish to Axminster. The only speed restriction used to be one at Yeovil Junction; but this applied only in the earliest of the runs in the accompanying table. In 1908 the layout was improved, and from that time onwards there was virtually no limit for down expresses in the entire 88 miles. Up expresses usually eased through Seaton Junction, and a more pronounced slack was required at Wilton.

In the accompanying table full details are given of the principal maximum and minimum speeds, and the fluctuations from point to point are a reflection of the switchback character of the gradient profile. The first two runs provide an interesting comparison between the 6 ft. 7 in. and 6 ft. 1 in. varieties of large boilered 4-4-0. Charlewood's notes include very few speed details for the latter engine; but in the earlier stages of the run there seems to have been very little in it. The 'L12', No. 431, was hampered in having the Yeovil Junction check, and dropped about 2 min. on the 'S11' in consequence between Sherborne and Sutton Bingham. But after passing Hewish summit (milepost 133¼) the 'S11' seems to have struck a bad patch, and despite her smaller wheels she had much the worst of it in climbing Honiton bank. The gradient here is 1 in 80, and

No. 398 fell to 22½ m.p.h. against the 28 m.p.h. of No. 431. Although Charlewood did not quote any downhill speeds for the former engines after Honiton, it is evident from the times that she must have come down to Broad Clyst at a speed very little slower than No. 431, which reached a maximum of 80 m.p.h. The 'L12' kept time on a schedule of 98 min., but to make a true comparison one should treat the Yeovil Junction slowing as an out-of-course check. If this is done the net time of No. 431 becomes 95¼ min. The 'S11' lost 1¼ min. on the 96-min. booking.

The next four runs were also on 96-min. trains. The work of the 'G14' four-cylinder 4-6-0 was undistinguished in its early stages, and as far as Axminster it showed no advantage whatever over the efforts of the 'S11' 4-4-0. But just where the latter engine went to pieces the 4-6-0 excelled. She made a really splendid ascent of Honiton bank, with a minimum speed of 32½ m.p.h., from an initial speed of no more than 69 m.p.h. at Axminster; and a smart run down to Broad Clyst, with a top speed of 76½ m.p.h. brought the train into Exeter 2 min. early.

Then come the 'T9s'. Runs 4 and 6 in this sparkling trilogy were clocked by R. E. Charlewood, and No. 5 was recorded from the footplate by Cecil J. Allen, in 1912. Engine No. 289, without cross water tubes, made a brilliant start and was ahead of the other two engines at Crewkerne, though both Nos. 113 and 719 were also going very well. There was some level pegging between the equally loaded 289 and 113 right on to Axminster, with 289 leading by about ¾ min. But then No. 113 made a grand ascent of Honiton bank not falling below 26 m.p.h. at the entrance to the tunnel, and the descent to Exeter was a positive whirlwind, with speeds of 82 m.p.h. before Sidmouth Junction and 86½ m.p.h. at Broad Clyst. One would dearly like to have details of the engine working that produced such running; Allen certainly makes the significant comment that boiler pressure was maintained constantly at just below 175 lb. per sq. in. throughout the run. The signal check experienced on the run with engine No. 289 was a bad one. Charlewood records that the brakes were applied 'while going at a terrific speed'; but the check evidently took him by surprise, and he did not record the speed just previous to it. The net time was 95 min., or perhaps a shade under, while the 'flying 113', with a clear road, stopped at Exeter in 94 min. 40 sec. from Salisbury. In consideration of the heavier load of 265 tons, engine No. 719, with cross water tubes, also did very well, just finishing inside booked time. The climb of Honiton, with its minimum speed of 24½ m.p.h. was another great effort.

Against these brilliant 4-4-0s efforts the last two journeys in the table make disappointing reading, although the 'paddleboat' was being driven with the knowledge that the preceeding train was only a short distance ahead, and that an 'L12' 4-4-0 hauling a load of 320 tons was not likely to make very fast time on the banks. The huge four-cylinder 4-6-0 No. 335 made a poor showing until it came to the ascent of Honiton bank. There were some brisk downhill speeds at times, but the driver seemed disinclined to give the engine her head, and bad riding may have been the cause of this restraint. But the fact remains, that 2½ min. were lost on schedule. It is true that the Yeovil Junction slack was still in operation at the time of this run; but it was allowed for in the schedule, so that any loss of time on that account would have to be taken as part of the driver's 'terms of reference', and not be regarded as an out-of-course slack.

The last run, while disappointing from the viewpoint of overall times was probably a most artistic piece of enginemanship. The train had made good time from London and came into Salisbury right on the tail of the 11 a.m. to Padstow. Engines were changed, and the restart was made so promptly that the driver had to whistle for signals no further out than Wilton. The Padstow train had a load of 320 tons, and was hauled by an 'L12', and the driver of No. 445 would quite justifiably have been expecting to catch it up on all the severe uphill sections. He therefore drove easily out to Dinton, to let the other train get a chance to get ahead, but from there onwards there was some fine running. Such minimum speeds as 43 m.p.h. at Semley, 42½ above Templecombe, and 47 up Sutton Bingham bank were all excellent, with a 325-ton train. The driver was evidently expecting to catch up the Padstow express on the stiff climb from Crewkerne up to Hewish, and took things easily here, with a minimum speed of 31 m.p.h. and in anticipation of still more trouble on Honiton bank he did not hurry unduly down to Axminster. With no more than a moderate ascent of the bank, falling to 22¼ m.p.h. he managed to keep clear of checks. Having done this, and judging that the preceeding train would have gone 'thunder and turf' down from Honiton to Exeter he also ran hard, touching 82 m.p.h. at Broad Clyst. The Ilfracombe was eventually stopped outside Queen Street station, waiting for the Padstow to clear.

Taken all in all this was one of the most interesting runs in the entire collection. It suggests very intelligent work on the part of the driver in attempting to make the best of a rather unrealistic piece of timetable arrangement. All the same it would have been most interesting to see how one of these engines would have coped with the 96-min. schedule, with a load of 325 tons. On trains making a number of intermediate stops the smaller-wheeled 4-6-0s of the 'G14' class, did consistently well uphill; in particular No. 455 on the 11.7 a.m. from Salisbury with a load of 270 tons, passed Semley in the good time of 22 min. 20 sec. Later in the journey she ran the 48·9 miles from Yeovil Junction to Exeter in 57¼ min. climbing Honiton bank at a minimum of 26 m.p.h. It has been the custom to decry the work of the Drummond 4-6-0s on the L.S.W.R.; but while their performance could not be compared with certain contemporaries on other lines these notes alone are enough to show that the 'G14' and 'T14' could run fast and climb well. The basic design, particularly of the 'T14' was sound, and when R. W. Urie had removed the Drummond 'gadgets', and fitted normal superheaters the 'T14s' became excellent engines, as the next chapter will show.

XIII
Wartime Working

In past years it has very frequently been said that Britain was completely unprepared for war in 1914. So far as the nation as a whole was concerned that was largely true. From the military point of view, in sheer weight of manpower and armament there had certainly been no preparation for the titanic struggle that eventually developed on the continent of Europe. Public opinion was also manifestly unprepared. But so far as the naval and military policy followed by successive governments was concerned, the arrangement for mobilisation and transport of our small, but highly professional army had been rehearsed and perfected some years before that fatal August of 1914; and to this state of preparedness the London & South Western Railway had made a massive contribution. For any expeditionary force destined for a campaign overseas it had long been accepted that Southampton would be the principal port of embarkation; invaluable experience, both from the railway and the military point of view had been gained during the South African War, and the army manoeuvres of 1910 had been made the occasion for a very extensive combined railway and military exercise.

Then, in July 1911, came the dangerous German intervention at Agadir, Morocco, in what would ordinarily have been no more than a minor French colonial fracas. That intervention was quickly turned into a fiasco by the strong combined action of France and Great Britain; but the outspoken comments on the affair made in both London and Paris left Germany angry and resentful, and many responsible men in England realised how near to a European war events had been. Implications of modern war quite other than the transport of troops began to occupy the minds of senior Ministers of the Crown, and as early as August 1911, the Under Secretary of State for War, Sir John Seely, called a meeting with the general managers of six of the principal British railways, of which the L.S.W.R. was one, to consider transport problems in time of war. At that time the South Western was represented by Sir Charles Owens, but he retired at the end of the year, after 50 years service with the company, and in his place the directors made an appointment of the utmost significance. Instead of a South Western officer they chose Herbert Ashcombe Walker, then Outdoor Goods Manager, Southern Division, London & North Western Railway, and then 44 years of age. From the age of 17 he had been an L.N.W.R. man, and served directly under such famous railwaymen as G. P. Neele, and Sir Robert Turnbull.

In any preparations for wartime traffic it was realised that the L.S.W.R. would occupy a key position. When the Railway Executive Committee was set up in the late autumn of 1912 under the nominal chairmanship of the President of the Board of Trade, Sir Frank Ree, General Manager of the L.N.W.R., was appointed Acting Chairman; but on his death in February 1914 Walker was asked to take over the task, and it was under his chairmanship that the R.E.C. dealt with the crisis of August 1914. With the actual declaration of war, as from midnight on the 4th, the War Office gave the R.E.C. sixty hours to assemble all the locomotives and rolling stock to get the 'Expeditionary Force' to Southampton. But everything was ready within 48 hours, and on Sunday August 9, embarkation of the troops at Southampton had begun. Between that day and August 31 no fewer than 711 special trains had arrived at the docks, and the official records show the following number of men and supplies to have been conveyed:

5,006 officers
125,171 men
38,805 horses
344 guns
1,574 other limbered vehicles
277 motor vehicles
1,802 motor cycles
6,406 tons of stores

The busiest period of all was during the 20 hours from 10.12 p.m. on Friday August 21, when 73 special trains arrived at Southampton, an average of roughly one every quarter-hour. These trains conveyed approximately 12 per cent of the entire expeditionary force.

From the official announcements made it would seem that news was released to an anxious public long before the task of transportation was complete. For example, as early as August 18, the Press Bureau announced:

> "The Expeditionary Force, as detailed for foreign service, has been safely landed on French soil. The embarkation, transportation, and disembarkation, of men and stores were alike carried through with the greatest possible precision and without a single casualty."

Again, in his first despatch from France, dated September 7, the Commander in Chief, Sir John French said that "the concentration was practically complete on the evening of Friday, the 21st ultimo." In the light of what we now know was happening at Southampton on that very evening that report appears to be optimistically premature. But in its issue of September 1914 *The Railway Magazine* commented:

> "One of the most remarkable features—a decidedly commendable one in the circumstances—is the fact that the public, as a whole, has seen little of what has been going on. Indeed on one or two railways there was little indication of anything abnormal until the mobilisation of the Navy and the regular forces had been completed, and it was only when the Territorial and reserve contingents came to be dealt with, and then largely owing to the development of other factors, that the general public began to realise what feats of transport were being carried out, largely by night, but also while dealing with a great deal of ordinary traffic."

It was remarkable that the L.S.W.R. was able to maintain cross-Channel services for passengers from Southampton to Havre and the Channel Islands, though at the peak of intensity of embarkation of the

Expeditionary Force, a Cunard liner, the *Ascania*, sailed from Newport (Mon) for Montreal, instead of from Southampton. A special working of a different kind fell to the L.S.W.R. in November 1914. In that cheerless month the best beloved of all British war leaders, Lord Roberts, had been to France to visit the Indian contingents, and had died of pleurisy. His home was at Ascot, and after his body had been conveyed thence from Folkestone the L.S.W.R. had the task of working the funeral train to London, for the burial service at St. Paul's Cathedral. But the London terminus chosen was *Charing Cross*, not Waterloo, and the train was worked over a most unusual route to get there. From Ascot it travelled on the up Windsor line to Clapham Junction, and then transferred at Factory Junction on to the former London Chatham & Dover line. At Brixton it took the western spur towards Blackfriars, and was there halted. The train was then backed over the South Eastern spur to Metropolitan Junction on the London Bridge–Charing Cross line, and then proceeded, still with the South Western engine, through Waterloo Junction into Charing Cross. It might at first have been thought that this was a case for using the connecting line direct to the South Eastern from Waterloo station; but had that been done the engine would have been at the wrong end on arrival on the S.E. & C.R. line. A contemporary report of the journey gives the engine number as 772, but a doubt arises here, as the L.S.W.R. then had no engine of that number. The most likely guess is that the engine was a 'T9' No. 722.

Many unusual engine workings were to be seen on the L.S.W.R. in the war years, particularly on the lines converging on Southampton. In April 1915 an observer at Eastleigh who sent his notes to *The Railway Magazine* saw a complete L.B.S.C.R. train both engine and stock; a North Eastern train hauled by a G.W.R. 'Duke' class 4-4-0, and a North Western train hauled by a G.W.R. 'Flower'. Then he had the extraordinary experience of seeing an up train of empty stock hauled by a Great Eastern 0-6-0 pass a loaded troop train hauled by another Great Eastern engine, this time a 4-4-0 of the rebuilt 'T19' class. Some extremely sharp turn-round times were being worked at Southampton, for later on that same day another G.W.R. 4-4-0, the *Begonia*, was seen on a loaded troop train passing Swaythling, and then returning north only 33 min. later, with the same rake of coaches, empty! Another foreign working noted by the same correspondent was a South Eastern train worked by the first of the Borsig built 'L' class 4-4-0s of the S.E.C.R., No. 772. Mention of this engine raises the doubt as to whether it was, after all, this engine, and not one of the L.S.W.R. that worked the Earl Roberts funeral train through from Ascot to Charing Cross. The contemporary report is however quite definite that a South Western engine was used.

Locomotives or not, the part played by the L.S.W.R. in the early months of the war was widely acclaimed, and it was signalised by the award to the General Manager not only of a knighthood in the New Year Honours of 1915, but also the added distinction of a K.C.B. in

1917. In 1916 Sir Herbert received a further recognition of the remarkable place he had so quickly achieved in the British railway world, when his former railway, the London & North Western, named one of their newest express locomotives—No. 2204 of the 'Claughton' class—*Sir Herbert Walker*. A gigantic project that had been initiated soon after he came to Waterloo, the suburban electrification of the L.S.W.R., was no more than slightly retarded by the onset of war, and an important piece of civil engineering work was planned in readiness for the more intense suburban services that were to come when electrification was completed in the autumn of 1915; this was the new 'flyover' at Hampton Court Junction, carrying the down branch over all four main running lines. The electric services were inaugurated in October 1915, and the project as a whole is described in the next chapter.

In the meantime, on the mechanical side R. W. Urie was acting vigorously to modernise the locomotive stock. His first innovation, so far as the L.S.W.R. was concerned was the construction at Eastleigh, during 1913–4, of the 'H15' class two-cylinder mixed traffic 4-6-os, with 6 ft. diameter coupled wheels. These engines included several departures from Drummond practice, rather in the omissions than otherwise. The steam dryer and the firebox water tubes were discarded, and Urie provided a high raised running plate giving much more ready access to the motion. Outside frames were also used on the large double-bogie tenders. Above the running plate the appearance was traditionally Drummond, but internally instead of the steam dryer Urie tried no fewer than three different types of superheater on this first batch of 10 locomotives. Originally two engines of the class used saturated steam; four had the Schmidt superheater, and four the Robinson. But the outcome was that Urie, like Churchward at Swindon, developed his own type of superheater, the 'Eastleigh', and the last two engines which were originally saturators had the last mentioned apparatus.

The first use of the Eastleigh superheater was however not on one of those engines but on a Drummond 'D15' class 4-4-0 No. 464. This important conversion took place in 1915 when the engine in question was no more than 3 years old. The steam dryer and firebox tubes were removed, and the conversion proved so satisfactory that all the remaining nine engines of the class were similarly treated in 1915–7. The same principles were applied to the 'L12' class, also in 1915, with the rebuilding of engine No. 421, which in 1906 was involved in the terrible accident to the American boat special at Salisbury. Finally Urie completed his application of superheating to the three principal Drummond express passenger locomotive classes, again in 1915, by the rebuilding of a 'Paddleboat', No. 458. The original and revised heating surfaces of the three engines is given in the accompanying table.

It will be seen that as originally built the 'L12' had the largest firebox heating surface, and the 'T14' had the smallest—a most curious inversion of the proportions one would expect. As originally built the

DRUMMOND–URIE PASSENGER LOCOMOTIVES

Heating surfaces in square feet.

Class	'D15'		'L12'		'T14'	
	Original	Rebuilt	Original	Rebuilt	Original	Rebuilt
Small tubes	1406	782·5	1222	682	1580	873
Superheater flues ..	—	357	—	311	—	407
Firebox water tubes..	170	—	165	—	200	—
Firebox	148	144·5	163	161	140	158
Superheater	—	231	—	195	—	269
Total	1724	1515	1550	1349	1920	1707

'D15' and 'T14' classes carried a working pressure of 200 lb. per sq. in. but in the rebuilding both had the pressure reduced to 175 lb. per sq. in, as on the 'L12' class. But although all three classes had the nominal heating surface considerably reduced in the process of conversion all three became far better engines for the change. The 'L12s' in particular came to do some really splendid work on the Bournemouth trains; and although they always played the part of 'second fiddle' to the 'D15' class they were nevertheless no mean deputies. Aesthetically one must admit that the change did not improve the appearance of any one of the three classes; but although Urie did not keep their original chimneys he had not then adopted the stove-pipe fashion of his later designs. It was a great pity that the decelerated schedules of wartime had begun to appear on the L.S.W.R. by the time the superheater 4-4-0s took the road, because it would have been most interesting to see how they could have tackled the two-hour Bournemouth non-stops. With the lower water consumption resulting from superheating they should have shown up to considerable advantage. By the summer of 1915 only the 2 p.m. down was left with a non-stop run of more than 100 miles.

Despite the war there was still some splendid running to be recorded on the London & South Western Railway; indeed, two runs published in 1916 in *The Railway Magazine* were considerably finer than anything that had previously appeared in print at that time. Both runs were made on the forerunner of the late, lamented Atlantic Coast Express—the 11 a.m. from Waterloo to Salisbury, which retained its old 91-min. schedule for some little time after the outbreak of war in 1914. These two runs are tabulated herewith, and the first of them, remarkable to relate, features the large boilered four-cylinder 4-2-2-0 No. 720, This most beautiful of all South Western engines was usually worked by one driver, a man by the name of Geare, and he took immense pride in the appearance and work of the engine. The companion run was made by the first of the superheated 'Paddleboats', and was also a grand piece of running.

Engine No. 720 did extremely fine work from the outset, gaining steadily on the brisk point-to-point times laid down for this train, and with this substantial load of 260 tons the minimum speed at Milepost 31 was as high as 50 m.p.h. This was far better work than that of any of the eight-wheeled engines described in Chapter Twelve, and an average speed of more than 60 m.p.h. was made between Farnborough and Basingstoke. In preparing this chapter I have naturally been looking over some of my own logs of runs over this route, and the best I ever clocked from Waterloo to passing Basingstoke with any type of engine up to September 1939 was 52 min. 40 sec., and that was with a 'King Arthur'. This certainly highlights the performance of No. 720, when Basingstoke was passed in 51 min. 17 sec. with a load of 260 tons. Very little detail was given in the original published account of the work beyond Basingstoke; but after so splendid a start over the harder part of the journey the rest was easy. The maximum speed on the run was 75½ m.p.h. at Andover Junction.

L.S.W.R. WATERLOO–SALISBURY

		Engine No. Engine Type Load, tons full	720 4-2-2-0 260	458 4-6-0 370
Dist. miles		Sch. min.	Actual m. s.	Actual m. s.
0·0	WATERLOO	0	0 00	0 00
3·9	Clapham Junction	7	6 37	6 52
7·3	Wimbledon		10 18	10 28
13·4	*Hampton Court Junc.*	17	16 32	16 22
24·4	WOKING	28	27 02	26 55
33·2	Farnborough		36 42	36 56
39·8	Winchfield		—	43 20
47·8	BASINGSTOKE	54	51 17	51 06
			—	sigs. p.w.s.
59·2	Whitchurch		—	67 01
66·4	ANDOVER JUNC.	73	70 05	73 48
72·8	Grateley		—	79 55
78·3	Porton		—	85 24
83·8	SALISBURY	91	88 15	91 12
Net times	min.		88¼	87

The work of the superheated 'Paddleboat' was also very fine. When I was travelling regularly to Bournemouth on the 6.30 p.m. from Waterloo the load was usually about 370 to 380 tons; but never, in the whole of the 'King Arthur' reign did I ever log a run like this wartime effort of No. 458, on a bad day, with a greasy rail. In making the very excellent time of 51 min. 6 sec. to Basingstoke the principal variations of speed were 66½ m.p.h. as Esher; a minimum of exactly 50 m.p.h. at Milepost 31, and 63½ m.p.h. on the level at Winchfield. Then came a bad signal check at Winklebury box—intermediate between Basingstoke and Worting Junction—and the speed had not recovered to more than 31½ m.p.h. when the 1 in 249 gradient was topped at Battledown. The driver had evidently been getting some time in hand to offset the effect of a permanent way check that was in store for him at Overton; but the combined effect of the two checks was to cause a loss of 3¾ min. in running between Basingstoke and Andover. But the last mentioned station was passed at 70 m.p.h. and a brilliant finish brought the train into Salisbury virtually on time. In that fast finish the stiff rise to Grateley was climbed without speed falling below 51½ m.p.h., and the final dash down Porton bank produced a sustained maximum of 82 m.p.h.

War conditions led to the making of two of the most interesting runs with the Adams 4-4-0s that I have ever seen. On the 12.30 p.m. from Waterloo to Bournemouth a non-superheated 'L12' 4-4-0, No. 420, had an absolutely packed train of 375 tons gross behind the tender, and for some unexplained reason became a total failure and had to come off the train as early as Surbiton. An Adams 'Jubilee' 0-4-2 was quickly substituted; but she was obviously unprepared and unequal to the task, and took a rather laborious 23¼ min. to get the train on to Woking, 12·3 miles farther on. There however, probably obtained from Guildford, an Adams 6 ft. 7 in. 4-4-0 No. 565 was waiting ready, and she made what was in the circumstances, quite a remarkable run to Southampton. The log is tabulated herewith, and I have added to the times the average speeds from point to point. With this heavy train the start up to Milepost 31 was slow, and the recovery towards Winchfield on the level still on the laborious side. But by that time this hastily requisitioned engine was evidently going in first class style, as witness the average speed of 59·5 m.p.h. from Winchfield to Basingstoke. The climb to Wootton Box, with its five miles of 1 in 249 took its toll, but then the engine was taken downhill to Southampton in tremendous style with an average of 72 m.p.h. over the 15·4 miles from Micheldever to Eastleigh.

L.S.W.R. WOKING–SOUTHAMPTON WEST

Load: 375 tons gross
Engine: Adams 6 ft. 7 in. 4-4-0 No. 565

Dist. miles		Actual m. s.	Av. speed m.p.h.
0·0	WOKING	0 00	—
8·8	Farnborough	17 45	30·0
15·4	Winchfield	25 55	47·8
23 4	BASINGSTOKE	36 05	59·5
33·8	Micheldever	51 50	39·3
42·3	Winchester	59 00	71·1
49·2	Eastleigh	64 40	73·1
54·9	SOUTHAMPTON WEST	72 30	

Drummond 4-cylinder 4-6-0 No. 333 of Class "F13" at Exeter; built 1905.
[*L.G.R.P.*

Drummond 4-cylinder 4-6-0 No. 452 of Class "P14" at Waterloo; built 1911.
[*L.G.R.P.*

Close-up of the pull-out levers of the interlocking frame, and covers below removed to show the interlocking.

A view below the level of the operating floor, showing the complicated arrangements of air piping. [*British Railways*

Top. Joseph Locke—Engineer of the London and Southampton Railway.

Centre. Sir Charles Scotter: General Manager from 1885 to 1897, Director from 1897 to 1904, Chairman from 1904 to 1910.

Bottom. Sir Herbert Walker, K.C.B.: General Manager L.S.W.R. from 1912 to 1922, General Manager S.R. from 1923 to 1936.

A gantry of four two-arm automatic signals between Winchfield and Hook.
[*British Railways*

Pneumatic point operating mechanism showing the very large diameter cylinder. [*British Railways*

One of the Metropolitan type 4–4–0 tank engines, No. 323, built by Beyer, Peacock and Co. 1875.

Adams 4–4–2 suburban passenger tank engine No. 424, built by Beyer, Peacock and Co. in 1882.

An Adams 0–4–4 passenger tank engine Class "F6", in original condition, but painted in first type of Southern Railway Livery. [*All L.P. Co.*

The L.S.W.R. steamer *Hilda* at Guernsey pier. This packet steamer was lost off St. Malo in a snowstorm in November 1905. [*British Railways*

Whitchurch station, looking west. [L.G.R.P.

Broadstone station, looking north. [L.G.R.P.

Top. One of W. G. Beattie's "348" class, of 1876–7, here shown as numbered in the duplicate list. [*L.P. Co.*

Centre. An Adams 6 ft. 7 in. 4–4–0 of Class "T3" No. 562, built 1893. [*L.G.R.P.*

Bottom. Two Adams 4–4–0s on a London express preparing to leave Salisbury. The leading engine is a "T3" No. 574, and the train engine a 7 ft. "X6" class. [*L.G.R.P.*

At Southampton such was the crowd of passengers waiting to join the train that three more coaches were added, making up the exceptional load of 460 tons. Yet the Adams 4-4-0 carried on unassisted, and ran the 13½ miles to Brockenhurst in 22½ min. start to stop. The observer who logged this remarkable run alighted at Brockenhurst; but on returning by the 5.42 p.m. up express to London he was surprised to see No. 565 again at the head of the train, though in this direction with a much more manageable load of 275 tons. The run to Southampton was made in 18 min. 55 sec., and then came a very laboured ascent to Micheldever after a good start to Eastleigh. A special stop was made at Basingstoke to change engines, presumably to work No. 565 more readily to her home shed, and for the last stage of this unusual round an Adams 7-footer, No. 682, was put on. She was clearly a properly prepared engine, for she got away smartly and continued in fine style all the way to Clapham Junction. The accompanying log gives some interesting detail of an excellent performance.

L.S.W.R. BASINGSTOKE–VAUXHALL

Load: 275 tons gross
Engine: Adams 7 ft. 0 in. 4-4-0 No. 682

Dist. miles		Actual m.	s.	Av. Speed m.p.h.
0·0	BASINGSTOKE	0	00	—
8·1	Winchfield	10	30	46·3
14·6	Farnborough	16	55	60·8
23·4	WOKING	25	05	65·4
28·7	Weybridge	29	35	69·3
35·8	Surbiton	36	20	63·1
43·9	Clapham Junction	45	30	53·7
46·5	VAUXHALL	49	55	

In the later years of the war maximum speeds on the London & South Western Railway were limited to 60 m.p.h., and a typical schedule of that period was a non-stop allowance of 88 min. from Waterloo to Winchester 66·7 miles. Much finer work was done on the two up journeys tabulated from Winchester to Waterloo on which the work of a non-superheater 'T9' No. 773, the Dübs engine shown at the Glasgow Exhibition of 1901, and a superheated 'D15' are compared. Both engines did remarkably well in starting up the long 1 in 250 gradient from Winchester, with attained speeds at Litchfield summit of 35½ m.p.h. by No. 773 with 350 tons, and 34½ m.p.h. by No. 472, with 390 tons. On the fast stretch from Basingstoke to Clapham Junction, 44 miles, the respective average speeds of the two engines were 59·1 and 58·3 m.p.h. though engine No. 472 was checked by signal at Raynes Park, and had the additional disadvantage of a slack to cross from slow to fast lines at Basingstoke East instead of the usual full speed crossover from the Bournemouth to the main line at Worting Junction.

L.S.W.R. WINCHESTER–VAUXHALL

	Engine No.	773	472
	Engine Class	'T9'	'D15'
	Load tons full	350	390
Dist. miles		Actual m. s.	Actual m. s.
0·0	WINCHESTER	0 00	0 00
10·4	*Litchfield Box*	20 40	20 34
16·3	*Worting Junc.*	28 51	27 48
18·9	BASINGSTOKE	31 08	30 55
—		—	slack
33·5	Farnborough	45 44	45 12
42·3	WOKING	54 51	53 38
54·7	Surbiton	66 48	65 30
—		—	sigs.
62·8	Clapham Junc.	75 42	75 15
—		sigs.	—
65·3	VAUXHALL	80 59	80 00
Speeds	m.p.h.		
	Litchfield	35½	34½
	Fleet	65	63½
	Milepost 31	53	56
	Byfleet	67½	68
Net times	min.	79½	77

Before leaving the subject of the locomotive department in wartime some further mention must be made of the Uries, father and son. Although Robert Urie, on becoming Chief Mechanical Engineer of the L.S.W.R., came to change a good deal of Drummond's design practice, in his reversion to two-cylinder propulsion for the largest locomotives and by the abandonment of such Drummond specialities as the cross-water tubes and the steam dryer, in the vital matter of constructional detail and in workshop practice Robert Urie continued entirely in the Drummond tradition. He it was who had been the leading member of the Glasgow contingent that followed Drummond to Nine Elms, and eventually to Eastleigh. He had been Chief Draughtsman at St. Rollox, and came south to be Works Manager at Nine Elms. In reverting to the two-cylinder method of propulsion, with all the motion outside and exposed by use of a high running plate, Urie was one of the very first British locomotive engineers to break away from the tradition of concealing as much of 'the works' as possible. In 1913–4 it would have seemed that Gresley, on the Great Northern, was going the same way; but in later years he forsook simplicity for the attractions of three-cylinder propulsion with a derived valve-gear for the middle cylinder. Urie was therefore the true, if not the original advocate of the engine layout that became standard on the British Railways locomotives for which R. A. Riddles was responsible from 1951 onwards.

Robert Urie's son, D. C. Urie, had been a pupil of Dugald Drummond, and joined the L.S.W.R. at Nine Elms in 1901. By the year 1910 he had risen to the post of Leading Draughtsman, and after his father had become Chief Mechanical Engineer he was appointed Assistant to the Works Manager, with special duties concerning running and testing of locomotives. He carried out all the tests in connection with the introduction of superheating on the L.S.W.R. In this connection it is interesting to find that his father, in applying the 'Eastleigh' superheater to the various Drummond engines, used only a moderate degree of superheat. The heating surface of the superheater used on the 'T14' 4-6-0s for example was only 269 sq. ft.—a close parallel to the 262 sq. ft. of the Great Western 'Stars'. In 1915 however David Urie left the L.S.W.R. to take up the appointment of First Assistant to the Locomotive, Carriage and Wagon Superintendent of the Midland Great Western Railway of Ireland. But after 7 years he returned to his native Scotland, as Locomotive Superintendent of the Highland Railway, in succession to Christopher Cumming. In still later years he became Superintendent of Motive Power for the entire L.M.S.R.

Although it does not refer strictly to the activities of the war period it is necessary to mention the stage to which the reconstruction of Waterloo station had progressed by the time the outbreak of war put an end, temporarily, to further rebuilding. As in the great reconstructions proceeding at the time of writing this book, at Euston and Birmingham New Street, the civil engineers worked gradually across Waterloo, taking a group of platforms at a time. The traffic department arranged for the diversion of trains to other platforms so as to enable the engineers to have clear possession of successive areas. An interesting stage had been reached by the summer of 1913, by which time 8 out of the 21 platforms in the completed station were in service. It will be realised by this that the picturesque, but inconvenient main line platforms of the old station had at last been replaced. The complicated structural work had been carried out with a minimum of interference to traffic, though during the summer months work that involved the occupation of additional running lines had to be suspended.

One is so used to the solid durability of an institution like Waterloo Station that its origin and foundations are sometimes apt to be forgotten. The original station was built upon marshy ground lying immediately to the south of the Thames, and indeed the entire area of the original and the enlarged station was carried on arches. There is, in fact, a tributary of the Thames running underground beneath the actual station. Beneath the old station, while traffic was flowing normally, foundations had to be dug for the new and palatial buildings incorporated in this fine project.

Unseen from travellers excavations were in progress far below, and pumping operations to keep the working clear of water from that tributary of the Thames. The foundations had to be carried down to the London clay, which in many cases was 20 to 30 feet below street level. Over some platforms the new roof of the station was constructed over the top of the serried profiles of the old ones, to which additions had been made piecemeal, as traffic demanded successive enlargements of the original station.

As the reconstruction of the station progressed there gradually emerged tangible evidence of what the completed station was going to look like, in the magnificently spacious concourse between the platform barriers and the half-moon of buildings rising between the cab arrival yard and the concourse itself. It was evident that there were to be no half measures in the reconstruction. All the station buildings, like the platforms and track layout, were to be entirely new. In the summer of 1913 the new refreshment rooms were opened. This was far from a group of new buffets, where the traditional railway fare of stale buns and curled-up sandwiches was served. It was a refreshment 'suite', containing a handsome buffet at platform level, and a dining and tea room on the first floor. The walls of the buffet were lined with various marbles, and the floor was laid with Roman marble mosaic. Upstairs the dining room was panelled in English oak of Georgian design. The entire effect, in buffet and upstairs rooms alike, was to give a light and dignified atmosphere quite different from the general impression of hurried and unappetising snacks obtainable on a railway station. The dining room opened in 1913—the 'Surrey Room' in the Waterloo station of today—is still one of the pleasantest restaurants on British Railways.

It is sad to recall that the man who was, above all others, the architect of the new Waterloo did not live to see it finished. It was under the direct and expert supervision of the Resident Engineer, J. W. Jacomb-Hood that each stage of the reconstruction was planned and executed. He was among the London & South Western officers present in the summer of 1913 when Hugh Drummond, the Chairman of the company presided at a lunch given to some 80 railway and journalistic guests to celebrate the partial completion of the station, and the opening of the new refreshment 'suite'. In March of the following year he was out hunting at Dulverton when he was seen to drop from the saddle; other members of the hunt hurried to him, only to find him dead by the side of his horse. He was succeeded by Alfred W. Szlumper, who took the title of Chief Engineer.

XIV
Suburban Electrification

In the first decade of the 20th century the London & South Western Railway was already handling the heaviest suburban traffic of any railway running into London. But as with Waterloo Station itself, with Southampton Docks, and with the Locomotive Works, the South Western Management considered the problem on the broadest possible scale, and on the recommendation of the new General Manager, Mr. H. A. Walker, as he was then, a programme of electrification was decided upon. It was planned so as to be capable of steady expansion; and how well the scheme was conceived in those years just before World War I has been shown subsequently by the many extensions made to the system, including now the electrification to Bournemouth which is being engineered at the time this chapter is being written. In view of the numerous extensions to the system that have been made subsequent to that first installation, which was brought into service in the autumn of 1915, it is interesting to review some of the considerations that led the engineers and Management of the London & South Western Railway to adopt the low voltage d.c. system, with power supply through a third rail and return through the running rails.

The system adopted was in strong contrast to that already installed on the neighbouring London, Brighton & South Coast Railway, on which the single phase a.c. system with overhead wires and a voltage of 6,600 had been chosen largely on the recommendation of the Company's consulting engineer, Sir Philip Dawson. The Management of the Brighton Railway was also thinking far beyond the area covered by its suburban train services. Electrification to Brighton and other South Coast resorts was clearly in view, and for that reason Dawson recommended single phase a.c. at high voltage in order to minimize transmission losses when the system was applied to the main lines radiating from London. The engineers of the London & South Western Railway had doubtless watched with considerable interest the problems experienced by their Brighton neighbours, and observed the amount of overhead structure that had to be installed, and the time and cost of installing it.

Viewing the Brighton project in retrospect, and particularly in view of more recent developments on British Railways there is no doubt that the argument advanced by Sir Philip Dawson was eminently sound. As an engineering graduate in my post-graduate year at the City & Guilds Engineering College I had the good fortune to attend a number of lectures by this great authority, and heard then his strong advocacy of single phase a.c. traction systems. At the time I was at College the future of the Brighton system was very much in the melting pot. My year on post-graduate work was 1924-5, when both the South Western and the Brighton railways had been merged into the Southern, and plans were being made for the electrification of the suburban area of the former South Eastern & Chatham Railway. At that time from being a pioneer in British railway electrification, Sir Philip seemed to be fighting a rear-guard action in defence of the Brighton system. It was all very interesting, all the more so through hearing it from his own lips.

In view of the undoubted advantages, in many respects, of the overhead system at 6,600 voltage a.c. single-phase, it may be questioned whether the engineers and management of the London & South Western Railway took the right decision in 1913 in adopting 'third-rail' at low voltage d.c. In so doing they introduced into Great Britain a system of their own. The London underground lines, while also using low voltage d.c., used a fourth rail return, and this latter system was also being adopted by the London & North Western Railway. The South Western system involved a current return through the running rails. It was, of course, cheaper and simpler to instal, and as many extensions of the system since 1925 have shown, it can be installed with a very minimum of interference to ordinary traffic on almost any line of railway. Of course, as is well known, any third or fourth rail system has the disadvantage that it can be put out of action by icing on the conductor rails; on the other hand I have heard of very severe weather conditions having just the same paralysing effect on overhead wire systems, where freezing fog has solidified on the catenary wires.

Another problem in connection with a third or fourth rail system, which did not become apparent until the electrified area spread into the country well beyond the suburbs of London, was the frequency of level crossings encountered in country districts. These crossings necessitated a break in the conductor rails, and very careful provision had to be made to ensure that children or animals did not stray beyond the confines of the crossings themselves to where the live rail began again after the crossing. But one can quite imagine that to the management of the London & South Western Railway, in 1913, the third rail system appealed on the score of simplicity and cheapness of the provision that had to be made for the electrical pickup. It is true that sub-stations for feeding the live rail had to be closer together than would have been necessary with the Brighton system, but this point was more than off-set by simplifications in other directions.

There was another feature that had to be given consideration arising from the use of a traction return through the running rails. The extent to which the L.S.W.R. had adopted quite advanced techniques in signalling has been mentioned in earlier chapters; a considerable mileage of the line was track circuited, but with the traction return through the running rails different methods would have to be adopted to avoid interference with signalling apparatus from traction currents. In the electrified areas a change was made from d.c. to a.c. track circuits. The relays could be readily designed so as to be immune from operation by d.c. current, but there remained the matter of the block joints. While the line had to be divided up into sections of approximately one mile for track circuiting purposes, continuity in the running rails was required for the traction return currents. The problem had already been experienced on the Central London Tube Railway, 'The Twopenny Tube', which differed from the other underground lines in London, by having a third rail and traction return in the running lines.

On that line the problem of the block joints had been overcome by the use of what are called 'impedance bonds'. These consist, in effect, of a large coil of heavy copper rectangular section, enough to carry the traction return currents, and bond connections are provided from the running rails so that where there is a block joint for track circuiting purposes the traction return currents are diverted from the rails through the coils of the impedance bonds. These coils, because of their large cross-section have a very low resistance to the passage of d.c., but because of their design, in helical form, they offer a substantial impedance to a.c. and provide an effective 'insulation' between one section of the line and another. Impedance Bonds have had to be provided therefore at all track circuit block joints in the d.c. electrified area.

At that time in history electrical power supplies were few and far between. There was no such thing as a national 'grid', and the London & South Western Railway built their own power station at Durnsford Road, Wimbledon, beside the main line and adjacent to the River Wandle. The generators were driven by steam turbine, and the proximity of the main line was necessary for ease in bringing supplies of coal for the boilers. Water was pumped from the river for the surface condensers associated with the turbines. The layout was cleverly contrived, so that from a long gantry coal could be discharged direct from railway trucks into overhead bunkers in the boiler room. By this means the need for a coal conveying plant was obviated. There were sixteen boilers of the Babcock & Wilcox type, each having an evaporative capacity of 20,000 lb. of water per hour—each roughly equal to the output of an 'H15' locomotive working at maximum capacity.

The installation of turbines included five main and three auxiliary generating sets, and the main sets generated 11,000 volts a.c. three-phase. This supply was distributed to nine sub-stations, where it was transformed down to 600 volts d.c., and as such delivered to the conductor rails. The section of line first electrified was that from Waterloo via Wandsworth and East Putney to Wimbledon. Then, in January 1916 came the Kingston roundabout: from Waterloo down the main line as far as New Malden, then via Kingston and Strawberry Hill to the junction with the Windsor line at Twickenham, and so back to Waterloo via Barnes and Clapham Junction. This second 'opening' from January 30, 1916, also included the Shepperton branch. To supply this first group of electrified lines substations were built at Waterloo, Clapham Junction, Raynes Park

Kingston, Sunbury-on-Thames, Twickenham and Barnes. At the same time two others were finished ready for the further extensions that were nearing completion. These were at Isleworth and Hampton Court Junction. By March 1916 work on the Hounslow loop had been completed, and by June 1916 the electrified area had been extended from New Malden along the main line through Surbiton to Hampton Court Junction, and thence over the branch to Hampton Court terminus.

Although the Southern 'third-rail' electrification is such a familiar feature of railway working today the details of the track work, as originally installed in the autumn of 1915 are worth recalling. About 150 single-track miles were involved in the work brought into service in 1915–16. The third rail was laid at one side of the track 16 in. from gauge, and 3 in. above rail level; it was rolled in a special high-conductivity steel, and weighed 100 lb. per yard. The return circuit was formed by the running rails, the joints of which were bonded—except at track circuit block joints—by two copper bonds placed under the fishplates. The running rails were cross-bonded at frequent intervals to equalise the current returning by the different rails.

The trains themselves were not new. Existing bogie non-corridor carriages were taken and the necessary alterations made to fit them for the electrical apparatus. All trains were equipped for multiple-unit working, and made up into three-car sets, close coupled, with a trailer car between two motor coaches. Each three-car set was equipped with four 275 h.p. motors, arranged in pairs on the bogies underneath the driving compartments at opposite ends of the set. With 1,100 h.p. for a three-car train it was not surprising that the acceleration could be very rapid. The motor equipment on each coach was controlled during the accelerating periods by its own relay, which was independent of the other relays on the train; thus the motors on the different coaches were notched up in accordance with their individual requirements, which were in a measure, dependent upon the diameter to which the wheels might be worn and the slight inherent difference in the characteristics of the motors. That system, therefore, helped to equalise the load on the different motor coaches, and gave a low energy consumption.

With the introduction of these trains there came also a new conception, on the L.S.W.R., of the functions of a locomotive engineman. With steam the driver, from long experience, had a good working knowledge of the boiler and machinery of his locomotive. In the event of trouble he was expected to be able to render first-aid to his charge, and to get to a station where relief could be obtained, albeit not without some loss of time. But for the motorman on one of the new electric trains it was different. With the system of operation installed the master controller became a very simple piece of apparatus, and this was important because it was the only piece of apparatus handled by the drivers, who were generally non-technical men. The operation of the controller was extremely simple, the driver merely having to move the controller right round to the full 'on' position, and the relays automatically did the rest.

The master controller was of the drum type, and was provided with both main and reversing handles so interlocked that the reversing handle had to be either in the forward or reversed position before the driver could operate his controller. The main handle embodied the 'dead man' feature, the arrangement being such that in the event of the driver releasing the handle the supply of control current was interrupted, thus opening all the main contactors, and the brakes were automatically applied. Should the driver have allowed the handle to move upwards at any time, he had to bring the operating handle to the 'off' position again before he could release the brakes. When coasting, and when making ordinary service stops the driver moved the main handle to the 'off' position, and kept his hand on the handle, thereby preventing the automatic application of the brakes. In passing it may be added that in these 3-car electric trains the old carriage colours of the L.S.W.R. were abandoned, and a livery of engine-green adopted, very pleasantly lined out in gold.

When the new service was introduced in the late autumn of 1915, although the war situation was getting manifestly more serious and the prospects of an early conclusion were becoming more and more remote there was still a strong disposition in railway, as well as in business circles, to adopt the attitude 'Business as usual', and the new electric services were very extensively advertised, both by poster and in the daily press. One cannot criticise the Management of the London & South Western Railway for this, because in pressing on with the first stage of their great electrification project they were making a major contribution towards the transport situation in South West London at a time when private transport and means of getting about were becoming steadily more difficult. One of the posters advertising the new services included a pictorial representation of one of the new trains, but some present-day readers viewing this would be interested, and perhaps mystified to see a form of saloon carriage in the first-class accommodation. All the coaches provided for the original electrification were adapted from steam stock, and some of those taken did include saloon compartments. It was well known that many season ticket holders travelled regularly in groups, as a series of unofficial clubs, and it was thought that these saloon compartments would be very much to their liking. The new trains were first and third class only. This itself was an innovation on the London & South Western Railway, which at that time provided accommodation for all three classes. The omission of second class accommodation on the electric trains was, of course, a pointer towards future practice, and arrangements were made for the conversion of any long-term second-class season tickets either to first class, on payment of the necessary difference, or to third class, in which case a refund of the difference was made.

What was then considered quite a novelty however, was the arrangement of the timetable with trains on the various routes scheduled leaving at regular intervals. This was the first time that such a timetable had been applied on any of the main line railways in Great Britain, and the London & South Western Railway inaugurated in these electric services of 1915–16 a practice which has been followed in every subsequent extension of the d.c. electrified system south of the Thames, whether under the auspices of the Southern Railway, or of the Southern Region of British Railways. The main point was that regular interval services did away with any need for looking up a train before one made a journey. Of course, season ticket holders all had their regular trains for travelling to and from business; but in between times one knew that with the electric trains there was, for example, a service from Waterloo to Kingston every 10 minutes throughout the day. It was the same on other routes, though the actual service intervals varied naturally according to the destination. The Shepperton and Hampton Court branches for example, each had a train from Waterloo every half-hour of the day.

With the electric trains there was naturally a very considerable speed-up in service. When something like 1,100 h.p. was provided for every three coaches it was no more than natural that acceleration would be incomparably faster than with a Drummond or an Adams 0-4-4 tank engine, hauling anything up to ten non-corridor bogie coaches; and the following table shows the difference in time between Waterloo and Teddington.

Station	Steam Schedule	Electric Schedule
	Time min.	Time min.
Waterloo	0	0
Vauxhall	5	3
Clapham Junction ..	11	8
Earlsfield	16	12
Wimbledon	21	16
Raynes Park	25	19
Malden	29	22
Norbiton	33	26
Kingston	arr. 35 leave 40	28
Hampton Wick ..	43	31
Teddington	47	34

So that the new trains could be readily identified as to route, by signalmen, a system of letter codes was devised and carried on the front of the trains. During daylight these letters appeared in large white characters in the central panels of the coach ends, and at night they were similarly shown in illuminated characters. These destination codes were very simple to identify from the railway operating point of view, and much more easily read than destination head boards. But in reading contemporary accounts of the introduction of the new trains one is rather amused to see the attention paid to what was then an almost unprecedented step by the London & South Western Railway, in what was described as 'taking the passengers into their confidence' by revealing by poster what these purely operational head codes signified. At that time in railway history there was a disposition on the part of many railwaymen, in both senior and intermediate positions, to regard everything appertaining to the running of trains as a completely closed book. Destination boards were placed on the trains and that was all the passengers were told. One recalls also the practice of the North British Railway which used destination boards on the smokeboxes of its express locomotives. But these were not for the edification of the public at all; they merely indicated where the engine itself was going, so that an express leaving Edinburgh for England via the Waverley route would merely be labelled Carlisle.

All eight running lines into Waterloo were electrified, and it is interesting to recall the following details of the very intense service provided from the outset, during every hour of the day from Waterloo:

Min. past hour	Destination	Headcode
	VIA MAIN LINE	
3 (a)	Kingston 'Roundabout' via Malden	V
13 (c)	Kingston 'Roundabout' via Malden	V
18	Hampton Court via Surbiton	H
25 (e)	Shepperton via Malden	S
33 (a)	Kingston 'Roundabout' via Malden	V
38	Hampton Court via Surbiton	H
43 (c)	Kingston 'Roundabout' via Malden	V
55 (e)	Shepperton via Malden	S
58	Hampton Court via Surbiton	H
	VIA WINDSOR LINES	
8 (b)	Kingston 'Roundabout' via Richmond	$\overline{V}$
14	Wimbledon via Southfields	P
18 (d)	Kingston 'Roundabout' via Richmond	$\overline{V}$
22 (f)	Hounslow via Chiswick	O
28 (g)	Hounslow via Richmond	$\overline{O}$
34	Wimbledon via Southfields	P
38 (b)	Kingston 'Roundabout' via Richmond	$\overline{V}$
48 (d)	Kingston 'Roundabout' via Richmond	$\overline{V}$
52 (f)	Hounslow via Chiswick	O
54	Wimbledon via Southfields	P
58 (g)	Hounslow via Richmond	$\overline{O}$

(References to letters in brackets)

(a) Does not stop at Queen's Road (outwards) and returning passes Wandsworth Town and Queen's Road.
(b) Does not stop at Queen's Road and Wandsworth Town (outwards), and in returning passes Queen's Road.
(c) Does not stop at Queen's Road (outwards), and in returning passes Queen's Road and Vauxhall.
(d) Does not stop at Vauxhall and Queen's Road (outwards), and in returning passes Queen's Road.
(e) Passes Queen's Road, Earlsfield and Hampton Wick.
(f) All stations outwards, passes Wandsworth Town and Queen's Road in returning.
(g) Passes Queen's Road and Wandsworth Town (outwards), and all stations in returning.
(h) Passes Queen's Road, Earlsfield and Raynes Park.

The new services got into their stride with very little in the way of teething troubles and in a very few days all was running very punctually. To anyone who had known the L.S.W.R. at the height of its steam operated suburban services the transformation was quite extraordinary, and it could, perhaps be appreciated most vividly from a sojourn on the platform of Clapham Junction station. From the above details of departures from Waterloo, and realising that there must also be a corresponding number of arrivals, there would be 20 trains an hour in the down direction and another 20 in the up passing through Clapham Junction; and if one added to these the electric services of the London Brighton & South Coast Railway on the adjoining tracks it was possible to count the passage of about 50 electric trains through Clapham Junction in a single hour. These 50 trains were spread over 10 running lines, 4 on the Windsor section of the L.S.W.R.; 4 on the main line section of the L.S.W.R.; and 2 representing the slow lines of the Brighton. At that time the Brighton main lines were also electrically equipped, but they were not normally used for the electric suburban trains. Even so, keen observers were able to sight simultaneously between 6 and 10 electric trains at once, while standing on the platforms of Clapham Junction station and looking towards Waterloo. It should be appreciated also that amid all these electric services, which were providing such a relatively dense traffic on the South Western lines, the longer distance residential trains running to Woking, Guildford, Aldershot, Windsor and Reading had still to be worked by steam. The majority of these latter trains were run fast through the suburban areas, and only took up a stopping train character once they were clear of the electrified area.

At the time the first stage of electrification was brought into service the extension of the scheme was also announced. This was designed to cover all three routes to Guildford:

(a) via the main line, as far as Woking.
(b) via Oxshot.
(c) via Epsom and Leatherhead.

But work on the extension of the scheme was postponed on account of the war and this work, together with the further extensions contemplated, were not put in hand until several years later. It is nevertheless important to appreciate that the first phase of electrification covering the 'Kingston Roundabout', the Hounslow loop, and the Shepperton and Hampton Court branches provided the pattern on which all subsequent electrification work on the Southern railway was carried out. Its immediate success was a lasting tribute to Sir Herbert Walker, and to the various officers of the L.S.W.R. who carried it through so successfully.

XV

Prelude to the 'Southern'

The end of the war found the London & South Western Railway in a strong position. Its engineering departments were poised ready for immediate post-war developments; its operating department had won great distinction by its flexibility and success in handling its huge wartime traffics; but above all there was the personality of the General Manager. Not long before the outbreak of war, owing to the untimely death of Sir Frank Ree, then General Manager of the L.N.W.R., Mr. H. A. Walker, as he was then, was appointed Acting Chairman of the secret Railway Executive Committee, and he continued as Chairman throughout the war period. He had with him, as Secretary, another distinguished South Western officer in Major, now Major-General Gilbert S. Szlumper, son of the L.S.W.R. Chief Engineer. The partnership of Sir Herbert Walker and Gilbert Szlumper in this vital task was a most fortunate and happy one, both for the railways and for the Allied cause.

But it was upon Walker himself that the immense burden of responsibility mainly fell. During the war he was, literally, executive chief of the whole British railway system under Government control. When he retired from the General Managership of the Southern Railway, in 1937, *The Railway Gazette* referred thus to his work with the R.E.C.:

> "This meant long and tedious days at Westminster, in addition to the management of the South Western Railway, which, owing to its geographical position, had a large share in the war transport. Only a man physically strong could have withstood the strain; and throughout this trying period, whatever he may have felt, he always gave the impression of unruffled imperturbability and being endowed with extraordinary patience. This characteristic he has displayed throughout his career and it has been particularly noticeable when he has taken the chair at important conferences at the Railway Clearing House and elsewhere. After the war came the necessity of facing conditions and crises such as pre-war railway general managers never had to encounter."

Fortunately, under his wise administration the South Western house was very neatly in order, and the last four years as an independent concern show a truly splendid record of development all of which was to contribute notably to the eventual build-up of the Southern Railway of which Walker himself was the principal architect.

With one exception the chief officers of the Company who had carried the burden of the working in wartime continued in office. That exception was Arthur H. Johnson, the Signal and Telegraph Engineer, who retired on account of ill-health at the end of 1918. I have referred earlier to his genial personality and fine work for the L.S.W.R., but during the time he was in America, in the nineties of last century he had the great distinction of being invited to lecture on signalling to Harvard University. This was probably the first lecture on signalling ever to be given to a university. It was certainly the first to take place in the United States. Johnson was succeeded by W. J. Thorrowgood, a very able engineer, but one of a very different temperament. He took a leading part in the work of the Committee set up by the Institution of Railway Signal Engineers on 'Three Position Signalling', and as Signal Engineer of the Southern Railway had the distinction of installing the first four-aspect colour light signals in this country—and indeed in the whole world. These were however not on one of the former South Western lines, but on the one-time London, Chatham & Dover line, at Blackfriars.

Another appointment of great importance made shortly after the end of the war, was that of Major Gilbert S. Szlumper, as Deputy Docks and Marine Manager. After a varied career in the engineering departments before the war Major Szlumper was appointed Assistant to the General Manager in February 1914, and as previously mentioned served as Secretary to the Railway Executive Committee throughout the war. The association between Sir Herbert Walker and Gilbert Szlumper, which had been such a close one during the war years, continued throughout Sir Herbert's long and distinguished career; and when he retired from the General Managership of the Southern Railway in 1937, it was Gilbert Szlumper who succeeded him.

Returning however to the years immediately following the end of World War I, news of a great project, on which work had been steadily proceeding despite the war, was released at the end of 1919—the huge freight marshalling yard at Feltham. In its conception, which was largely due to Sir Herbert Walker himself, this yard was in principle a definite prototype of the yards recently brought into service on British Railways, at Temple Mills, Middlesbrough, Margam, Carlisle, and elsewhere, in that its over-riding purpose was to concentrate marshalling work in one large yard, instead of a number of small ones, and to eliminate trip working between such yards. The location of Feltham, on the Windsor and Reading line was in itself a stroke of genius. It was ideally situated for receipt of traffic from the London & North Western, from the Midland, the Great Central, the Great Northern and the Great Eastern, via the various connections at Willesden and Acton. Furthermore, it virtually eliminated freight train working on the busiest part of the main line, between Weybridge and Clapham Junction. Trains to and from the main line would henceforth be diverted at Weybridge via the connection to the Reading line at Virginia Water, while traffic between Feltham and Nine Elms Goods Station could be worked entirely on the Windsor lines.

One of the most important advantages that were derived from this new yard was the elimination of duplicate freight services. Hitherto, because of the lack of any concentration, or classification centre in the London area, freight from the south and west for the north and for London had to be conveyed in separate trains, whereas with Feltham Yard available heavy goods loads could be worked thence, and there remarshalled. The yard was laid out on the hump principle, with through working for both down and up traffic. This practice is familiar enough today, but it was novel, if not necessarily unique in 1919. As originally laid out there were 6 reception and 17 sorting sidings in the 'down' section of the yard, and 8 reception and 16 sidings in the 'up' section. A comprehensive scheme of track circuiting, together with power operation of points was installed to facilitate the working. At the time the news of the yard was first published the work was not finished, but in October 1920 the 'down' section of the yard was brought into service, and from that time onwards the practice of marshalling L.S.W.R. trains at Willesden was discontinued.

An interesting outcome of the establishment of this new yard was the introduction of two new types of heavy tank locomotive—one a 4-8-0 for humping duty in the yard itself, and the other a 4-6-2 for working interchange traffic with the London and North Western and Midland railways. The basic dimensions of these two new classes were as follows:

Type	4-6-2	4-8-0
Cylinders dia. × stroke: in. ..	21 × 28	22 × 28
Coupled wheel dia.: ft. in. ..	5–7	5–1

The boilers were the same in both classes, being somewhat smaller than those fitted to the 4-6-0 express goods locomotives of the '498' class. The comparative dimensions were:

Class	4-6-0 Express goods	4-6-2T 4-8-0T
Heating surface in sq. ft.		
Large tubes	464	357
Small tubes	1,252	910
Firebox	162	139
Superheater	308	231
Total	2,186	1,636
Grate Area sq. ft.	30	27
Boiler pressure p.s.i.	180	180

Four tank engines of the 4-8-0 type were built for service on the Feltham humps, and five 4-6-2 tanks for the interchange traffic.

These tank engines are naturally considered at the same time as Feltham yard; but in appearance and general features of mechanical design they followed in the traditions established by Robert Urie, in his express passenger 4-6-0s of the 'N.15' class. It was in anticipation of a rapid development of post-war holiday traffic on the L.S.W.R. that authorisation for the construction of the first few of these engines was given before the end of the war, and in them Urie developed his own practice in locomotive design which had been foreshadowed by the 'H.15' engines of 1913. After the flowing elegance of the Drummond era, and the gadgets that came to be associated with it, there was an austere simplicity about 4-6-0 No. 736 and her sisters, with their high raised running plate, only two cylinders, and everything outside and get-at-able. A touch of individuality was provided by the stove pipe chimney. These engines were followed, in 1920, by the express goods version, with 5 ft 7 in. wheels, and cylinders 21 in. diameter. Urie had certainly surprised the locomotive world on the '736' class, by using cylinders of no less than 22 in. diameter.

So far as maximum haulage power and high speed were concerned I cannot honestly say that the original 'N.15' class represented a great advance over the superheater 'Paddleboats'—in fact I have not been able to turn up any run with them, recorded personally or by anyone else, that is the equal of that splendid performance of No. 458 referred to in Chapter 13 of this book. But the original 'N.15' class has a special place in locomotive history as the foundation—and a very solid one at that!—of the very celebrated 'King Arthurs' of the Southern Railway. How R. E. L. Maunsell and his team from the South Eastern & Chatham Railway transformed an ordinary work-horse of a locomotive that was very sound mechanically, and was reliable and free from trouble in day-to-day maintenance, into one of the most brilliant medium-powered engines the country has ever seen is another story. The fact remains that as originally built the engines did not steam too freely, and in consequence they were not capable of sustained high power output. Like all South Western express engines they had a tremendous turn of speed when their drivers gave them their heads downhill.

In the years immediately after the war my own journeys on the L.S.W.R. were all made on the Bournemouth trains, and the 'N.15s' worked only those trains allocated to Nine Elms shed. Bournemouth Central then had nothing larger than the superheated 'D15' 4-4-0s, and as that shed had all the fastest trains, with the exception of the 6.35 pm up, there was little chance for the 4-6-0s to show their paces on the Bournemouth expresses. At that time I used to spend part of my college holidays with an uncle who lived in a quiet part of the town near to the Central station, and to Meyrick Park, and I passed many happy hours watching the train working of those days, and taking photographs. Although it was a very dull train from the stop-watching point of view the old 9.30 a.m. from Waterloo was a photographer's 'scoop'. One never knew from day to day what class of 4-6-0 Nine Elms would put on, and I have 'snapped' 'N15s', 'Paddleboats' and the original Urie 'H.15s' on the regular return working, which left Bournemouth around 3.30 p.m.

It was in 1921 that the L.S.W.R. caused something of a surprise by introducing the new 5-coach 'Tea Car' sets on to the Bournemouth service. Until that time very few trains on the service included restaurant cars, and a considerable amount of non-corridor stock was still in regular use. Many of my own journeys at that time were made in the rather spartan, and straight-backed L.S.W.R. non-corridor 'thirds', which had been the rule, rather than the exception in pre-war days. The 'crack' 2 p.m. down, with its fast non-stop run to Christchurch was entirely a non-corridor train. The new set trains consisted of 'brake third', 'third', 'pantry third', 'first' and 'brake third'. The pantry accommodation was very small, amounting to the space normally taken up by one third class compartment and one lavatory; but the ordinary compartments adjoining were designed so that tables could be set out in them for meals, and although designated 'tea car trains' the pantries were equipped to serve egg dishes and a variety of grills.

Quite apart from the welcome service they provided, in these four 5-coach trains Mr. S. Warner, the Carriage Superintendent of the L.S.W.R., created something of a prototype towards the Southern Railway standard corridor coach of the future. Until that time the South Western had remained faithful to the older traditions of British railway carriage construction, with a relatively narrow body; a roof raised very little above the 'flat' style of the nineteenth century, and much panelling work on the sides and ends. Warner, in 1921, produced one of the first British carriage designs to have a smoothed exterior, carried out to the limits of the loading gauge both in its overall width and in the high elliptical roofs. The outside panelling was entirely galvanised steel, screwed to the framing. It is however significant of the traditions then still persisting in carriage construction that the body framing was entirely of timber. The bodies and the underframes were entirely separate structures, the latter being constructed of steel channels and angles. The complete change from the older traditions of the L.S.W.R. was emphasised by the exterior painting, in dark green, lined out in yellow and picked out in black.

The summer services of 1921 marked another great step forward in the development of the L.S.W.R. under Sir Herbert Walker's guiding hand. From July 10 in that year the main line departures from Waterloo were arranged systematically, so that expresses to the West of England left at the even hours; those to Bournemouth and Weymouth at the half-hours, and those to Portsmouth, for Southsea and the Isle of Wight at 50 min. past the hour. On the Bournemouth route there was a train every hour from 9.30 a.m. to 7.30 p.m., and to Portsmouth every hour from 7.50 a.m. to 6.50 p.m. In the latter case however the 8.50 a.m., 10.50 a.m. and the 2.50 p.m. departures were Saturdays only. The Bournemouth service was accelerated to an overall time of 2¼ hrs. by the best trains, with an intermediate stop at Southampton West. Here again the departure times were systematised, in that the fastest trains, calling only at Southampton, left at the even half hours from Waterloo—10.30, 12.30, 2.30 and so on. The other Bournemouth-line departures gave a very good service to intermediate stations such as Basingstoke, Winchester, Eastleigh, Brockenhurst, and Christchurch. On the West of England service the old arrangement of having a 'bunch' of trains around 11 a.m. went by the board, and during the summer there were, instead, expresses at 10 and 11 a.m., and 12 noon—all running non-stop to Salisbury. Other West of England departures, serving intermediate stations, left Waterloo at 8 and 9 a.m., 1, 5 and 6 p.m. There was also a fast afternoon train at 3 p.m. non-stop to Salisbury.

The pattern of train services inaugurated by the L.S.W.R. in the summer of 1921 was indeed a national prototype. It was followed by the Great Western, with all the publicity then usually associated with any developments on that line, so much so that many simple souls might have thought that regular-interval departures were a Paddington idea! The irony of it was that after grouping, when the Southern applied the same principle to some of the old Brighton services there was a general howl of protest, although the previous South Western and Great Western timetable changes had been acclaimed as strokes of genius. The famous words of John Bright must have found many a sympathetic echo at Waterloo in the early days of the Southern, when Sir Herbert Walker was steadily rationalising, and co-ordinating the practices and train services of the South Western, of the Brighton, and of the South Eastern & Chatham:

> "Railways have rendered more service and received less thanks than any other institution in the country".

Although there was so much that was new on the South Western in those years just after the war, with the new Urie locomotives, the new carriages and the new services, in actual quantity there was not enough of the new equipment to take away much of the old atmosphere of the railway, and a great deal of the express working still devolved upon the Drummond 4-4-0s. In my experience, provided they were not too heavily loaded the superheated 'L12' 4-4-0s did very good work. We frequently had one on the old 8.45 a.m. $2\frac{1}{4}$ hr. up express from Bournemouth to Waterloo, and with the usual load of about 300 tons, they kept excellent time. Incidentally, a memory of those days is the old porter at Bournemouth Central who, the moment the engine appeared round the curve from Talbot Woods cutting, used to roar 'SOUTHAMPTON WEST and WATERLOO' in a voice that bade fair to rival old Sandy Grant at Forres, on the Highland. Unlike some modern public-address systems one could always hear quite distinctly what he said!

I look back with particular pleasure to the Bournemouth expresses of 1921–3, because on them some of my earliest attempts at stop-watching were made. I never managed to catch any of the really brilliant runs that were at times made by the 'D15' engines, but the Rev. L. A. Garrard has been kind enough to give me some of his own recordings of that same period, and these make impressive reading. I have tabulated first two runs on the up Southampton non-stops—one of my own, on the 8.45 a.m. from Bournemouth, and one of Mr. Garrard's with an extraordinary load on the 10.35 a.m. On my run, with No. 468, the driver was clearly spinning out his time so as to effect an arrival exactly on-time. We were going splendidly up the earlier part of the Micheldever bank, sustaining 45½ m.p.h. for mile after mile past Winchester; but then either steam or water must have been concerning the driver, for there was a pronounced easing to 39½ m.p.h., and a recovery to 41 m.p.h. at Litchfield. To this point engine No. 470 hauling the tremendous load, for this service, of 440 tons, had done wonderfully well, not falling below 39½ m.p.h., and she recovered much more rapidly from the summit than No. 468 had done on

L.S.W.R. SOUTHAMPTON WEST–WATERLOO

Run No.		1		2	
Engine 'D15' 4-4-0 No.		468		470	
Load tons E/F		301/325		416/440	
Dist. miles	Sch. min.	Actual m. s.	Speeds m.p.h.	Actual m. s.	Speeds m.p.h.
0·0 SOUTHAMPTON WEST	0	0 00	—	0 00	—
1·1 *Northam Junc.*	3½	3 20	—	3 30	—
5·6 EASTLEIGH	10	9 50	50	10 42	48
9·5 Shawford		14 30	45½	15 51	—
12·5 WINCHESTER		18 35	45½	20 16	—
21·1 Micheldever		30 00	39½	32 38	—
22·9 *Litchfield Box*		32 35	41½	35 38	39½
28·9 *Worting Junc.*		40 45	—	42 30	—
31·4 BASINGSTOKE	42	43 10	68½	44 44	—
37·0 Hook		48 05	70	49 41	72½
39·5 Winchfield		50 15	65½	51 51	—
42·7 Fleet		53 20	64	54 57	—
46·0 Farnborough		56 20	63½	58 09	—
48·2 *Milepost* 31		58 35	58½	60 25	57½
54·8 WOKING	64	64 21	70½	66 38	—
57·5 Byfleet		66 40	72	69 00	69
60·1 Weybridge		68 55	69	71 21	—
62·1 Walton		70 45	62/64	73 28	56/63½
67·2 Surbiton		75 45	58	78 30	51½
71·9 Wimbledon		81 05		83 56	56½
		sigs.			
75·3 CLAPHAM JUNC. ..	84	85 20		87 46	
		sigs.		sigs.	
79·2 WATERLOO	92	93 35		96 40	
Net times min. ..		91½		95	

my run. Then the two engines made average speeds of 66 and 63·7 m.p.h. over the 35·8 miles from Basingstoke to Surbiton. Both engines were checked in the final stages; but the net times of 91 and 95 evidenced good work.

Mr. Garrard has also sent me details of a run on the 6.30 p.m. down on which No. 471 tackled a load of 425 tons. On this occasion time would have been more than kept, but for heavy delays. Because of signal checks it took no less than 23¼ min. to pass Surbiton, 12·1 miles; but the 61½ miles from there to Eastleigh were covered in the remarkable time for a 'D15', with this load, in 66½ min. The minimum speed on the 1 in 249

L.S.W.R. BOURNEMOUTH–SOUTHAMPTON

	Run No. Engine 'D15' 4-4-0 Load tons E/F	1 472 245/270			2 470 278/290			3 469 282/300			4 470 416/440		
Dist. Miles		m.	s.	m.p.h.	m.	s.	m.p.h.	m.	s.	m.p.h.	m.	s.	m.p.h.
0·0	BOURNEMOUTH CENTRAL	0	00	—	0	00	—	0	00	—	0	00	—
1·2	Boscombe	3	18	—	3	27	—	3	58	—	3	44	
3·7	Christchurch	6	10	63½	6	19	66	7	04	61/53	6	44	60
6·9	Hinton Admiral	10	04	—	10	01	—	10	51	—	10	30	—
9·4	New Milton	13	10	42½	13	33	39	14	04	44	14	02	41
12·4	Sway	16	14	61	16	55	59/53	17	20	57/55	17	38	56/51
15·2	BROCKENHURST	18	49	79	19	44	70	20	10	67½	20	29	65½
19·8	Beaulieu Road	22	55	62½	24	07	56	24	39	53	25	05	61
22·6	Lyndhurst Road	25	22	69	26	50	62	27	28	60	27	52	58
26·0	Redbridge	29	16	39*	30	33	35*	31	10	42*	31	29	—
28·7	SOUTHAMPTON WEST	33	45		35	15		35	32		35	20	

* Speed restriction

L.S.W.R. DORCHESTER–WAREHAM

		Run. No.	1		2		3		4	
		Engine No.	431		424		431		558	
		Engine Class	'L12'		'L12'		'L12'		'T3'	
		Load tons E/F	108/115		107/115		112/120		162/170	
Dist. Miles		Sch. min.	Actual m. s.	Speeds m.p.h.	Actual m. s.	Speeds m.p.h.	Actual m. s.	Speeds m.p.h.	Actual m. s.	Speeds m.p.h.
0·0	DORCHESTER	0	0 00	—	0 00	—	0 00	—	0 00	—
5·5	Moreton		7 03	67	7 20	63	7 50	—	7 19	66-63
10·0	Wool		10 47	82	11 13	75½	11 50	80	11 13	75½
—			sigs.		—		—		—	—
13·9	*Worgret Junc.*	15	13 59	—	14 31	—	14 55	—	14 34	—
15·0	WAREHAM	17	15 43	—	16 35	—	16 50	—	16 16	—

from Basingstoke to Wootton box was 40½ m.p.h., and the maximum afterwards 74 m.p.h. After Eastleigh the train was involved in a further series of checks, and eventually Southampton was reached 14½ min, late. But the net time was no more than 90 min. The Bournemouth enginemen of those days included some great runners in the persons of Drivers Bullard, Harding, Lowman, and Penton—to mention only a few. The section through the New Forest, with the need for moderating the speed a little through Christchurch before tackling the Hinton Admiral bank, and the severe slack over the River Test bridge at Totton, made the allowance of 37 min. for the 28·7 miles from Bournemouth to Southampton none too easy. Four runs clocked by the Rev. L. A. Garrard are tabulated herewith. The first three are typical of ordinary load running, while the fourth is the magnificent effort of Driver Bullard with No. 470, of which I have already described the continuation to Waterloo.

Some exciting running used to be made with the Weymouth portions of the Bournemouth expresses on the up road, and a 60-m.p.h. timing was once in operation between Dorchester and Wareham. The gradients are slightly downhill to Moreton; steeply downhill for a mile at 1 in 100 towards Wool and then gradually easing out. In post-war years the allowance was 17 min., but with loads of 4 coaches the drivers used to hop along merrily. The Rev. L. A. Garrard has sent me details of four runs, on three of which superheated 'L12' 4-4-0s were used; of these No. 431 would have come very near to the old 15-min. timing but for the final check. Of course, by far the most interesting run of the four was the last, which not only had two extra coaches, but had an Adams 6 ft. 7 in. 4-4-0 instead of a Drummond. This was a splendid run, with a load of 170 tons.

One of the most interesting locomotive events in the last years of the L.S.W.R. was the rebuilding of one of the 'T9' 4-4-0s with a new boiler and Eastleigh superheater. This alteration was applied first to No. 314 and the total heating surface was changed from 1,500 to 1,258 sq. ft. The change was highly beneficial and between 1922 and 1929 all the remaining 65 engines of the class were similarly rebuilt. Two runs on the Bournemouth service show clearly the effects of the alteration. I should mention that the non-superheated No. 313, used on a 390-ton train, was not a hurriedly arranged substitute. She was in the regular link at Bournemouth Central and worked turn and turn about with the 'D15' and 'L12' superheaters then at the shed. It was in her uphill work out to Basingstoke that the superheated engine No. 336 showed up to such tremendous advantage, with such speeds at 48 m.p.h. at Milepost 31, and 44½ m.p.h. beyond Battledown. A similar form of rebuilding was applied to one of the Drummond 0-4-4 tanks, No. 126, and one of the '700' class 0-6-0 goods; but while all of the latter were subsequently rebuilt the 0-4-4 tank No. 126 remained the only one of her kind.

And so I come to the autumn of 1922, when the end of the London & South Western Railway as an independent concern was drawing near.

L.S.W.R. WATERLOO–SOUTHAMPTON WEST

	Run No.	1		2	
	Engine No.	313		336	
	Engine class	'T9'Ns		'T9'S	
	Load tons E/F	370/390		361/380	
Dist. miles	Sch. min.	Actual m. s.	Speeds m.p.h.	Actual m. s.	Speeds m.p.h.
0·0 WATERLOO	0	0 00	—	0 00	—
3·9 CLAPHAM JUNC.	7	7 25	—	7 10	—
7·3 Wimbledon		12 06	—	11 18	—
12·0 Surbiton		18 10	56	16 38	60
19·1 Weybridge		26 13	57	23 59	60½
24·4 WOKING	29	31 55	50	29 28	—
31·0 *Milepost* 31		40 53	42½	37 31	48
33·2 Farnborough		43 50	—	40 03	—
36·5 Fleet		47 12	57	43 24	—
42·2 Hook		54 05	48	49 22	—
47·8 BASINGSTOKE	56	60 35	55	55 04	—
50·3 *Worting Junc.*	59	64 05	—	58 05	44½ (min)
56·3 *Litchfield*		72 11	—	65 31	—
58·1 Micheldever		74 10	—	67 29	—
66·7 WINCHESTER		82 55	—	75 25	—
69·7 Shawford		85 55	71	—	70
73·6 EASTLEIGH	83	89 10		82 24	
78·1 *Northam Junc.*	88½	94 00		87 33	
79·2 SOUTHAMPTON	92	96 00		90 23	

T9NS = Non-superheated 'T9' 4-4-0
T9S = Superheated 'T9'4-4-0

In that last year the great reconstruction at Waterloo had been completed and the impressive new frontage of the station was consummated by inclusion of the magnificent 'Victory Arch' war memorial. The new station—for completely renewed it had been in the preceding 15 years—was formally opened by Her Majesty Queen Mary, on March 21, 1922; but it is unfortunate that this splendid façade is not seen to advantage by the great majority of those who travel from Waterloo. They arrive either by Underground, or round the back way, by taxi; and by far the best view of the grandly impressive Waterloo 'block' is obtained from passing trains on the South Eastern & Chatham line. The station was rightly described by *The Railway Magazine* of the day as 'The Largest Railway Terminus in Great Britain'. It was also unquestionably the finest, and the completion of the work certainly epitomised the distinguished position the London & South Western had attained among the railways of Britain. From being a ramshackle concern, parsimonious in badly-needed expenditure in order to provide its shareholders with a dividend, it had risen to become one of the best and most vigorously managed railways in the country.

It had been very fortunate in having in succession, three such General Managers as Sir Charles Scotter, Sir Charles Owens, and Sir Herbert

Walker, and the esteem in which the two first named were held is shown by their long association with the Company as directors after their retirement from executive management. Of Sir Herbert Walker it is enough to say that he was one of the greatest managers in British railway history. His work for the London & South Western alone was outstanding in itself; but he continued for another 15 years as General Manager of the Southern Railway, and building upon the South Western edifice he created the largest suburban electrification in the world—a system which he proved readily adaptable to expansion on a longer-distance basis, and which, as I write, is now in process of extension to Bournemouth. The success of the South Western, in its last twenty odd years lay in the skill with which expenditure was confined to the things that most mattered. An example of this was the signalling at Waterloo. No company was more forward thinking in signalling techniques, and it might have been thought that the completion of the new station would have been the occasion for a grand new installation. Instead, with each successive stage of the reconstruction of the station the plant in 'A' box had been adapted, and it was not until the time came for the Portsmouth electrification, in 1935, that this most famous mechanical signalling installation was at last replaced. This in itself was a great tribute to the apparatus itself, and to the foresight used in the original design and layout.

At the time of the grouping, in January 1923, some of the greatest of the former railway companies immediately began to lose all their old individuality and character, and in a few years they were no more than memories. Some of these traits, and cherished features were perhaps overdue for modernisation; but on the South Western, under Walker's skilful hand, the process of modernisation was already in full swing by 1922, and in the grouping era the Brighton and the South Eastern were gathered into the flowing tide. Both had much to contribute to the eventual build-up of the closely-knit Southern Railway system, and I have told elsewhere how the men of the South Eastern & Chatham came to dominate steam locomotive affairs. But the greatest legacy bequeathed to the railway system of this country by the L.S.W.R., is the 'Southern Electric', and all that it has come to mean, in its mass handling of passengers in the London area, and the smooth clock-like precision of its operating as its boundaries have extended to Brighton, Portsmouth, Dover, and now, in the near future, to Bournemouth. In retrospect we can now see the inauguration of the 'Riverside Electric' by the L.S.W.R. in 1915 from which the huge modern system has directly developed, as one of the greatest railway events of the century.

Index

Bibliography

History of the Southern Railway (1936) C. F. Dendy-Marshall
Express Trains English and Foreign (1889) Foxwell and Farrer
A Royal Road, (1882) Sam Fay
A Manual of Locomotive Engineering (1899) Pettigrew and Ravenshear
London and South Western Railway Locomotives, 1873-1922 F. Burtt
Proceedings of Institution of Civil Engineers (paper on Waterloo by A. W. Szlumper)
The Railway Magazine: numerous articles by John Bosham
Life and Labours of Mr. Brassey (1872) Arthur Helps
Life of Joseph Locke (1862) John Devey
Lectures on the Locomotive (1921) Dugald Drummond and R. W. Urie